A History of
ST ALBANS

James Corbett

Phillimore

1997

Published by
PHILLIMORE & CO. LTD.
Shopwyke Manor Barn, Chichester, West Sussex

ISBN 1 86077 048 7

Printed and bound in Great Britain by
BOOKCRAFT LTD.
Midsomer Norton, Avon

Contents

List of Illustrations vii
Acknowledgements xi
Foreword xiii

I Verulamium 1
II Saint and Saxons 11
III In this Town 18
IV Knights, King and Royal Pawn 26
V From Retribution to Revolt 33
VI Dangerous Times 41
VII Changes 49
VIII Civil War 60
IX Remarkably Clear and Fine 68
X Mysterious Ways 77
XI Full Steam Ahead 88
XII Sober Excitements, Comical Exertions 96
XIII Enlargement 104
XIV 'Nice Quiet Place' 113
XV Energetic Steps 121
XVI Aftermath 129
XVII War and Peace 136
XVIII A Need that Never Ends 144

Bibliography 153
Index 155

List of Illustrations

1. Devil's Dyke, Wheathampstead 1
2. Boudicca, her two daughters and troops (*Herts Advertiser* supplement, 20 July 1907) 5
3. Venus (*FestAlban 77* souvenir brochure, St Albans, 1977) 6
4. Scallop-shell mosaic (J. Watkins, *The Alban Guide*, St Albans, 1938) 6
5. London Gate 7
6. Cernunnus (*FestAlban 77* souvenir brochure, St Albans, 1977) 7
7. Portrait of Carausius 8
8. Verulamium theatre (J. Watkins, *The Alban Guide*, St Albans, 1938) 9
9. Kingsbury mount 12
10. King Offa holding model (*Register of Benefactors of the Monastery of St Alban*, Corpus Christi
    College, Cambridge) 13
11. The building of St Albans Abbey (facsimile of a drawing by Matthew Paris: Charles Ashdown,
    St Albans: Historical and Picturesque, London, 1893) 13
12. A coin of King Offa (Charles Ashdown, *St Albans: Historical and Picturesque*, London, 1893) 14
13. St Michael's Church (J.W. Comyns Carr, *The Abbey Church of St Alban's*, London, 1877) 14
14. St Peter's Church, drawn by Frederic Kitton (Charles Ashdown, *St Albans: Historical and
    Picturesque*, London, 1893) 15
15. St Stephen's Church (H.M. Alderman, *A Pilgrimage in Hertfordshire*, London, 1931) 15
16. The Battle of Hastings (R. Chambers [ed.], *The Book of Days*, vol.II, London, 1886) 17
17. South aisle of presbytery (J. Watkins, *The Alban Guide*, St Albans, 1938) 18
18. An extract from Domesday Book, 1086 19
19. A 12th-century water-carrier (Adolph Goldschmidt, *Der Albanipsalter in Hildesheim*, Berlin, 1895) 20
20. A man with a bird (Adolph Goldschmidt, *Der Albanipsalter in Hildesheim*, Berlin, 1895) 21
21. Ivory book-cover 23
22. Matthew Paris 28
23. Henry III charter 30
24. St William of York mural 33
25. Teazle (Anon., *The Journal of a Naturalist*, London, 1829) 37
26. Memorial brass of Abbot Thomas de la Mare 39
27. Abbey Gateway 40
28. French Row 42
29. The chantry chapel of Humphrey, Duke of Gloucester (*The Graphic*, 10 June 1871) 44
30. The *Antelope Inn*, drawn by Frederic Kitton (Charles Ashdown, *St Albans: Historical and
    Picturesque*, London, 1893) 44
31. The *George Inn*, drawn by Frederic Kitton (Charles Ashdown, *St Albans: Historical and
    Picturesque*, London, 1893) 45
32. Henry VI 46
33. Hall Place, drawn by Frederic Kitton (Charles Ashdown, *St Albans: Historical and Picturesque*,
    London, 1893) 47
34. St Albans Abbey before its suppression 48
35. Misericord 49
36. Remains of the cloisters 51
37. The *Fighting Cocks* 51
38. The Holyrood lectern (H.M. Alderman, *A Pilgrimage in Hertfordshire*, London, 1931) 52
39. Lee Hall 52

40.   The Lady Chapel (*The Graphic*, 10 June 1871) 53
41.   Death by burning (Anon., *The Days of Queen Mary*, London, n.d.) 53
42.   George Tankerfield plaque, Romeland Garden 53
43.   Francis Bacon memorial (R. Chambers [ed.], *The Book of Days*, vol.I, London, 1896) 56
44.   Pemberton almshouses 57
45.   Map of St Albans, 1634 58
46.   Alban Roe anniversary 59
47.   Trade tokens, drawn by Frederic Kitton (Charles Ashdown, *St Albans: Historical and Picturesque*,
        London, 1893) 59
48.   Abbey church passageway entrance, Sumpter Yard 63
49.   Abbey church passageway interior 65
50.   Waxhouse Gate Lane 65
51.   John Townsend pamphlet, 1662 66
52.   Sarah Jennings, Duchess of Marlborough (from an engraving of the portrait by
        Sir Godfrey Kneller, *c*.1705) 70
53.   Marlborough almshouses 70
54.   William Hogarth (a 19th-century engraving) 71
55.   Nathaniel Cotton (St Albans and Hertfordshire Architectural and Archaeological Society
        Transactions, 1936-8) 72
56.   William Cowper (*Poems*, London, n.d.) 72
57.   Collegium Insanorum, drawn by Frederic Kitton (Charles Ashdown, *St Albans: Historical and
        Picturesque*, London, 1893) 73
58.   Nathaniel Cotton's grave 73
59.   St Michael's bridge 74
60.   The east end of the abbey church (Peter Newcome, *The History of the Abbey of St Alban*,
        London, 1793) 75
61.   Methodist meeting house steps 76
62.   Market Place, St Albans (engraved from a drawing by G. Shepherd for *The Beauties of England
        and Wales*, John Harris, London, October 1812) 78
63.   Gorhambury House 79
64.   Silk Mill 80
65.   St Albans in 1700 and 1822 (*Hertfordshire Past & Present*, no.2, 1961) 81
66.   The Clock Tower 81
67.   William Cobbett (William Cobbett, *A History of the Protestant Reformation*, London, n.d.) 82
68.   The Holyhead Road (*Hertfordshire Past & Present*, no.2, 1961) 83
69.   Road repairs (Thomas Bewick, *History of British Birds*, vol.I, Newcastle, 1832) 83
70.   Town Hall 84
71.   Dalton's Folly (William Oldfield, *Views in Hertfordshire*, *c*.1806) 85
72.   *Turf Hotel*: an engraving of a painting by J. Pollard 86
73.   A map of St Albans, *c*.1840 (drawn by R. Creighton, engraved by J.&C. Walker) 89
74.   The *Wonder* coach, drawn by Frederic Kitton (Charles Ashdown, *St Albans: Historical and
        Picturesque*, London, 1893) 89
75.   Harvesting 91
76.   Electoral corruption cartoon 92
77.   Buckingham's 'Guardian of the Morals' 92
78.   Sopwell House (William Oldfield, *Views in Hertfordshire*, *c*.1806) 93
79.   Christ Church (*Herts Advertiser*, 16 April 1859) 93
80.   The west front of the abbey church 98
81.   The Wooden Room, Lattimore Road 101
82.   The drinking fountain 102
83.   Pedestal of the restored shrine (*The Illustrated London News*, London, 4 January 1873) 105
84.   Vintry garden 106
85.   The Cathedral and Abbey Church of St Alban (*The Quiver*, vol.XXI, London, 1886) 106
86.   Lord Grimthorpe 107
87.   Building workers, 1880 108
88.   Lord Grimthorpe as an angel 108
89.   Ground plan of the abbey church (*Murray's Handbook*, London, 1895) 109
90.   Sandpit Lane 110

 91. William Hurlock 111
 92. Joseph Halsey 113
 93. Cottage Hospital 114
 94. Boy wearing a smock 116
 95. City railway station 117
 96. Area map (*Murray's Handbook*, London, 1895) 118
 97. Arthur Ekins 120
 98. Market Place 122
 99. Bryant and Son's store (*Herts Advertiser*, 26 November 1904) 123
100. Charles Henry Ashdown (St Albans and Hertfordshire Architectural and Archaeological Society
      Transactions, 1924) 124
101. Farm workers, *c.*1910 127
102. Sopwell Lane 1914-18 war memorial 128
103. Women and war work (*Punch*, 20 June 1917) 129
104. Ver bridge 132
105. Camp Road School pupils 134
106. High Street 135
107. Ballito Hosiery Mills (*St Albans*, St Albans City Council, 1949) 137
108. St Peter's Street (*St Albans*, St Albans City Council, 1949) 137
109. Sander's (*St Albans*, St Albans City Council, 1949) 140
110. Cyril Swinson (*Souvenir Programme*, St Albans Millenary Pageant, 1948) 142
111. St Albans, 1875-1960 (*Hertfordshire Past & Present*, no.2, 1961) 143
112. Lord Runcie (*FestAlban 77* souvenir brochure, St Albans, 1977) 146
113. The Maltings shopping centre 148
114. Peace tower 148
115. Elizabeth II in St Albans (*St Albans Review*, 15 July 1982) 149
116. Dagnall Street Baptist Church (*Church Magazine*, June 1992) 150
117. Jim Greening 151
118. Crown Court 151
119. Beryl Carrington 152
120. Harry Javeleau 152

Illustration Acknowledgements

Illustrations are reproduced by permission of the following:

Cathedral and Abbey Church of St Alban, 21, 23, 24, 26, 34, 50, 75, 80, 86, 87; Julian Eve, 32; Pam Forster, 42, 58; Dolly King, 66, 92, 94; The Maltings Management, 113; Geoffrey Miller Collection, 5, 27, 28, 37, 59, 64, 70, 82, 84, 98, 104, 106; Museum of St Albans, 72, 97, 120; Geoff Place, 119; Private Collection, 7, 62, 101; St Albans Central Library, 22, 44, 45, 48, 49, 51, 53, 63, 71, 76, 77, 90, 91, 93, 95, 105; Rev. David Williamson, 46.

Acknowledgements

IT IS A PLEASURE to acknowledge with grateful thanks the many kindnesses of the librarians and staffs of the British Library, Collingwood, the Hertfordshire County Record Office, Hertford, the Hudson Memorial Library, St Albans, and the St Albans Central Library. Practical and informed help also was given generously by the Museum of St Albans and by the Verulamium Museum, and I am indebted respectively for their kind help to the St Albans and Hertfordshire Architectural and Archaeological Society, the Press Office of the Campaign for Real Ale, St Albans, the Deacons of Dagnall Street Baptist Church, St Albans, and to the management of The Maltings, St Albans. Particular help was generously provided by Mr. Adrian Allan, University Archivist of the University of Liverpool, Mr. Peter Barnes, Mr. William Bond, Dr. Julian Eve, Pam Forster, Rev. Canon Christopher Foster, Mr. and Mrs. J. Greening, Dr. David Kelsall, Mr. Frank Kilvington, the late Miss Dolly King, Mr. John King, Mr. Patrick McDermott, Mr. Gerard McSweeney, Mr. Geoffrey Miller, Mr. Barrie Morley, Mrs. Elsie Newton, Miss Susan Newton, Ms. Bernadette Nolan, Mr. Noel O'Hanlon, Mr. Malcolm Smith, Mrs. Brenda Swinson, Mr. Roger Talbot, Mrs. Maggie Telfer, Mr. and Mrs. H. Tomlinson and Mrs. Margaret Young. I am especially indebted to Dr. Alan Hooper, Mr. Eric Hopkins, Miss Vivienne Prowse and Miss Mary Willson for having taken the trouble individually to read a draft of the text, offering many suggestions for improvements of style and content. The mistakes are my own, and the opinions expressed are not necessarily shared by any helper or patient adviser. As usual, I owe to Mary, my wife, much more than words can say.

Foreword

THE FOCUS in these pages is, wherever possible, on the hopes, apprehensions, disappointments and endeavours of the people of St Albans. It is a history remarkable for the stubbornness with which, from time to time, they have defended their best interests during a variety of social, civic and urban changes. And as it is a local history, events of a national or, indeed, international dimension are referred to only insofar as they relate to St Albans or provide a necessary point of reference. In any case, the future, too, has a past and, for a city as venerable as St Albans, that past has a potentially inexhaustible future.

But it is a past with a future made more vulnerable by the rate and size of modern developments. Because of that, particularly since the middle of the 19th century, there have been repeated occasions when it has been felt necessary by people in St Albans—as by others throughout Great Britain—to spring to the defence of their local past. Threatened buildings especially, beginning with the Clock Tower, have found their defenders, though not always successfully. Nevertheless, the continuing dialogue between past and present, and the manner in which the residents have recorded, or reflected upon, the city's past, and taken action, provide another strong and persistent theme in the history of St Albans.

Verulamium

ST ALBANS inherits a written history that begins more than two thousand years ago with the Romans, although its prehistory is much older. The first traces of human activity date back to a warm interval during the Ice Age, from when a flint hand axe, found at Flamstead End, reveals the fleeting presence of those few, nomadic people of the Old Stone Age who hunted wild animals on the higher ground of the Vale of St Albans.

Long after the glaciers had melted, and forests covered the country, people of the Middle Stone Age entered the area in about 6000 BC. They ate fish, wildfowl, deer and pigs. Their flint implements—scrapers, blades, arrowheads, axes—are found in and around St Albans and worked cores of flint confirm some local manufacture. But, like the earlier hunters, these wandering food-gatherers lived off the land, not on it. The people responsible for making the crucial change from temporary to permanent settlement were those of the New Stone Age who, by 3500 BC, had become Hertfordshire's first farmers. One of their chiefs was cremated at Colney Street in a dug-out canoe dragged from the then wider and deeper river Ver. A broken flint dagger, found in St Albans, and a polished flint axe from Harpenden, are shapely reminders of those agricultural pioneers.

Around 1400 BC knowledge of the making of bronze spread to Britain, with the arrival, perhaps, of people from across the Channel skilled in the alloy's production. A hoard of scrap bronze, probably buried by a smith, was found at Watford, and at an allotment off Verulam Road, St Albans, there surfaced a badly-damaged bronze razor of later date.

Celts invading from what is now northern France settled down to farm on hillsides in the south and west before more Celts, arriving after about 600 BC, and armed with the superior knowledge of iron crossed the narrow seas and established themselves upon the well-drained gravel soil around St Albans. Five miles north-west of St Albans a double rampart and ditch at The Aubreys, Redbourn, surrounds one of their defensive sites.

Fiercer Celts, related to Teutonic people, sailed up the Lea valley around 75 BC, and built a huge fortified enclosure at Wheathampstead. Devil's Dyke, originally a 30ft. deep ditch on the edge of the present-day village, still is an awesome part of its remaining defences. These Celts, known as the Belgae, rapidly carved out separately organised and mutually hostile kingdoms throughout the south-east, where the dominant kingdom became that of the Hertfordshire Catuvellauni. Their chieftain, Cassivellaunus, led the armed resistance to the invasion in 54 BC of Julius Caesar, whose pretext for the invasion, as for that of its forerunner the previous summer, was to prevent the Belgae from helping their Celtic cousins in Gaul resist Roman occupation. In Britain, Caesar's decisive battle against the Belgae during the second expedition may have been fought at the Wheathampstead stronghold of Cassivellaunus. In any case, Cassivellaunus agreed terms and the Romans withdrew with first-hand information likely to be useful should the island on the north-west fringes of their empire demand further military intervention.

1   Devil's Dyke, Wheathampstead, is part of the defences of a first-century BC fortified enclosure.

But for almost a century there were peaceful relations. Trade flourished, partly because the Belgic chieftains already had acquired a taste for opulent furniture, silverware, delicate glass, fine pottery, jewellery and indispensable wine obtainable only from Roman Gaul. At first, lacking a coinage, the best that the Belgae had been able to do was to barter, obtaining the coveted luxuries in exchange for wheat, cattle, hunting dogs, hides and slaves. Their wars against neighbouring kingdoms were a ready provider of the slaves, though not every prisoner necessarily ended up abroad, if an iron gang-chain discovered on the site of a Belgic farmstead at Park Street signifies the presence of a local taskmaster. All the same, the luxuries were arriving on an unprecedented scale.

Money, too, began to flow. Gold coinage from Gaul had been introduced into Britain as early, perhaps, as 150 BC. Copies were made until, gradually, native forms developed in gold and silver for the luxury trade and, eventually, lower denominations in bronze were issued for everyday transactions, many of them imitating Roman coins.

Tasciovanus, the new ruler of the Catuvellauni, changed strongholds around 25 BC, moving from Wheathampstead to Prae Wood, a plateau south-west of St Albans. The scattered site, which slopes down to the southern bank of the river Ver, was called Verlamio and its establishment is likely to have been prompted if Wheathampstead had been the site of Caesar's victory and, therefore, no longer a propitious location; equally, the new site may have provided strategic advantages. Boundary ditches in Prae Wood and the Devil's Dyke at Gorhambury, on the western boundary of present-day St Albans, indicate its extent. Beech Bottom ditch, north west of St Albans, connects the new settlement with its predecessor five miles away at Wheathampstead. There were at least three farmsteads and houses, other structures and a large, rectangular enclosure, possibly a temple or royal residence, occupying the lower slopes near the Ver. Coins inscribed VER (for Verlamio) were produced after about 20 BC, and mint moulds and crucibles have been found at the site.

Coins accompanied the ashes of some of the inhabitants of Verlamio buried in a cemetery functioning from about 15 BC to AD 40 at what is now the western end of King Harry Lane. Costly grave goods, such as silver mirrors, were provided in seven of the 472 burials excavated, but most consisted of burnt bones in a pot accompanied by one or two other vessels while the ashes of poorer people were buried in leather bags without grave goods. Previously, until about 50 BC, the Belgae had buried their dead; then, with Roman influence extending to the grave, cremation before burial became favoured. Of those buried in the Belgic cemetery only 17 had family or friend so unfashionable as to ensure inhumation.

A richly-furnished royal cremation grave, found near St Albans City Hospital, confirms the ever-extending influence. Buried with the human ashes were valuable chain-mail, bronze horse harness and Roman silver vessels. The grave may be that of Tasciovanus or, more likely, that of Adminius, a puppet king installed by the Romans at the time of their invasion in AD 43. An associated temple built next to the great grave mound survived for more than two centuries to encourage veneration by Britons of a British leader loyal to Rome.

The last and most powerful of the Catuvellaunian warlords was Cunobelin—Shakespeare's Cymbeline and the Old King Cole of the nursery rhyme—who minted coins at Verlamio, which remained important, although Camulodunum (Colchester) became his capital. Bronze coins of his bear the title *Rex:* king of the Britons, according to the Roman historian Suetonius, who was exaggerating since the kingdom directly controlled no more than south-east Britain. Other of Cunobelin's bronze coins symbolised military success by a winged Victory and an elaborately equipped soldier. On a gold coin an ear of barley proclaimed his kingdom's agricultural wealth, confirming, perhaps, to Roman eyes that Britain, if taken over as a province, could reasonably be expected to offer choice pickings. Cunobelin's death, and the kingdom's renewed hostility, gave Rome its chance to invade in AD 43. Shortly before the invasion, a clay and wattle hut appears to have been built in what is now the back garden of 8 Salisbury Avenue. The brown or black pieces of pottery pots, bowls and cups found at the site suggest a permanent structure.

No united opposition faced the invaders and, despite fierce fighting, Camulodunum fell in the presence of the Emperor Claudius. By AD 47, most of Britain south of a line from the Humber to the Severn estuary was occupied, although campaigning would take another 30 years before the rugged western and northern regions were subdued. Meanwhile, the Romans transformed haphazard Verlamio into rectilinear Verulamium.

At first, a four-acre fort was built on the northern slopes above the Ver, commanding the strategic road to Camulodunum, but it was on the south bank of the Ver that Verulamium was established. Like Camulodunum and Londinium, it developed rapidly into a recognisably Roman town. Flanking Watling Street, the main route to the Midlands and the north-west, it had been carefully sited to meet military, political and economic needs. A day's march from Londinium, it supplanted the native settlement, inheriting, maybe, its loyalties, even though its name had been Romanised, and continued as the focus of a relatively populous and productive countryside. Soon, Verulamium covered 50 acres enclosed by a bank and a ditch with straight, gravelled roads laid out in the standard grid pattern. Timber-framed buildings, some with plastered interior walls and glazed windows, lined the roads. One of the few masonry buildings was a public bath-house: its absence would have been a serious deprivation to Roman soldiers and civilians alike. The shops included that of a bronze-smith; another may have been a tavern. An early malting oven, found behind the *Black Lion*, Fishpool Street, operated for almost two centuries and processed, most likely, the plentiful barley supplied by the surrounding farms.

Development was so fast and extensive that around the year AD 50 Claudius raised Verulamium to the status of a self-governing *municipium*: a rare honour in Britain, probably shared with Londinium and, perhaps, Ratae Coritanorum (Leicester). Slaves excepted, the privilege did not exclude the inhabitants from paying taxes although everybody in Verulamium could marvel at the changes. For the first time the Catuvellauni lived in a planned town. The richer of them had long enjoyed Roman luxuries; adjusting to Roman rule as well is unlikely to have been unpleasant, and the poorer inhabitants would not have found life any worse, at least, than previously; besides, the interminable Belgic warfare had been ended.

There was a price to pay. The wealthiest of the wealthy were compelled to accept loans from Roman speculators to pay for the developments. In parts of Britain the rapacity of the speculators, the taxes and the forced labour of those doing the hardest work combined to provide an inflammable tinder. The spark was the humiliation by Roman officials of Boudicca, queen of the East Anglian Iceni who, in the ensuing uprising of AD 60, put to the torch Camulodunum, Londinium and Verulamium. Burnt debris, uncovered during excavations, records the storm in which the farm at Park Street (where the gang-chain was found) and another farm at Gorhambury went up in flames before the uprising was crushed.

Among others in Verulamium who died around that time were seven men and a woman, whose bodies were tossed carelessly into a shallow ditch on the eastern edge of the town. All had long been unhealthy and the condition of their skeletons indicated lives of unremitting hard labour. Some of them, for lack of a bench on which to sit, had squatted habitually: it is supposed that they were slaves. Other slaves were more fortunate. For instance, men who might have been household slaves in Verulamium scratched their nicknames on domestic pottery: Bonus, Sacer, Similis, Celer. Coincidentally, the Emperor Hadrian had a secretary called Celer. In English, the names become Goody, Holy, Likely, Speedy. But, slaves or not, the luckier hewers of wood and drawers of water in Verulamium, unlike those of Verlamio, were literate.

After the uprising recovery took more than a decade, but was helped by wiser methods of government. The farms at Park Street and Gorhambury were re-built as Roman-style villas, appropriate for profitable estates, with costly mortared stone-walls to enclose their ultimate luxuries of private bath-rooms. In Verulamium the charred ruins of houses were cleared to be replaced by superior buildings, most of which were again of the half-timbered kind, but containing tesselated floors. The town doubled in size as trade revived and one of the shops appears to have sold the highly-prized red-glazed samian ware from Gaul.

Beyond the town, tile and pottery kilns at Potters Bar, Aldenham, Elstree and Brockley Hill worked at full blast to keep up with the demand. The Brockley Hill kilns also produced wine amphorae which, perhaps, were containers for wine made in the south-east of Britain. Most of the wine drunk in the province came from Gaul or what is now Spain. As for the Brockley Hill potters, the names of some are known because they are stamped on their wares: Martinus, Marinus, Maricamulus.

By AD 79 an exceptionally large forum and basilica had been built in the area now partly occupied by St Michael's Church. Fragments survive of a magnificent carved inscription commemorating the completion of the forum during the governorship of Agricola. A market hall was built and a new bath-house, followed by a triangular temple dedicated to an oriental goddess, Cybele, whose devotees practised ritual mutilation.

2   Boudicca, her two daughters and troops in 61 BC as portrayed in the St Albans pageant of 1907.

At the turn of the first century Verulamium's importance as a busy market town increased further, already having attracted potters, builders, stonemasons, cobblers, carpenters, plasterers, painters, brewers, butchers and metal workers. The old enclosure bank was levelled in about AD 120; another appeared, incompletely enclosing a greater area. Twenty years later,

a theatre with seating for 1,500 spectators was built alongside Watling Street in the western half of the town. New public baths opened outside the town, where the quantity of oyster shells found at the site, in Branch Road, suggests an accompanying bar or an inn.

A fire, an ever-present danger, broke out in *c.*AD 155, destroying almost half the town, and causing a devastating setback, but upon its ashes arose a new, more substantial Verulamium. The market hall was remodelled and the forum rebuilt with two adjacent temples. Hollowed lengths of timber, connected by iron collars, supplied drinking water to public fountains; private wells supplemented the supply. Sewers emptied into the Ver. At the end of the second century, the new private houses were flint and mortar mansions with wall-paintings and mosaic floors. On one of the floors a lion crunches a stag; another depicts what could be the head of the sea god Oceanus or, as likely, that of the Celtic god Cernunnos, lord of animals and nature. Worshipped also in Gaul, his association with the house would imply a well-off Briton as the owner. The furniture in one of the mansions included a splendid Italian-style table with carved, stone legs.

The residents were witnessing a period of prosperity. For a few of them, who doubtless were viewed with suspicion, the prosperity was questionable if it became a cause of avarice. According to their incomprehensible beliefs, the love of money was the root of all evil and, nonsensically, the same believers declared that free men and slaves were of equal worth; treasonably, they denied the divinity of every god except their own. But those Christians and their strange beliefs attracted Alban, a citizen of Verulamium who, when confronted by the authorities, did not mince his words. 'Those whom you call gods are idols,' he told them and, almost as blasphemously to their ears, spurned the offer of a bribe to renounce his new-found faith: 'I couldn't care less about money.' Condemned to death, his public beheading on 22 June 209 or, according to a revised reckoning, about forty years later, made him Britain's first Christian martyr. His grave near the place of his execution

3 (far left) Bronze statuette of Venus from Verulamium; height 8 inches.

4 (left) Scallop-shell mosaic: Verulamium, second century AD.

5 (right) The foundations of Verulamium's London Gate after excavation in 1930. The gateway itself had long been razed to the ground.

6 Cernunnus: a Verulamium mosaic, c.AD 200.

became a shrine around whose site, during successive centuries, arose the abbey and the town which bear his name.

A year or so after 209, a tomb, found in Verulam Hill Fields, commemorated a private tragedy. Wrapped in a carefully-sewn woollen cloak, the body of an infant boy had been placed in a lead-lined coffin; beside him, his parents had placed a small wooden box containing his favourite possessions: coloured beads, a bronze-handled toy, a lucky charm. Accompanying them, and buried with the child, were his two treasured sea-shells from the Mediterranean.

Another who died around the same time as Alban and the child was a youth aged between 15 and 18. His shattered skull, found at the city hospital grave mound site, showed he had been battered to death and beheaded. The skull, its flesh scraped off, would then have been displayed on a pole at the nearby temple. It is unique evidence of the Celtic head cult persisting in Britain until, perhaps, the official recognition of Christianity early in the next century.

By 230 or somewhat later a two-mile long defensive wall surrounded a 200-acre town, making it the third largest in Roman Britain. Impressive gateways spanned either end of the main thoroughfare; eventually, three monumental arches straddled the thoroughfare. The theatre was reconstructed and enlarged. Shops, a public latrine and a private house were built in a central lane between the forum and the theatre. Other new houses testified to the town's continuing prosperity during the first half of the third century.

But the empire was under internal and external pressure. Saxon pirates, who already had raided Britain's east coast, were a widespread nuisance by the end of the third century. At the same time there was a general upheaval as rival military commanders fought for regional power, and the disturbances were accompanied by inflation and the disruption of trade. In Verulamium and the surrounding countryside neglect and decay left houses deserted, hypocausts fallen. Outside the city's south-west wall beyond the Silchester gate, a suburb was abandoned, and in one of the houses a chisel, a bradawl and a hammer were left behind. Someone forgot, or did not think it worthwhile to take, a reaping hook. Is it possible that the occupants had been forced to leave in a hurry? Four styli, pointed metal instruments for writing on wax-surfaced wooden tablets, suggest the presence of a literate resident. The rooms were candle-lit and one of the candle-holders came with a handy spike for sticking into the wall or a post. Table lamps, using imported olive oil, cost too much for most people's use. All the same, good quality glassware graced the tables of the suburban citizens.

Their security proved to be elusive. The Saxon pirates continued to harry the south and east; the Irish raided in the west. The attacks, random, spasmodic and not full-scale invasions, were unsettling. For instance, discontented peasants may have reacted by venturing to abscond or revolt and traces of disrepair at the Park Street villa hint at a shortage of slave labour. Indeed, the troubled period when many coin hoards were buried throughout Britain (including a hoard hidden at Verulamium) overlaps an uprising of Gaulish peasants in 286, for a clamour in either province tended to resonate in the other. Prominent in helping to suppress the Gaulish uprising was an ambitious military commander, Carausius, who was rewarded by being given command of the Channel fleet. Shortly afterwards he arrived in Britain, pro-claimed himself emperor, and seems to have been made welcome: especially welcome if his unresisted arrival had prevented, or suppressed, a British uprising. Significantly, coins he issued describe him as the *Restitor Britanniae*—Restorer of Britain.

Britain was only a stepping-stone for Carausius, who returned to Gaul in pursuit of imperial ambitions and after an uneasy truce with the central authorities was murdered in AD 293. But he is credited with improving Britain's coastal defences by means of great bastioned fortresses built from the Wash to the Isle of Wight and smaller forts to protect the west coast. Inland, out of reach of the wild raiders, and in the wake of the Emperor Diocletian's administrative reorganisation, eco-nomic activity began to revive at the end of the third century. Verulamium benefited.

7 *Portrait of Carausius (AD 286-93) on a bronze coin.*

Mansions and smaller houses were built, old houses repaired or enlarged, and more improvements made to the theatre and market hall. A temple was enlarged and, most indicative of economic optimism, large new shops went up along Watling Street. A corresponding renewal in the countryside included improvements at the Park Street villa: three rooms received new underfloor heating; the baths were extended. A kiln nearby produced building, roofing and flue tiles for the busy builders in Verulamium, which had never looked so grand, so affluent, thanks in part to the increased agricultural exports to Gaul, where wars and barbarian invasions had devastated the farms.

A prosperous, peaceful Britain acclaimed Constantine, the first Christian emperor, in 306. Seven years later an edict granted freedom of worship to the Christians, whose religion quickly became the empire's official religion. In Christian Verulamium there may have been a small church in the southern corner of the town and another outside the

8 *Verulamium theatre (Gorhambury Drive) was built around* AD *150 and is one of only six Roman theatres in Britain.*

London gate, but the evidence is flimsy. On the other hand, circumstantial evidence points to militant Christians as being responsible for the fate of Verulamium's theatre. Adjacent to a temple, and associated with that temple's cult, its abandonment could be ascribed to intolerance or to an absence of private sponsors willing to finance shows. Whatever the explanation, the theatre became a rubbish dump.

Two further generations enjoyed the late summer of Roman Britain until in 367 simultaneously invading Picts, Irish and Saxons overran Hadrian's Wall, penetrated the defences in the west and east, and plundered as far south as Londinium. The raiders were dispersed and order restored by an expeditionary force under a Spanish commander, Count Theodosius. Verulamium, possibly having escaped the turmoil, resumed its quiet life with a confidence strong enough to justify the building of new houses. One of them, although small, was elegant. Underfloor heating kept a living room comfortably warm and ornate painted plaster adorned the walls. Floors were carefully tesselated. Later, about 380, a great mansion built near the London Gate contained 22 ground-floor rooms in three wings around a central court. Its interior complemented its external grandeur with a mosaic floor and elaborate wall plaster. A wealthy landowner, perhaps, had decided to substitute the perils of rural isolation for the assurance of strong town walls. He, or his successor, felt sufficiently at home to sanction extra expenditure: two mosaic floors were added and rooms extended at the turn of the century.

By then, military adventurers had again depleted the army in Britain to fight abroad for a bigger slice of the falling empire, leaving the province, militarily weakened, to suffer more raids and invasions. In such circumstances security remained a dream despite its brief realisation in the late 390s, after which Britain, like the rest of the empire, came under renewed attacks by the barbarians. When Rome itself was captured by Visigoths in September 410 the Emperor Honorius, unable to hold out any prospect of assistance, authorised the Britons to look to their own defences.

Verulamium seems to have tried. Although the least Romanised part of the empire, because it was the least urbanised, Britain fought to retain its Roman identity longer and harder than any other province in the West. At risk from the Saxon invaders were not simply the localised advantages of piped water and gravelled streets, but the faith for which Alban had died.

II

Saint and Saxons

THE PAGAN Saxon invaders of Britain, unlike the invaders being assimilated in Gaul or Spain, regarded a church as a place for plunder not prayer, while for Verulamium, as for the rest of what survived of Roman Britain, Christianity signified that civilisation, no matter how ramshackle, would prevail.

An indication of the success of Verulamium's defensive measures is the building shortly after 410 of three huts with ovens, apparently with fenced yards, boldly located outside the north gate. About the same time a small timber house was built in the shadow of the by then delapidated basilica. A fragment of pottery from the eastern Mediterranean found inside the excavated remains of the house suggests that trade links, even if weak, remained unbroken. For some time, too, important and welcome foreign visitors could continue to arrive. Most famously, in 429, Bishop Germanus of Auxerre prayed at Alban's shrine. According to a later description, the shrine had been 'reddened' by the martyr's blood although a likelier explanation is that its old wall plaster was damp and crumbling. Roman-British mausoleums, such as Alban's probably resembled, are known to have contained decorated wall plaster. In any case, Germanus, a former general, went on to lead a British Christian army to victory over a force of pagan Picts and Saxons.

Soon afterwards a mosaic in the mansion near the London gate was replaced by a large corn-drying oven which, after frequent use, had to be repaired. The mansion itself remained occupied until about 440 when, on its ruins, a vast barn was built. Despite the unsettled times, and the surrounding farm villas having been deserted, agricultural produce was still available in amounts worth storing safely in quantity. Ten or twenty years later subsidence affected the barn, which was abandoned, and its foundations were used to support a timber water-main of an aqueduct, which had long supplied the town, and which had been kept in working order. Nevertheless, although Verulamium was increasingly derelict, and its inhabitants had reverted to barter in the absence of coinage, it somehow managed to continue resisting the Saxons.

But for how long? Besides, not all Britons had resisted. In fact, rather than resist, so many had migrated to Armorica that it became known as Little Britain—Brittany. And did one party of the migrants, invoking the name of their patron saint, come from Verulamium? A village ten miles east of St Brieuc is called St Alban, though various French churches and villages were named after him due to the influence of Germanus.

By the year 500 the Saxons had settled on the northern and eastern borders of Hertfordshire; evidence of their settlement for the rest of the county is lacking until after 571. In that year they captured the Luton and Aylesbury area; shortly afterwards they took control of ruinous Verulamium, burying 39 of their dead outside the neglected Silchester gate, at the western end of what is now King Harry Lane. A shroud fastener for one of them was a Roman bronze pin, though whether booty or barter is a matter of conjecture. The cemetery remained in use till about 620, by which time most of the former province of Britain, except for Cumbria, the south-west and Wales, had fallen to the Saxons.

Their crushing impact on Hertfordshire was such that none of the Roman place-names survived and only a few of the Celtic place-names: Chiltern, for example, and the names of the rivers Beane, Colne, Lea and Mimram. On the other hand, Wall Hall, five miles south of St Albans, suggests a pocket of stubborn British *weala*—Saxon for 'foreigners' and understood to mean Britons.

Verulamium half-survived in name as Verlamchester but, by the eighth century, the name had become Watlingchester in recognition of the dominance near the Roman site, a 'chester', of a group of Saxon settlers, the Waeclingas. It is after them that the old Roman road through Verulamium was named Watling Street, lined on either side with ruins. But on the hillside opposite, on or near the site of Alban's shrine, stood 'a beautiful church ... where,' according to Bede (673-735), 'sick folk are healed and frequent miracles take place to this day'.

When that church was built is unknown: it could have been after the conversion of the English following the arrival in 597 of Augustine as leader of the mission sent by Pope Gregory the Great (540-604). Augustine, who died *c.*605, is reported to have repaired churches surviving from Roman times and to have built new ones. Almost two centuries later the 'beautiful' church attracted the attention of Offa, King of Mercia and overlord of most of England south of the Humber. He took care to maintain friendly relations with the pope in Rome not only as a religious duty but as a component of a statecraft which sought the legitimisation of papal support for his own expansionist schemes. The older Rome to which he looked for the mantle of imperial authority led him to style himself in Latin on a silver penny as king: 'Offa Rex'.

9 Kingsbury mount from New England Street playing field, 1995.

The old Roman style had been set for him by his dazzling contemporary, Charlemagne (*c*.742-814), King of the Franks and Lombards, Patrician of Rome and, in 800, Emperor of the West. Their negotiation of a commercial treaty was the first to be agreed by a king of England.

Offa visited the site of Alban's martydom in 793. He had already, perhaps, caused nearby Kingsbury—the 27-acre hill-top between the present-day Verulam Road and Fishpool Street—to be fortified as a royal stronghold, hence its name. His plans for the church were similarly impressive. In fulfilment of a vow he seems to have re-founded the church as a double monastery of monks and nuns, each living in their own enclosure, and endowed his foundation with extensive lands to finance its various undertakings. He placed it in the hands of the Order of St Benedict, the foremost monastic institution of the day, with a relative, Willegod, as the monastery's first abbot. Three years later Offa died, traditionally at Offley (Offa's clearing or wood), near Hitchin, north Hertfordshire, where he is supposed to have had a palace.

His monastery, like Benedictine foundations throughout western Europe, was designed to be an island of peace and light where learning and literature would be preserved and education promoted on the rock of prayer and praise. In England, Westminster Abbey and the cathedrals of Canterbury, Durham and Norwich were Benedictine houses; others included Bury St Edmunds and Glastonbury. St Benedict (*c*.480-*c*.547), in the writing of his rule of monastic life, had taken pains to ensure that prayer, manual labour and study should be integrated. The combination attracted men and women to the religious life and, in St Albans, the shrine attracted pilgrims, too. The new town, whose name proclaimed its Christian rather than Roman origins, took shape as a cluster of buildings on the higher ground north east of the monastery. Thereafter, the history of both abbey and town would long remain intertwined.

10 *A 15th-century* Register of Benefactors of the Monastery of St Albans *shows King Offa holding a model of the abbey.*

11 *The building of St Albans Abbey as conjectured by Matthew Paris in the 13th century.*

That connection had found early expression in the careful dedication to St Andrew of a chapel, now vanished, at the north-west end of the abbey church. Its name constituted an elegant allusion to Gregory the Great, who in Rome had founded the Benedictine monastery of St Andrew, from which came Augustine and his fellow missionaries. Subsequently, the readily identifiable St Andrew's cross became the arms of the abbey, was transferred to St Alban as his arms and today, on the shield of the arms of the city, perpetuates the ancient associations.

Ten years before the start of the ninth century an age of disasters began as heathen Viking raiders from Norway and Denmark plundered and burned around the coast. A hoard of 41 Saxon silver pennies and one halfpenny, buried south of the abbey in *c*.865-75, may have been hidden in fear of the raiders. Their easiest and most rewarding targets were the defenceless churches and monasteries, although St Albans seems to have been spared until about 890, when the Danes are believed to have sacked the abbey.

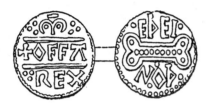

12   A silver coin of King Offa (d.796).

In the meantime, the abbey and the town had increased in size. A chapel in honour of St Germanus was built against the outside of the Roman city wall north of the London gate. Another chapel, further north but inside the city wall, and dedicated to St Mary Magdalen, was built by Abbot Ulsinus (*c*.860-70). Credited with having founded St Albans School, he encouraged people to settle in the little town by giving them money and timber for building, and established the Saturday market to make the place more convenient and attractive. His masterstroke for the town's success was the closure of Watling Street through the ruins of Verulamium which, in any case, were occupied by lawless squatters. The road's closure served notice to quit on those undesirables and, more enduringly, compelled all travellers entering St Albans to pass near the abbey and the market place. Watling Street was diverted up Holywell Hill, around the

13   St Michael's Church as it was in 1877—before Lord Grimthorpe's re-building in 1896.

abbey and down the other side to the ford at St Michael's.

Ulsinus is believed to have been responsible for the building of a church at each entrance to the town: St Peter's to the north, St Stephen's beside Watling Street in the south, and in the west, St Michael's, above the ruins of the great Roman basilica. Roman tiles from Verulamium were re-used in the building of two of the churches and, probably, in St Peter's, although repeated restorations have obliterated the evidence. Ulsinus' successor, Alfric (*c.*870-90), was a scholar, writing commentaries as well as translating parts of the Bible, but he did not neglect everyday matters. One of them concerned Kingsbury.

Its inhabitants were at loggerheads with the monastery and, perhaps, the townsfolk. The Kingsbury people had an advantage in that from their royal stronghold they overlooked a very large fishpool, whose stocks

14   St Peter's Church before the restoration of 1893.

they regarded as their own. Although by no means outlaws, the Kingsbury fishermen were irregular and uncontrolled, and the monastery resented their independence. Alfric's answer was conclusive. He persuaded the king —Ethelred I, possibly—to sell him the pool, drained it except for a corner, which he kept as the monastery's fishpool, and had the satisfaction of

seeing good farming land increased while, at the same time, punishing insolent Kingsbury.

The next abbot, Ealdred (*c.*890-c.910), focused his attention on the undislodged squatters of Verulamium. Outside the law, they set, perhaps, a bad example to the obedient taxpayers of St Albans. Besides, lawlessness could not be countenanced on the town's doorstep when there was danger enough from the Danes, a group of whom had settled no further away than Bedford. Some of the squatters may, as was alleged, have been thieves and robbers, but none was allowed to remain even though the ruins were their home. Two of their loomweights and ninth-century coins were lost or left in the remains of the forum. But the squatters' clearance made Ealdred's next task all the easier: the quarrying of the ruins to provide the material for the building of a new monastery.

The work was continued by Abbot Eadmer (*c.*910-30). Stone slabs, columns and

15   St Stephen's Church, 1931.

tiles were amassed, but pagan altars and statues, as well as glass funerary urns containing human ashes, were smashed to dust on Eadmer's orders. Idolatry was, he knew, forbidden by the Scriptures, which also commended the throwing down of the altars of false gods: 'And ye shall overthrow their altars, and break their pillars,' Deuteronomy 12:3 instructs, 'and burn their groves with fire; and ye shall hew down the graven images of their gods, and destroy the names of them out of that place.'

A second Alfric took over at the abbey around 970, about forty years having passed without there being a properly constituted abbot. The interregnum years had been turbulent. Norsemen had raided far and wide over the Midlands, followed by a Viking invasion in about 946 and, half-a-dozen years later, another Norse invasion. It was not a time for building a new monastery and it is likely that the preparatory work of gathering materials was suspended. On the other hand, Alfric II clearly was not the kind of man to pass up an opportunity of tackling unfinished business, and Kingsbury, the fortified royal enclosure, had remained defiant. Its continuing insolence challenged the abbot's authority.

Alfric had an advantage over and above that of his position as abbot. He was a friend of King Ethelred II (978-1016), having been his chancellor before coming to St Albans, and was granted permission to buy the hilltop site. At once, he evicted the residents, demolished the buildings and levelled the area. Kingsbury would no longer defy the abbey. Today, some of the houses on the north side of Fishpool Street, which stand two or three feet above the level of the road, are built on the remains of the old stronghold's ramparts.

Alfric is credited with having another trick up his sleeve. Fearing a raid by the Danes, he had the bones of St Alban hidden in a wall of the abbey, placed other bones in a chest and, for the benefit of the Danes, declared them to be those of the saint, which he sent as such to be kept in the fen-surrounded, secure Abbey of Ely. The danger there, however, came from within. Tempted irresistibly, the abbot and monks of Ely, believing that they had received relics both holy and profitable, kept them, substituting other bones, and returned the chest and its apparently original contents to St Albans when the Danish alarm was over. Alfric, behaving impeccably, treated the substitute bones reverently, retrieved the genuine bones from the hiding place in the wall and put them back in the saint's shrine. A less likely story claims that Christianised Danes did manage earlier to steal Alban's bones, taking them to Odense in Denmark, from where they were rescued by two resourceful St Albans monks, who restored them to the abbey. The Danes claimed that the monks had been outwitted because the rescued bones were substitutes. The fact is that places possessing relics could rely on a ready and reliable way of raising money: pilgrims.

The ways in which that money was spent ranged from building works to hospitality and charity. And in at least one winter during the long abbacy of Leofric (c.990-1042), a son of an Earl of Kent, the need for charity was great, and his response was correspondingly great: too great, said some of his monks, but the harvest in 1005 had failed and people throughout England were starving. Leofric sold everything he could to raise money for relief: the building materials which had been collected so painstakingly, the monastery's gold and silver liturgical vessels and its superfluous tableware. He was unable to find a buyer for the monastery's gemstones and deliberately kept back from sale several cameos, which may have been discovered during the quarrying of Verulamium, and which he hoped would be used to decorate the shrine when the new monastery was built.

Building was delayed further by a Danish attack in 1009 and by more than a half-century of intermittent war, although successive abbots persisted in trying to make the monastery and the town better places. Abbot Leofstan (c.1042-64) improved the safety of the roads by

granting the manor of Flamstead to a knight, Thurnoth, on condition that he and his retainers patrolled Watling Street north of St Albans to keep it clear of robbers and outlaws, and wild beasts such as wolves and boars. Arrangements for Watling Street to be protected south of St Albans were made by Abbot Fritheric (*c*.1070-77), but, by then, the Battle of Hastings in October 1066 had made the Normans under William I (1066-87) the rulers of England.

16   *A scene from the Battle of Hastings, 1066, on the Bayeux Tapestry, which dates from shortly after the Norman Conquest of England.*

III

In this Town

ALTHOUGH castle-building came first for the Normans, as a strategic necessity, they did not long delay the building of churches. Common to both castle and church was a version of the romanesque architectural style—semi-circular arch, sturdy column, zigzag decoration—which unambiguously proclaimed power and confident majesty. At St Albans, a demonstration of that power and majesty would in a comparatively short time create a romanesque abbey church of a size almost unrivalled throughout the Christian world and the largest in England.

17   St Albans abbey church: south side of presbytery with, facing, re-used Saxon baluster shafts and Roman tiles and, right, the 14th-century abbot's doorway.

Designed to replace the smaller and, to Norman taste, meaner Saxon monastery, the tremendous work was put in hand when Paul de Caen (1077-93), a monk, and nephew of another monk, Archbishop Lanfranc of Canterbury, became abbot in 1077. Eleven years later most had been re-built except for the bakehouse and buttery. Some of the construction material used was that quarried from Verulamium by the Saxon abbots for their intended rebuilding, which wars and invasions had prevented, and much more of the material was gathered by Paul to complete the abbey. Incorporated high above both transepts of the new abbey church were eight lathe-turned baluster shafts of Saxon origin, possibly survivals from the old monastery. Inconspicuously re-using them had combined thrift and thoroughness. As Robert the Mason's re-building was so thorough, and the foundations made so strong, the abbey church is the only one in England with its 11th-century crossing tower still standing.

Among Robert's rewards was the gift of a house, free of rent and taxes, in the little town of St Albans. A clue to the house's possible location, and elegance, came to light during archaeological excavations east of Chequer Street in 1982 when part of an 11th- or 12th-century stone window was found.

Elaborately decorated with a carving of a human head, the fragment displays an attention to detail that could be in keeping with the residence of a Norman master mason. Robert, working to the end, died in 1114.

Paul de Caen undertook the beautifying of the interior of the abbey's newly finished church. He gave a silver bowl to contain a light at the high altar, arranged for an adjacent recess to be adorned with a mural and donated many devotional books as well as establishing a scriptorium for scribes and artists. Their copies of texts, and their new manuscripts on sacred or secular subjects, each ingeniously decorated in gold-leaf and brilliant colours, won admiration and high praise which, by the time of Paul's death, ensured that the Abbey of St Albans was widely known for the artistic accomplishments of its 56-strong community. Pilgrims, too, were unlikely to be disappointed by the beauty they found enclosed by the hospitable walls.

Outside those walls details about the lay people of St Albans were contained in Domesday Book. Produced in 1086 by order of William I, it provided a census, county by county, of the adult males of the population, gave the value and ownership of the country's productive resources and listed taxable buildings. Religious houses, such as the abbey, were exempt from taxation. The survey disclosed:

> The town of St Albans answers for ten hides. Land for 16 ploughs. In lordship three hides; two ploughs there; a third possible. Four Frenchmen [Normans or their French-speaking allies] and 16 villagers with 13 smallholders have 13 ploughs. Forty-six burgesses. From tolls and other payments of the town, £11 14s. a year; three mills at 40s.; meadow for two ploughs; woodland, 1,000 pigs and 7s. too. Total value £20; when acquired £12; before 1066 £24. In this town there are a further 12 cottagers, a park for woodland beasts and a pond for fish. The said burgesses have half a hide.

A hide in the Domesday Survey was used as a basis for tax assessment and, being equal to approximately 120 acres, the 10 hides of St Albans amounted to 1,200 acres. Plough signified the implement itself and eight oxen. A lordship was a holding which included ploughs, land, men and villagers reserved for the lord's use. A villager usually farmed more land than a smallholder, who was a cultivator of inferior status, while cottagers sometimes held a little land but were obliged to labour on a lord's land either free or for a fixed sum. Burgesses

Villa S *ALBANI* p.x. hid ſe defđ. Ťra. ē.xvi.car.

Ťra. ē. xvi.car. In dñio. iii. hidæ. 7 ibi funt. ii. car. 7 tcia

pot fieri. Ibi. iiii. franciġ 7 xvi. uiłłi. cū. xiii. borđ

hñt. xiii. car. Ibi. xlvi. burġſes. de theloneo 7 de

alijs redditis uillæ. xi. liƀ 7 xiiii. fot. p annū. 7 iii.

molend de. xl. fot. p̃tū. ii. car. Silua miłł porc.

7 vii. fot. In totis ualent ual. xx. liƀ. Qdo receƥ:

xii. liƀ. T.R.E. xxiiii liƀ. In eađ uilla fuȷ̃ adhuc

xii. cot. 7 un parcus ibi. ē beſtiarū ſiluaticarum.

7 unū uiuariū piſciū. Ƥdicti burġſes dim hid hñt.

18 An extract from Domesday Book, 1086, describing St Albans.

were the citizens of a borough with full municipal rights, which included the levying of tolls and also, as in St Albans, payments from the market. Unlike Hatfield or Sandridge, there were no slaves recorded among the town's 500 or so inhabitants. And land in the county held by the abbey included that at Shenley, Sandridge, Redbourn, Napsbury, Rickmansworth and Aldenham. Later, its spiritual dependencies included two notable houses in Norfolk, Binham Priory of St Mary and the Holy Cross, and Wymondham Priory of St Mary and St Alban; in Northumbria, it held Tynemouth Priory. Each of these daughter-houses gave successive abbots trouble and to the latter house the abbey sometimes sent its own troublesome monks as a punishment.

Another of the abbey's holdings, Abbots Langley, was the birthplace in about 1100 of Nicholas Breakspear, the only Englishman ever to become pope. As Adrian IV (1154-9) he granted great privileges to the abbey, which resulted in it becoming the premier abbey of England. Instead of such generosity, Adrian could have been spiteful because, as a young man, applying at the abbey for admittance to the Order, he was considered unsuitable and rejected. Fortunately for the abbey, he then was accepted at a monastery in France and from there, via Norway, where he reorganised the Church, went on to be elected pope. The privileges he so richly granted were, perhaps, more out of respect for his father, Robert, than fondness for the abbey, where Robert had become a lowly monk, and upon whose death the abbey avoided the risk of attracting papal displeasure by laying him grandly to rest in the chapter house rather than obscurely in a common grave.

Earlier, in 1115, while Breakspear still was struggling over his vocation, the completed abbey church was dedicated in the presence of Henry I (1100-35) and Queen Matilda, accompanied by many of their nobles and ecclesiastics. Those of them not accommodated at the abbey were lodged in the town.

The St Albans Psalter survives from around that time as a sumptuous example of the kind of work which made the abbey's scriptorium famous. Created for Christina of Huntingdon before she became prioress at Markyate, eight miles north west of St Albans, it depicts in 43 full-page pictures the biblical story from the Fall to the day of Pentecost, and contains devotional texts as well as the oldest surviving illustration of Alban's martyrdom. Scenes of contemporary everyday life appear in the psalter's calendar of feast days and may relate to scenes observed in and around St Albans. A barefoot labourer holds a sickle, carries water, or wields an axe, while recreation is represented by a man holding a branch on which perches a bird as though being encouraged to sing.

For the monks, recreation is likely to have been a more serious matter. 'Idleness is the enemy of the soul,' wrote St Benedict, 'therefore, the brethren should be occupied at certain times in manual labour and again at fixed hours in sacred reading.' He condemned 'boisterous' laughter and warned against 'much' talking, but there was no reason to forbid a chuckle. Time and again, illustrations of monks at play appear in the pages of the manuscripts produced in their own scriptoria.

Bread and vegetables formed their basic diet accompanied by ale or, sometimes, wine. No flesh meats or eggs were eaten, except by invalids and the old, during Lent's 40 days of fasting and abstinence, when fish was eaten instead; beef and mutton tended to be reserved for invalids or special occasions. Some of the provisions came from

19 A 12th-century water-carrier from the St Albans Psalter, *produced at St Albans for Christina of Markyate, friend and adviser of Geoffrey de Gorham (1119-46).*

20 *A man with a bird: from the 12th-century St Albans Psalter.*

London, but cheese was supplied from Langley, Sandridge and Walden, chickens from Rickmansworth and Codicote and 1,000 eels a year from the abbey's water-mills at Sopwell and, southwards along the Ver, Stanefield and Park Street. Eggs and pigs were provided from local sources according to the season.

The monks fared better under Abbot Geoffrey de Gorham (1119-46), who was invited as a priest from his home in Normandy to take charge of the school in St Albans belonging to the abbey. Because he arrived late, he lost the job, but found work at St Catherine's, a school attached to Dunstable priory. There, in 1110, he wrote a play for the boys, *The Miracles of St Catherine*, and borrowed gorgeous copes from the abbey to dress the cast of his play—the first recorded theatrical presentation in England—but the costly vestments were destroyed afterwards when his house was accidentally burnt down. By way of contrition he became a monk in the abbey and already was prior when elected abbot. His improvements to the abbey's income enabled him to allocate more money for the monks' food.

Catherine, a popular saint and patron of chastity and learning, had miraculously escaped torture on a wheel, according to the legend, and as a consequence was especially dear to those, such as wheelwrights and millers, whose work required the use of a wheel. Her feast day was accorded particular honour at the abbey by order of Gorham and with the introduction of the spinning wheel she became the protectress of the spinners.

A reminder of the trade's importance in St Albans, where the textile industry brought prosperity, is the district known as Osterhills: Sheepfold Hill. But sheep in the 12th century were as useful as they remained until the 19th when Thomas Bewick, in *A General History of Quadrupeds* (1811), wrote, 'There is hardly any part of this animal that is not serviceable to man: of the fleece we make our cloaths [*sic*]; the skin produces leather, of which are made gloves, parchment and covers for books; the entrails are formed into strings for fiddles and other musical instruments, likewise coverings for whips; its milk affords both butter and cheese; and its flesh is a delicate and wholesome food.'

Ten years after election Gorham succeeded at his second attempt to replace the old reliquary containing the bones of St Alban with a costlier version made of silver gilt encrusted with jewels. His earlier attempt had ended when a famine compelled him to sell—as it had his predecessor, Leofric—the specially collected gold and silver to raise money for the relief of the hungry.

Gorham's further improvements to the abbey's income financed the regular purchase of medicine and refreshments for the sick or aged monks in the infirmary; alms for the poor, withheld by the previous abbot, Richard d'Albini (1097-1119), were restored. Gorham reserved a third of the provisions from some of the abbey's manors for the benefit of guests, for whom he built a 'handsome' apartment. Male lepers were accommodated in the hospital of St Julian he built (*c*.1130) on the southern outskirts of the town. As the disease was greatly feared, and its victims shunned, the provision of a secluded shelter was merciful to them and a relief to their former neighbours. Corn tithes from St Stephen's and St Michael's parishes helped support the hospital.

Similar help was arranged by Gorham for Sopwell convent in 1140. According to tradition, the Benedictine house, half a mile south west of the abbey, was built on the site where two devout women had erected a hut in which to follow the religious life. They were provided with the convent as a more suitable dwelling for themselves and 11 other nuns, and were limited to 13 because that number, referring to Christ and the 12 apostles, was considered lucky.

The establishment of the convent and of St Julian's were signs of the town's continuing development. Another sign was the construction, by 1143, of a bridge over the Ver at the foot of Holywell Hill, while the town's earliest defensive ditches may have been dug around that time, coinciding with a period of national anarchy. Stephen (1135-54), a nephew of Henry I, having disregarded the right of succession of Matilda, Henry's only surviving offspring, seized the throne, unleashing nearly twenty years of a civil war neither side was able to win. Massacre, torture and plunder persisted until, in 1153, a compromise was reached by the exhausted contestants: Stephen could reign during his life, and the first son of Matilda and Geoffrey Plantagenet, the future Henry II, would succeed him.

Both town and abbey suffered during the civil war when, at one stage, the abbey's high altar was stripped of its gold, silver and jewels to ransom the town from being burnt down; on another occasion, the peace of the town was broken by a skirmish between the rival groups. Stephen himself put in a timely appearance shortly before the death of Abbot Geoffrey's successor, Ralph de Gobion (1146-51), and authorised the monks to elect a new abbot, Geoffrey's nephew, Robert de Gorham (1151-67).

The chapter house Robert de Gorham built indicated the abbey's continuing expansion and, probably, that of the town. Completely replacing the chapter house built ninety or so years earlier by Paul de Caen, and on the same site south of the abbey church, it doubled the monks' seating on facing stone benches along the two longest walls. The monks occupied the benches every day to hear a chapter of their monastic Rule and to discuss the abbey's affairs and their own shortcomings. Their hide-shod feet rested on ledges between which stretched a magnificent floor of nine-inch square relief-decorated glazed tiles. Exceptionally, because, unlike those found anywhere else, the tiles might have been made at a local kiln. Set among the tiles, carved marble slabs marked the graves of Robert de Gorham's four predecessors, among whom he himself would be buried.

His practical and artistic additions to the abbey kept him busy. He repaired St Alban's shrine, built a grand reception room in which to entertain important guests, a chapel, granary, laundry, larder, stables, the side of the cloisters in front of his new chapter house and two sunny rooms, solars, to 'soften the rigour of the winter weather'. His most startling addition was to have the outside of the abbey church plastered and lime-washed. In sunshine or cloud, the effect on a traveller approaching St Albans would have been dazzling.

None of Robert de Gorham's building activities, or the miles he travelled by sea and land, deterred him in his efforts to protect and promote the abbey's interests. Travelling to Rome, he secured from the English pope, Adrian IV, self-government for the abbey, gaining for it exemption from ecclesiastical authority other than that of the pope himself and, at a general council of the Church in France, obtained confirmation of the abbey's pre-eminence in England owing to Alban being the country's first martyr. In 1160, he went to Normandy, where he successfully petitioned Henry II (1154-89) for the settling of a dispute with a baron over the ownership of profitable woods at Northaw, eight miles east of St Albans. A notable occupant of the woods earlier in the century had been a hermit, Sigar, who reputedly banished the nightingales because they disturbed his meditations. With another hermit, Roger of Markyate, he shared burial in a tomb recess at the abbey.

The woodland ownership dispute, although comparatively minor, was part of a larger one in which the king, the Church and the barons had long jockeyed for dominance and whose conflicting claims and shifting alliances were a threat to the realm's stability. There were savage events and the Abbey of St Albans was caught up in them following Robert de Gorham's death. Henry, in a bitter struggle with the Archbishop of Canterbury, Thomas Becket (1118-70), grasped the opportunity to assert his own position by invoking his right to appoint the abbey's new abbot, Simon (1167-83). Two weeks before Christmas 1170, Becket, resting at his manor of Harrow, sent for Simon to discuss the political situation. Simon, bringing gifts and provisions, stayed several days in unavailing argument before returning to St Albans, and Becket, unwilling to compromise the rights of the Church, returned to Canterbury, where he was murdered by four of the king's men. Three years later the martyr was declared a saint by Pope Alexander III (1159-81) and his shrine at Canterbury became one of the most famous in Europe.

Becket's canonisation in 1173 coincided with a return to the offensive by some of the barons, for whom a bungled rebellion, soon crushed by Henry, ended with the defeated insurgents obtaining sanctuary at, among other places, St Albans Abbey. Treated leniently by the king, their stay was brief, enabling Abbot Simon to continue undisturbed in a costly programme of work. He had the scriptorium repaired, employed scribes at improved rates of pay to secure their skilled services, and increased the number of books owned by the abbey, including extra Old and New Testaments. The costliest of Simon's undertakings saw the shrine raised to make it more impressive and, thanks to the genius of a master goldsmith, John, brilliantly re-decorated in gold and silver embellished with jewels. Few other shrines were believed at the time to match John's work for splendour and nobility.

21   Part of a 12th-century ivory book cover found by a gardener in the grounds of Orchard House, 1921.

Its distinction may not have been fortuitous. Simon, friend though he had been of Becket and aware of the extraordinary appeal of his tomb, is likely to have done everything possible to make the most of Alban and to have pondered over other ways of obtaining an additional counterweight to Canterbury, thereby making more alluring the attractions for pilgrims at St Albans. Remarkably, as if in answer to a prayer, a resident of good character came forward in 1178 with an account of a vision. Robert Mercer claimed that he had been told by Alban where to find the grave of the priest in whose place he, Britain's first martyr, had died. The priest, Mercer said he was told, awaited disinterment at Redbourn common. Simon, having nothing to lose and with, perhaps, attractive holy relics to gain, ordered the designated spot, a prehistoric burial mound probably re-used by the Saxons, to be dug. Unremarkably, human skeletons were discovered. Some of the bones were supposed to be those of the priest—incorrectly known as Amphibalus owing to a misreading of an early text—and were identified as his because, as he undoubtedly had been martyred gloriously, an evidential spear and a knife accompanied the mortal remains. Obviously to a gratified abbot the other skeletons were those of unknown but equally heroic witnesses to the faith martyred at the same time as their venerable companion. Simon had found his counterweight.

He needed the help. An increase in the number of pilgrims would be good for the abbey's finances and good, too, for the town's trade. Everyone could benefit; besides, Simon's costly undertakings, including the founding of a commemorative priory at Redbourn, left the abbey so deeply in debt to moneylenders that after his death some of them came in person to dun the new abbot, Warin (1183-95). Among the importunate callers was a Jew, Aaron of Lincoln (d.1186) who, when shown the brilliant shrine, exclaimed with excusable testiness that he had built it out of his own purse.

Warin was well acquainted with Jews: they had been his fellow students at Solerno, southern Italy, where men flocked from Europe, Asia minor and northern Africa to attend a renowned medical school. Studying medicine with Warin were his brother, Matthew, and their nephew, also called Warin who, like his uncles, came from Cambridge. After their return to England they settled in St Albans: the brothers as monks at the abbey, where they became abbot and prior respectively, and their nephew as head of the school which, under his guidance, enjoyed a reputation second to none for the usefulness of its curriculum. Headmaster Warin died in the house he occupied near Sopwell convent.

A previous head, the scholar and scientist Alexander Neckam (1157-1217), who was born in St Albans, taught theology at Oxford and published a textbook on instruments containing the earliest known European reference to the magnetic compass as a guide to navigators. Usefully, his description of how a magnetic needle showed mariners their course contributed to safety at sea at a time when England's maritime trade was expanding and the first English ships were entering the Mediterranean.

His life-long love of St Albans he made clear in a poem, translated from its original Latin by William Camden (1551-1623), which reads in part:

> Here my first breath with happy stars was drawn,
> Here my glad years and all my joys began.
> In gradual knowledge here my mind increased,
> Here the first sparks of glory fired my breast.
> Hail, noble town! where fame shall ne'er forget
> The saint, the citizens and happy seat.
> Here heaven's true soldiers with unwearied care
> And pious labour wage the Christian war.

Abbot Warin's greatest achievement was to provide in 1186 the long-desired additional attraction for pilgrims: a magnificent reliquary of gold and silver for the bones of Amphibalus and, in a separate compartment, those of the imagined martyr's equally imaginary companions. The relics until then had been stored in a chest near the high altar. But, although the abbot had kept an eye on the main chance, the honouring of those suppposed to have suffered death for the faith did not preclude honouring in the name of that faith those alive who were suffering. A year before his own death Warin founded the convent of St Mary de Pré for the care of 13 leprous women, locating it in the riverside fields midway between Redbourn and St Albans where the precious relics had been rested when first being carried to the abbey.

Earlier, he prevented the seizure of the abbey's silver chalices by giving money as a compulsory contribution towards an enormous ransom for the release from imprisonment in Austria of the Crusader king, Richard I (1189-99).

The size of the ransom reflected both the increasing wealth of the country and the rising prosperity of the towns, including St Albans, where changes for the better were evident. Clay-tiled roofs had been replacing inflammable thatch for half-a-century and the occupants of the houses had become accustomed to using locally-made pottery distinctively glazed in a rich shade of orange. Livings were earned from agriculture, brewing, the making of leather goods and, of course, cloth. John (1199-1216), soon after his accession to the throne, confirmed the townsmen's right to buy and sell cloth. Their tenterground for the stretching and drying of it lay beyond the Ver at the foot of Holywell Hill, though the clothiers were compelled to use the abbot's fulling mill to clean and finish the material. The traders at the market already had grouped themselves according to speciality and, by the end of the century, would occupy the same places every Saturday. Their stalls developed into permanent structures separated by passages, which remain as the alleys between Chequer Street and French Row. Inns, having recently opened in the town, showed that more travellers were on the move. Advantageous to inn and private house alike in the preparation of poorly ripened cereals was a corn-drying oven such as that unearthed at the site of The Maltings in central St Albans. The same site yielded evidence in the form of a sturdy bone knight to show that among the pastimes of the 13th-century town was chess. The game, known also at that time and until the 15th century as 'chequer', gave its alternative name to a nearby inn from which, coincidentally, Chequer Street took its name.

IV

Knights, King and Royal Pawn

KNIGHTS, king and royal pawn troubled the abbot and the people of St Albans. For a time there had been a semblance of harmony when King John, following his coronation, prayed at the shrine of St Alban in the presence of Abbot John de Cella (1195-1214). But the king's insatiable financial demands to pay for a botched defence of his possessions in France alienated the barons, the Church and the towns and, coupled with an unsuccessful struggle with the pope over authority, set in motion events leading via St Albans to the monumental Magna Carta, or Great Charter of Rights.

Abbot de Cella, born in Markyate, having studied grammar, poetry and medicine at Paris, returned to England with a reputation as a scholar of outstanding ability. While in charge of an abbey dependency, Wallingford Priory, Berkshire, he was elected abbot and soon began to extend the abbey nave westwards and, as a consequence, to build a new west front which, in any case, needed re-building as it was severely decayed. Trouble followed trouble. A miscalculation by the chief mason, Hugh de Goldclif, caused the collapse of the incomplete west front, the builders left the job and, though another mason was appointed, the work languished. Abbot de Cella did better with the delapidated refectory and the ruinous dormitory, replacing both with elegant buildings for which, to cover costs, the monks went without wine for 15 years. John de Cella ordered that the monks, who came from a variety of backgrounds, should be limited in number to 100, unless eminence of rank or power of sponsor made a refusal impossible. When he rejected a request by one of the monks, William Pigeon, for the admission of a nephew, there were mischievous consequences.

The aggrieved monk tried to obtain revenge by taking advantage of a renewed dispute over the abbey's ownership of Northaw woods. Pigeon forged a deed which purported to grant the woods to a baron, Robert Fitzwalter, but Abbot de Cella fought back tenaciously, refused to be intimidated, discovered the fraud and retained possession. The spurious deed was burned; Pigeon exiled to Tynemouth. Fitzwalter tried a similar fraud at the abbey's dependency of Binham Priory where in about 1212 he produced a forged deed stating that he had the right to appoint the prior and besieged the place in an attempt to enforce his claim to the patronage. The few resident monks, surviving on water from the drain-pipes and bran, resisted until relieved by an armed force sent from King John, eager to appear as a defender of the faith, and St Albans Abbey obtained the forged deed, although Fitzwalter never abandoned his fraudulent claim. Patronage, where the person appointed was compliant, meant influence and favours for the patron.

There were other ways of doing well financially by behaving badly. The struggle between the king and the pope had resulted in England being placed under a papal interdict, supposedly stopping most public worship, which remained in force for six years. In its last year, 1214, John commanded the abbot to ignore the interdict's restrictions and, when de Cella refused, John put the abbey into the hands of a royal pawn, Robert of London. Protected by soldiers, he did not leave until he had extorted a large sum of money for his ever needy master.

The conflict of interests between John and his hostile barons and the Church reached crisis point. In August 1212 the barons, including the shameless Robert Fitzwalter, failed in a plot to murder or desert John during a campaign planned against the Welsh, but in November, grasping at tactical advantages, John agreed to submit to the pope and called in July 1213 for his barons to muster their forces for an expedition against the French. They refused. Next month, hoping to placate his English opponents, John allowed a meeting to be convened at St Albans Abbey under the Archbishop of Canterbury, Stephen Langton (d.1228), for an announcement of royal concessions. To the meeting came the barons and the churchmen and, from the towns, the leading citizens for the first gathering of the three estates, which developed into an assembly, Parliament, for the airing of grievances and the listing of demands. After further discussions during 1214 at St Paul's, London, and at Bury St Edmunds, the demands as expressed in a list of clauses struck deep to become the root of Parliament—the Great Charter. It was sealed reluctantly by John at Runnymead, midway between Windsor and Staines, on 19 June 1215. Of special interest to St Albans and other places active in the textile industry was a clause stipulating throughout the kingdom a single measure for a width of cloth as a means of more fairly fixing a price.

If gratitude had been felt by the people of St Albans it turned sour for immediately following the barons' dispersal John repudiated the Charter, reviving a civil war that brought fear and violence to the town. He entered St Albans in December at the head of an army, held a council of war in the abbey's chapter house and, after his troops had pillaged Rickmansworth, Berkhamsted, Watford and Redbourn, clattered away to campaign in the north against his adversaries. A year later, December 1216, the troops were French and their leader the French king's son, Prince Louis. Called in as allies by the rebellious barons, the French troops plundered Abbots Langley while Louis, confronting Abbot William de Trumpington (1214-35), posed an alarming choice: allegiance to himself or the putting to the torch of the abbey and the town. Trumpington, a former monk of St Albans who owed his abbacy to John, extricated himself and the town by the payment of a ransom of 80 marks. The cost to him of a similar act of mercy early in the new year was increased by 20 marks when a cut-throat mercenary, Falkes de Breauté, acting in the name of the recently dead John, terrorised the civilian inhabitants. He imprisoned men and children, robbed townsfolk, murdered an abbey servant and randomly seizing a man burnt his unlucky victim alive. But the terror had the desired effect: richer by 100 marks, Falkes de Breauté departed with his fellow cut-throats although the outrages resumed. In April, French troops returned, pillaging and torturing in the town to extract money, and stealing food and drink from the victimised abbey. Again, Redbourn suffered, but intervention by the French in English affairs was doomed, forcing their withdrawal from England, after a conciliatory policy by able statesmen had won support for the young king, Henry III (1216-72), who in 1225 issued a revised and much welcomed Great Charter.

The civil commotions ending, workaday ways resumed and the town and the abbey adjusted to settled conditions. Abbot Trumpington, making up for lost time, conducted an overdue building programme as, among other defects, the roof of the abbey church leaked. A butt collected the intrusive rain-water which, providentially, was to hand when lightning set fire to the roof and threatened the entire church. The building programme included the completion of the great west front, repairing the transepts, extending the cloisters, strengthening and heightening the tower and finishing the rebuilding of lavatories and the dormitories, which Trumpington furnished with new oak beds. He bought a house in London for his own use and that of his successors when in the capital on Church or State business, and financed it by renting out other houses especially built on the same site. In Great Yarmouth, Norfolk, he acquired a store to ensure the regular supply of the salted herrings eaten in St Albans during Lent, on Fridays and fast days, and did not neglect the spiritual nourishment of his brethren but added many more books to their library and presented choice psalters to the priories at Redbourn and Wymondham.

Working on the abbey's refurbishment and decoration were artists of outstanding calibre. Walter of Colchester, a goldsmith, sculptor and painter, who died in 1248 after serving the abbey for almost fifty years, enriched it by painting murals and carving numerous statues. He was assisted by his brother, Simon, a nephew, Richard, and a lay brother, Alan. In between, Walter designed and made his long-acclaimed shrine of St Thomas Becket for Canterbury Cathedral.

Equally notable was Matthew Paris (c.1200-59), the historian and artist whose chronicles of events in England and Europe, as well as a history of the abbey, gave him an unrivalled reputation on the strength of the quality and quantity of his output. Succeeding as chronicler to Roger of Wendover, abbey monk and author of *The Flowers of History*, and continuing Roger's scholarly work, Paris had been admitted a monk at St Albans in 1217. A confidant of Henry III, and as much at home in a royal court as in his own cloisters, he represented Pope Innocent IV (1243-54) when visiting Norway to reform its Benedictine order. Paris declared that his chronicles were written 'for the benefit of posterity, for the love of God and in honour of the blessed Alban, protomartyr of the English, lest the memory of present-day events be destroyed by age or oblivion'. Furthermore, his maps of Britain, the Holy Land and the world secured for him, a brilliant figure in a brilliant company, a leading position among cartographers.

But treading on the heels of even the most brilliant company were the poor. Abbot Trumpington took seriously his daily duty to relieve the harshness of their lives and provided by way of thanksgiving extra food to those of them who waited at the abbey gates whenever he returned from a journey. And for the convenience of everyone in St Albans he obtained a sonorous angelus bell. Every day, morning, noon and evening, it rang out to remind the monks and the townsfolk to pause and recite the established sequence of prayers. The bell had been consecrated by John, Bishop of Ardfert, Ireland, who while travelling had called at the abbey and, finding it agreeable, stayed nearly twenty years before being able to wrench himself away.

The bell needed to be loud so as to be heard throughout the town which, from mid-century onwards, was developing steadily despite the occasional man-made and natural calamities. For instance, the house of Simon, the son of Alwin, was burned down after being struck by lightning, a plague in 1248 claimed up to ten victims a day and there was an earthquake on 13 December

22   Matthew Paris (d.1259) as imagined by a 19th-century illustrator.

1250, which caused little or no damage, but was, wrote Matthew Paris, remarkable for being accompanied by a noise like thunder underground, and the confused manner in which the roof-top sparrows and pigeons took flight.

The town's development called into question its security and, as a corollary, how best to achieve its improvement. The laborious answer was the mid-century replacement of a restrictive Norman earthwork by the protective Tonman Ditch, which although not continuous defined the town and remained the basis of its municipal boundary until the 19th century. The boundary ran for about three and three-quarter miles from a stone cross at the corner of Sandpit Lane to a red cross at Sopwell, incorporated the river Ver to St Michael's and went from there through Kingsbury to twist back to Sandpit Lane. Between the houses and the ditch on the eastern side of the town were the long and wide cultivated strips of the Town Backsides, which still exist between the rear of the *Peahen* and the *White Hart* at the top of Holywell Hill. Moveable barriers protected the entrances to the town and there were further obstacles beyond on the main roads; defence apart, their purpose was to make easier the collection of tolls and taxes. Behind the ditch some of the streets had acquired permanent names, first recorded around the latter half of the century: Dagnall Street, in 1248, Fishpool Street and Holywell Hill, 1250, and, in 1275, the street of the grocers, Spicer Street, and Romeland and St Peter's Street.

Two pious women provided the town with food for thought. The learned and eloquent Cecilia de Gorham, a widow and former teacher of the king's sister, who lived about a mile out of town, had taken a vow of perpetual chastity. Thereafter, until she died in July 1251, she wore a russet-coloured garment that signified her particular commitment. More dramatically, an anchoress occupying a cell in the churchyard at St Peter's had a vision in 1258 of a bearded old man on top of the church tower, from which he foretold a catastrophe; later that year incessant rain rotted the crops, causing a great famine. 'Apples were scarce and pears scarcer, while quinces, vegetables, cherries, plums and all shell-fruit [nuts] were destroyed,' wrote Matthew Paris.

The tree of man was never quiet. Shaking the branches were 'certain knights and others' trespassing on abbey land to hunt with dogs and catch hares in fields at St Albans, Rickmansworth, Codicote, Redbourn, Tyttenhanger and Barnet, among other places. They had for a limited time been given permission to enjoy their sport in the abbey's fields, but took advantage, impudently claiming the favour as an old custom. Remonstration having failed, Abbot John de Hertford (1235-63) wasted no more breath and prosecuted the huntsmen, who were found guilty, fined and ordered to pay compensation. Some of them, patiently biding their time for eight years, contested the verdict in 1248 only again to be defeated by the law.

Sir Geoffrey de Childwick was luckier. Married to the sister of a clerk in royal service, John Mansel, he obtained through him a charter from Henry III in 1250 which granted the freedom to hunt on abbey land around St Albans. The charter added insult to injury because Sir Geoffrey, a tenant of the abbey, had been educated at the abbey's expense and owed his social rise to the same source. His next move was outright theft when in 1251 he stole a horse and the gift of venison it was carrying to the abbot but, owing to the influence of his brother-in-law, escaped the legal consequences.

Abbot Hertford already had enough to worry about. Holy, prudent, hospitable, a former prior of Hertford, he was burdened like the rest of the Church in England, and the barons, with having to hand over on one pretext or another large sums of money to the king and donations to the pope. At the same time, he had to spend freely on urgent building tasks. Good oak timber was used to repair the abbey's water-mills, ruinously neglected by the

23 *A charter, dating from the reign of Henry III (1216-72) and bearing the Great Seal of England, granted St Albans Abbey free warren in all its lands. No one could enter them and hunt without the licence of the abbot on pain of forfeiture of £10.*

tenants and, south of the abbey, he built a mill to be worked by horses, the river Ver sometimes running dry in the summer. For guests, he erected a house with adjoining bedrooms, and built an entrance hall, beautifully decorated by a monk, Dom Richard, in place of a derelict, ugly and gloomy hall, and provided new accommodation for senior servants with a store below. Most popularly, perhaps, he arranged for the abbey's malt-house to increase the strength of the monks' ale.

The monks kept in touch with the wider world through their own journeys on abbey business and through visitors to St Albans. Three years before Matthew Paris visited Norway, abbey representatives attended a general council of the Church in Lyons and, in 1254, two monks visited Rome. A party of Armenians visiting the abbey in 1252 gave news about the terrifying Mongols, whose empire then was at its height, and the visitors astonished their hosts by declaring that the journey from Armenia to Jerusalem took about thirty days. One of the most frequent visitors to the abbey, and best informed, was Henry III. Combining piety with parasitism, he and his retinue stayed and prayed for days at a time, and fed at the abbey's expense, although the king always left expensive offerings at the shrine of St Alban.

But Henry's extravagance and incompetence, coupled with his repeated demands for money, had made him vulnerable. A rebellion broke out led by a Crusader hero, Simon de Montfort (c.1206-65), and Henry was defeated at the battle of Lewes in 1264. The following year, after a meeting of Parliament summoned by de Montfort, and to which the abbot was called, there was a reversal of fortunes at the battle of Evesham when de Montfort, an advocate of a limited monarchy, was defeated and killed by Henry's warrior son, the future Edward I (1272-1307).

Though Matthew Paris observed that the civil war inspired fear, there were also the war's occasions of fearlessness. During 1265, when troops of the rival armies threatened the tranquillity of town and country alike, St Albans, which sympathised with de Montfort, strengthened its defences. The measures annoyed Gregory Stokes, a supporter of the king and governor of Hertford Castle, who boasted that bolts and bars notwithstanding he would enter the town with only three youths, seize four well-off inhabitants and imprison them in Hertford as a surety for the loyal behaviour of the town. Underestimating the opposition, he dashed into St Albans with his bully boys, ran about wildly and inexplicably shouted, 'How stands the wind?' Hearing the question, a butcher present among the wary townsfolk supposed the wild intruder wanted to burn the town and, losing patience, punched Gregory Stokes in the face with such force that he fell down. At once, he and his trio were seized and chained until, next morning, they were with popular approval beheaded by the town's butchers and their heads stuck on long poles for display at the entrances to the town. The taking by the townsfolk of the law into their own hands could not, of course, be countenanced; besides, royal justice was a source of revenue, and needy Henry, snatching the chance, imposed a fine of 100 marks on the town. Its immediate payment suggests that the townsfolk believed they had had the best of the bargain.

More disturbers of the town's peace during 1265 also learned a hard lesson. A gang of armed robbers pillaged the convent at St Julian's and, making off towards Dunstable, were pursued by a man equal in fearlessness to the decisive butcher. Alone, blowing a horn, he roused the citizens, who attacked and struck down most of the thieves. In 1269 another thief, having taking part in the theft of 12 oxen from people in London Colney, was pursued to Redbourn, caught, brought to St Albans and beheaded on the spot in the presence of a bailiff. It would seem that the butcher, the baker, the candlestick maker had discovered that they, like the barons, could fight for what they believed were their rights.

At the beheading, the presence of the bailiff and not, as previously would have been the case, a reeve, an intermediary between the town and the abbot, implies that St Albans had won for itself a somewhat independent court of law. The step appears to have been taken a decade or so earlier when the burgesses obtained a charter giving the town court final jurisdiction in a range of cases. Irksome rather than oppressive for the burgesses, who enjoyed full municipal rights, were the restrictions imposed by the abbey: close-fencing of abbey land, its monopoly of hunting, fishing and grazing and, extremely irksome, the payments to the abbot for having to grind corn and full cloth at the abbey's mills.

Matters came to a head during the years of the scholarly Abbot Roger de Norton (1263-90). He had started the abbey's long connection with Oxford as a result of a decision by the English Benedictines to improve the level of education among their members and it became a point of honour at the abbey to maintain the largest number possible of its monks at the university. The clash with the town happened after some of the townsfolk, in 1274, set up domestic handmills, which were confiscated on the orders of Norton. One of the bolder burgesses, aided by his fellows, took the case to law by suing the abbot for trespass. Costs to fight the case were raised by the burgesses, contributions being levied from all inhabitants, rich and poor, and the money placed in a common chest. Norton riposted by fining the townsmen but, undaunted, they took the case on appeal to Westminster, where they lost, and were imprisoned and fined heavily. Frustrated, most of the townsmen gave way to a demand from the abbot that they should pledge their good behaviour, although the bitterness persisted until in March 1277, when, after promising not to sue the abbot again, the townsmen secured concessions. Norton, recognising that compromise was better than confrontation, gave an undertaking that the townsmen would be safeguarded against loss when their corn was ground at the abbey's mills, determined anew the town court's range of jurisdiction and, as a gesture of reconciliation, abolished the local tax on ale. Congratulating themselves, the people of St Albans could celebrate with cheaper drink, but their tussle with the abbey was far from over.

Charitably, in 1290, they offered prayers for the repose of the soul of Edward I's wife, Eleanor of Castile, and the town acquired, near where now stands the Clock Tower, one of the lovely stone crosses the king built at each of the places where her coffin rested overnight on its way from Lincolnshire to London.

V

From Retribution to Revolt

TUSSLES recurred between the town and the abbey, and tended to last longer and become more frequent throughout the 14th century in the wake of turmoil at home and abroad. A resumption of the friction occurred in 1297 when Abbot John de Berkhamsted (1290-1302) was found guilty of irregularities in his control of the market, but he turned the tables on his

accusers by obtaining a commission to enquire into infringements of his chartered rights. The town gained nothing. Emboldened, Berkhamsted in 1299 stopped the wardens of Hertford castle from usurping the abbey's rights to levy for the king's use its traditional tolls on travellers and traders. As a further assertion of the abbey's rights he denied hospitality to a cantankerous Archbishop of Canterbury, Robert de Winchelsea, who would have been welcomed had he promised that his admittance would not compromise the abbey's privileges but, after refusing to give such an undertaking, found himself compelled to stay at an inn. He retaliated by placing St Albans under an interdict which soon afterwards was lifted when the abbot died and the prior, his successor, John de Maryns (1302-9), smoothed the ruffled episcopal feathers.

Around the same time occurred a reminder, if any had been needed, that building work could be dangerous or, indeed, fatal. A Latin inscription cut into a pillar in the south aisle of St Stephen's Church memorialises a victim: 'Eustace Pearce was crushed under this very stone and killed here, pitiable fate! Death doth await mortal man.'

A century of war was already in full stride. Wales had been conquered by 1285 but not cowed; war with France, which broke out again in 1337, lasted until England's disastrous defeat (1372) interrupted hostilities; and

24 *A St Albans Abbey mural of the mild and conciliatory St William of York, painted about 1330, retains most of its original colouring.*

33

Scotland, invaded in 1296, continued fighting, sometimes on English soil, until 1360. In 1297 the barons had rebelled over exactions for the French wars and in 1327 they deposed and murdered Edward II after a reign of 20 years. War and the ways of conflict and killing were setting frequent examples of violence before a population increasingly burdened by higher taxation, rising prices, famine and, from 1349, bubonic plague.

There had been disturbances in the town from November 1313 to April 1314. Once again the declared cause of the trouble was over the question of handmills which, when several of the leading burgesses defiantly set them up in their own homes, resulted in Abbot Hugh de Evesden (1309-27) sending his officers to seize the millstones. His entirely legal and automatic attempt to defend the abbey's rights was clumsy and met with an entirely illegal response. The officers were resisted by force, a riot broke out and during it the abbot's close was entered, one of his houses destroyed and some of his trees felled. Among the culprits the names of Benedict Spichfat, Robert of Lymbury and Simon of Ikleford were particularly recorded.

Three years of successive bad harvests began in the following year. Edward II fixed the price of livestock in St Albans to alleviate the hardship, but owing to the famine could not himself be given enough bread to eat when visiting the abbot in August 1315. In 1317, because there was not enough barley, the supply of ale dwindled and, despite special enactments, its price soared. As a result, many people lacking fresh water were deprived of a daily necessity as well as a cheery means of nourishment. To cap it all, during 1322 the town was occupied briefly by armed supporters of the barons in revenge for the abbot's support of the despised king.

In the circumstances Abbot Evesden could, perhaps, be excused for supposing that the cross he had to carry was too heavy. His predecessor had re-arranged the saint's chapel to aesthetic advantage, but it was left to Evesden to complete the Lady Chapel with stained-glass windows set in delicate stone tracery. Alas, Evesden's cross was not to be lightened. Something went wrong with the abbey's sanitation and the collapse of a dormitory wall in June 1323 heralded worse to come: the fall, four months later of two great columns on the south side of the church, bringing down the aisle roof and the adjacent part of the cloister. The repairs would take years.

Across the Channel in Flanders other structures were under attack. In 1323 news of an uprising of peasants and artisans in Flanders would soon have reached St Albans. Strong links joined England and Flanders, where English wool was indispensable for Flemish industry, its importance recognised by treaty, and any disorder likely to be alarming or, maybe, inspiring. In 1324, the town's burgesses were again showing hostility to the abbey. Another tussle involving abbey officers and prominent burgesses led to the abbey being attacked once more. Forty or so townsmen broke into the abbey, forced the door off the treasury and took away goods and documents. It was an attempt to deny Evesden the records by which he claimed superiority over the town and the town's attack was renewed in January 1327, six months before the Flemish uprising's suppression.

Riots occurred in London and there was trouble in Abingdon and Bury St Edmunds. In St Albans, a resumed attack against the abbey was led by the poorer townsfolk, who forced their wealthier neighbours and the faint-hearts to take part. Together, the protesters accused the abbot of retaining some of their charters to deprive them of age-old rights and, so as to ensure that afterwards he could not plead failure of memory, handed him a list of audacious demands: election in the town instead of appointment by an abbot of the two burgesses who represented St Albans in Parliament; the right to pasture cattle on common land and the right to fish in the abbey's waters; a jury of 12 townsmen to judge minor court cases and arbitration by that court, not an abbot, in disputes over the weight, measure and price of bread and ale; the replacement of the abbot's bailiff by a town bailiff and, unsurprisingly, the right to possess handmills. In effect, the list set out the terms for a surrender by the abbey and the town's complete independence. Rather than haggle, Evesden played a waiting game, keeping the townsmen unanswered, but meanwhile took the precaution of hiring armed guards for protection. Their presence served only to provoke the townsfolk, who thereupon besieged the abbey until after ten days the county militia were called out by the sheriff at Hertford to restore law and order in St Albans.

The townsfolk were lucky. The coincident deposition of Edward II, the uncertainty in the country and the widespread unrest favoured a settlement of disputes, such as that at St Albans, if the task of a rapid re-assertion of central authority were to succeed. Representatives of the town and the abbey were called in Febrary 1327 to negotiate face to face at St Paul's, London, where pressure on the abbey delegation resulted in outright victory for the townsfolk except in the matter of the perennially troublesome handmills. The surrender stuck in the throats of the monks, who rejected the granting of the demands although Evesden had urged them to accept, in case worse should follow, and they accepted only under protest.

Self-government exercised the minds of the townsfolk because independence alone was insufficient: there had to be the machinery to implement it. The means settled on to conduct civic affairs was that of a commune consisting of townsmen, who obtained that important symbol of authority, a seal of office and, with that at the ready, had sanctioned the taxes with which to pay for the privileges of freedom. There were no complaints. Cattle were pastured as of right on common land at Bernard's Heath, townsmen blatantly pursued hares and rabbits on abbey land and, pending a legal settlement, 80 handmills were openly in private use. The occupation of Bernard's Heath had been celebrated by a large crowd, many of whom broke branches off the trees and waved them gleefully when all marched back into the town. Townsfolk also tore up the fences and hedges of enclosed land on the southern outskirts. Another sign of the changed order of things was a sedate but significant ceremony. Twenty-four burgesses beat the bounds, walking in formal procession along the town boundary to demonstrate, as clearly as possible according to the custom of the age, that civic authority belonged solely to the townsfolk. The town's independence was, they may have supposed, indivisible.

The supposition was similar in principle to that held by the new abbot, Richard de Wallingford (1327-36), for whom the abbey's independence, its authority, was necessarily indivisible. Wallingford had no doubt that power shared was power pared. The son of a blacksmith, and orphaned at the age of 10, he was adopted by Prior Kykeby of Wallingford, who sent him to Oxford, where he excelled in arithmetic, geometry and astronomy. His upbringing and the kindness of his foster-father made likely his decision to enter the religious life, which he did at St Albans before being persuaded to resume his studies at the university. As abbot, having inherited an institution almost bankrupt and deeply in debt, he spent as little as possible on himself, living in the humblest way until by better management of the abbey's affairs he had paid off most of the creditors and reached advantageous agreements with the rest. Patient, strict, he would judge to a nicety when and how to pounce upon the disrespectful townsfolk.

He bided his time for three years until John Taverner, a leading citizen with a roving eye, provided an opportunity in 1330 by laying himself open to a charge of adultery. And what better issue over which to fight than morals? An outburst of indignation would show the abbey on the side of right and call into question the trustworthiness of the townsmen who, after all, had not scrupled to rob the abbey of its rights. But the proceedings turned ugly. While Taverner was being served with a summons a crowd gathered, tempers flared and in the uproar he was killed by the abbot's representative, Walter Amersham. The crowd had had enough. Once again the abbey had gone too far and Amersham, guilty of murder in the mind of the town, was lynched.

From one side or the other it was certain that legal retribution would be sought. The first to make a move were the townsfolk. With breath-taking impudence they indicted Wallingford and his servants for the murder of both men, expecting to win the case by ensuring that the jury consisted only of men from the independent town, not from the abbot's countryside. The townsmen were outflanked by Wallingford: as overlord he had the right to summon a jury of his own liking, which he did, and it acquitted him and his servants and he, in turn, indicted 18 townsmen of complicity in the death of various abbey servants. Wallingford had pounced with startling agility. He pounced again. After the 18 were found guilty he brought actions against other men for failing to pay the corn-grinding tax even though their use of the handmills kept them out of the abbey's mills. Wallingford had not finished. The prey at which he clawed was the town's independence and he was closing in for the kill.

The townsfolk tried to escape, proposing terms, but Wallingford, certain of success, would not give way, threatening unrelenting persecution of the leaders unless resistance ended. For another three years the town and abbey struggled until the townsfolk, quelled rather than crushed, gave up their charter of liberties, handed over the common funds and allowed their dearly-won seal of office to be defaced although they directed that its silver should be used to decorate the shrine of St Alban: their quarrel was with the abbey, not the Faith. As for the townsfolk's handmills, which Wallingford demanded and obtained, he had the millstones set underfoot in his parlour as a permanent token of victory. Even so, there still were those who continued to resist. Some of the abbey's tenants defiantly, and dubiously, claimed that they had had the right to possess handmills from time immemorial, farming tenants again objected to paying the corn-grinding tax and in Redbourn 50 wildly hopeful tenants produced a forged charter exempting them from the abbey's taxation. But every one of the tenants was compelled to submit.

Wallingford's sweeping success came after he had put the abbey in a good state of repair and its finances under his own personal scrutiny. Appropriately for a mathematician his re-organisation of the administration, as well as increasing the income, restricted theft by the lay managers of the abbey's properties and improved the supervision of weights and measures in the town in an attempt to enhance the market's reputation, thereby attracting more trade and, as a result, obtain more revenue. Wallingford's many writings, including those on natural science, mathematics and astronomy, helped swell the abbey library while a weight-driven astronomical clock he designed and made was renowned, although his monks complained that its cost had been too high.

There was money to spare. Abbot Michael de Mentmore (1336-49), a distinguished academic and stickler for discipline, who had been born in a village near Aylesbury, seems to have found no difficulty in providing annual stipends of £10 for each of five abbey scholars at Oxford and built at his own expense a range of studies over the east walk of the cloisters. To avoid debt careful management was essential in the allocation of the abbey's revenues because, besides the expense of the occasional structural repair or renovation, the cost of new buildings or re-building, and the payments to the king and to the pope, there was the daily expenditure required to run the school, give hospitality to travellers, feed the poor and look after the sick and old. The lepers at St Julian's and the nuns at Sopwell placed further financial responsibilities on the abbey: for both houses Mentmore drew up new rules of conduct to improve their control and function.

His sudden death in April 1349, followed soon afterwards by the death of the prior and sub-prior, signalled the appearance in St Albans of the Black Death. Originating in Asia, and transmitted via the Mediterranean ports, the epidemic bubonic plague, recurring in the 1360s and 1370s, devastated Europe, killing between one-eighth and two-thirds of the population. In England it reduced the population by a quarter or a third, killed 47 of the 60 monks at the abbey, and cut the abbey's revenue by a quarter. How many of the townsfolk died is not known: one of the monks wrote that the plague had 'halved all flesh', and its impact nationally led to turmoil.

The surviving inhabitants of St Albans, like many of the other survivors throughout the realm, had attempted to make the most of the new conditions where too few people were available for too many jobs. As a result, wages rose until in 1351 the Statute of Labourers decreed that pay and prices should revert to what they had been before the Black Death. But the cost of living had risen and, though the pay clock could not be put back, resentment and discontent spread. In St Albans, the resentment is likely to have been reserved for the abbey's restrictive regulations as they affected tradesmen.

25 *The teazle, which now grows wild around St Albans, was cultivated from the 1330s for use by the town's clothiers as an indispensable means of giving their woollen cloths an even finish. Cloth manufacture throughout England could hardly have developed without this plant.*

A list dating from 1353 suggests a bustling town: four bakers, three taverners, seven hostellers, 11 butchers, 10 fishmongers, three cooked-meat sellers, six drapers, nine tailors, 14 tanners, eight skinners, one saddlemaker, 13 cobblers, two spicers, four smiths, four metalworkers, one plumber, 11 weavers, six fullers, five dyers, one cornmonger, two saltmongers and a thirst-defying 81 brewers. They occupied timbered properties, supported on low cill walls of flint bonded with clay and mortar, which lined the main streets. A few houses had upper storeys, two enjoyed the privilege of dovecotes and three at least of the houses were stone-built; south of the Ver lay a vineyard.

Flourishing around the same time was an author about whom little is known except that he claimed to have been born and educated in St Albans. Sir John Mandeville wrote *Travels*, a collection of travellers' tales to which he added imaginative adventures of his own, never letting the facts get in the way of a good story. He combined literary skill and creative imagination to provide a weary generation with an interlude of entertainment masquerading as information. It was none the less welcomed and heartily so, perhaps, by King John II of France who, taken prisoner in 1356 and held at the abbey, may have found life tedious between feasts at the abbot's table. By the time of the death of Edward III in 1377 the consequences of the plague and of the long war with France, which had brought defeat, forced the government to levy taxes harsher than ever before. The last straw, the imposition of a cruelly high poll tax in 1380, precipitated a widespread uprising in the following spring.

Observing and recording the uprising, Thomas Walsingham (d.1422), monk and chronicler at the abbey, described St Albans when it was in the grip of an unparalleled civic commotion. For a time it must have seemed to him and to the elated inhabitants that the town had broken free at last from the abbey's control and would enjoy the long-sought freedom.

The uprising had flared up in Essex, and spread quickly throughout Suffolk, Norfolk and Kent until by mid-June 1381 it had set alight the south-east, including Hertfordshire, and went on to generate outbursts in Dunstable, the Midlands and Cheshire. In St Albans, the uprising ignited when a large number of townsfolk, responding to a call from the rebels occupying London, set off for the capital at about one o'clock in the morning of Friday, 14 June. Led by William Grindcobbe, a property-owning townsman and resolute opponent of the abbey, they were joined at Barnet by more rebels and together they entered London alongside a contingent from Essex. Uppermost in the minds of the St Albans men, according to Walsingham, was 'how to achieve ancient aspirations, like new town boundaries, free pastures and fisheries, revival of lost sporting rights, freedom to establish handmills, the exclusion of the abbot's bailiff from the town limits and the return of bonds made by their sires to the late abbot Richard of Wallingford'.

Negotiations between ruler and ruled, including Grindcobbe, began immediately at Mile End. Richard II (1377-99), a fresh-faced, fair-haired 14-year-old advised by courtiers the rebels detested, promised to redress the grievances of St Albans and those of the other places involved. The royal promise did not save from the rebels' axe either Sir Robert Hales, the Treasurer, who was blamed for the poll tax or, having been judged equally responsible, the Chancellor, Simon Sudbury, Archbishop of Canterbury. Other prominent servants of the Crown, and foreigners, suffered similarly.

Grindcobbe, taking the king at his word, returned to St Albans with William Cadington, a baker, to prepare the town and abbey for the promised reforms. Among the rest of the returning rebels were those for whom there was no time like the present and they, without further delay, set about laying claim to their supposed rights. Down came the fences of enclosed abbey land; the proprietorial gates were broken. Assertive treatment likewise put paid to a house in St Albans owned by the abbey. Next morning, Saturday, 15 June, the energetic rebels, who had awoken refreshed after their 40-mile march to and from London, attempted to secure more reforms. They again demolished gates and fences before being joined by supporters from the surrounding countryside and together they confronted Abbot Thomas de la Mare (1349-96), producing as their warrant a letter from the king authorising the reforms.

Abbot de la Mare, a pastmaster of rhetoric, tried at first to confuse the rebels with legal objections and then, adopting a conciliatory tone, attempted to placate them with appeals to friendship. His eloquence was in vain and he had to surrender old charters, some of which were ceremoniously burnt, as well as allow the rebels the joyous revenge of ripping up the confiscated millstones from the floor of his own parlour. 'Smashing these,' wrote Walsingham, scandalised, 'they distributed fragments like holy bread in a parish church.' And, no doubt, revered them similarly.

But already the tide had turned in favour of the authorities. Wat Tyler, the overall leader of the rebels, had been killed during talks with King Richard at Smithfield. The disconcerted rebels, soothed by Richard, dispersed, although some continued to resist in East Anglia and

Kent until defeated by cavalry or, for smaller pockets of resistance, foot-soldiers. By the end of the month the uprising was over.

St Albans remained tranquil during the military actions and also while crowds of abbey tenants were in the town from, among other places, Redbourn, Watford, Abbots Langley, Sandridge, Tyttenhanger and Northaw to seek their own charter of rights from the abbot. The townsfolk of St Albans, having secured their charter on Sunday, 16 June, and trusting the king, had gone back to work unaware that a day of reckoning was near. In fact, Richard was making careful preparations. He appointed a Hertfordshire man, Sir Walter atte Lee, as a royal commissioner with the task of restoring to the abbey the surviving stolen charters, retrieving and cancelling the town's new charter and arranging for the leading rebels in St Albans to be punished. Lee's first move after arriving on 28 June was to appoint a jury whose job, he said, was to name those of their fellow townsmen guilty of wrong-doing. The jury refused to oblige and, for good measure, denied knowing the whereabouts of the stolen charters. Understandably, faced with such a reception, Lee planned his next move in secret: the arrest of Grindcobbe, Cadington and another of the leaders, John Barbour, who were taken under armed guard to prison in Hertford.

Angered by Lee's duplicity, the town erupted in a day of protest so threatening that Grindcobbe was released on bail for a week, although there was no doubt that he and his comrades were in great danger. Consequently, the townsfolk attempted to make restitution in an attempt to lessen the severity of the inevitable punishment, met the abbot and agreed to replace the millstones, rebuild the destroyed house and pay compensation to the abbey in return for which de la Mare promised not to complain to Richard and, should

26 *Memorial brass in the Cathedral and Abbey Church of St Alban of Abbot Thomas de la Mare (1349-96).*

the king persist in seeking retribution, to make every effort to secure pardons.

Richard entered St Albans on Friday, 12 July, at the head of an army and with, ominously, Sir Robert Tresilian, the Chief Justice of England. Two days later, John Ball of Colchester, a priest and spokesman of the rebels, was tried by Tresilian in the Moot Hall, and in the

27   The abbey gateway, built in 1362, had its gates opened by order of Abbot Thomas de la Mare to admit rebels in 1381. This photograph dates from the 1930s.

presence of Richard hanged, drawn and quartered on Monday, 15 July. On the same day, the town's charter was annulled, all the concessions were cancelled and protesters threatened with arrest. Grindcobbe and the other prisoners would have had no illusions about what to expect. Again the jury refused to indict until forced to do so by Tresilian, after which Grindcobbe, Cadington, Barbour and 12 more of the St Albans men were convicted of riot and hanged. Still there was resistance. A whispering campaign, in which the king and the abbot were, according to Walsingham, 'slandered', developed to the extent that a proclamation was issued threatening the men taking part with hanging and the women participants with burning.

Grindcobbe had remained defiant to the end: 'Fellow citizens,' he said before his execution, 'whom now a scanty liberty has relieved from long oppression, stand firm while you may, and fear nothing for my punishment, since I would die in the cause of the liberty we have won, if it is now my fate to die, thinking myself happy to be able to finish my life by such a martyrdom.'

There was more defiance. Richard had commanded that the bodies of the 15 hanged men should be left swinging on the gallows. Instead, the townsfolk took them down and gave them decent burial, whereupon Richard, 'amazed', ordered the bodies to be dug up and hung in chains for as long as they lasted. 'This reduced to a revolting slavery,' Walsingham gloated, 'the freedom-loving revolutionaries of St Albans, for none would do the work for them and with their own hands they had to hang up their fellow citizens whose decomposing bodies were full of maggots and stank.'

VI

Dangerous Times

INCIDENTS of arson, including the burning at Sandridge of a great barn filled with corn and the distribution of anonymous messages threatening the abbey with destruction, were an immediate aftermath of the crushed uprising.

Annoyed, perhaps, rather than alarmed, Abbot Thomas de la Mare turned his back on that disagreeable episode to concentrate on beautifying the abbey church. Aristocratic, well-connected, he had been admitted to the abbey when a youth, made progress in his vocation and was promoted steadily until after nine years as prior of Tynemouth he left that previously bankrupt house financially sound upon his unanimous election as abbot at St Albans. His efficient attention to administrative duty gradually improved abbey discipline as well as its finances, enabling him to increase the monks' allowances for food and drink while he himself lived in the grand style expected of a friend and confidant of kings. All the same, he found it compatible with his elevated status to supervise in person the care of the sick and to look after them with his own hands. At Redbourn Priory, which had settled into a kind of rest house for clergy, he built a new dormitory with rooms set aside for his own use during periods of quiet and study. But it was on the abbey, and on the abbey church especially, that he spent most freely for processional crucifixes, rich vestments, chalices of gold or silver, gilded candlesticks, crosses set with precious stones, silver censers with silver chains, silver patens, costly mitres, jewelled rings. The cascade of gifts continued: four books sumptuously illuminated, valuable ornaments for the shrine of St Alban, a devotional picture painted in Lombardy to hang over the great altar, velvet cushions for the choir, silver ewers, altar-cloths, tapestries.

And the people of St Albans, who kept clear in their minds what they loved and loathed about the abbey, freely gave their contributions. John Gale bequeathed his house in George Street for the use of the abbey's under-cook, John Pickborn gave a 'mansion' in French Row and two acres of land, Robert de la Chamore, his house opposite St Peter's Church, Agnes de Longford, her house in Sopwell Lane, Robert Heynot, his house in Romeland, Richard Eccleshall, his house on Holywell Hill and John Cheston gave three acres of woodland. There were also many gifts of money or plate.

Simultaneously, de la Mare had overseen the rebuilding of the abbey's great gatehouse, the replacement along part of the abbey's site of an earthern boundary bank with a stone wall easier to defend, the building of quarters for the abbey's copyists and, after the events of 1381, the laying down of new flooring at the abbey church's west end. In effect, the abbey's fame and fortune were fast approaching their height, but following the death of de la Mare, aged 88, expenditure started to exceed income, the famed monastic hospitality became a burden and the town, as usual, resumed hostilities.

The new abbot, John de la Moote (1396-1401), rebuilt the Benedictine college at Oxford and part of the abbey cloisters, but committed the abbey to the extravagance of

28 *French Row, a medieval street, is overlooked by the early 15th-century Clock Tower. This picture, dating from the 1920s, also shows a horse-drawn cart carrying a beer barrel.*

building a magnificent country house at Tyttenhanger which, having put the abbey deeply in debt, perforce was completed by his young and able successor, William Heyworth (1401-20). He cleared most of the debt by, among other devices, the well-tried expedient of living frugally at dependent priories, where he did not have to provide the kind of lavish hospitality he would as an abbot in his own abbey. He could not so nimbly avoid involvement in politics. Personally and socially, Church and State were intermingled, and Heyworth, as had his predecessor, supported the accession of Henry IV (1399-1413), whose claim to the throne rested on the consent of the clergy, the nobility and the commons, and their shared expectations of non-arbitrary, lawful government. The close involvement meant, for example, that by Henry's special request de la Moote had attended the secretive, midnight burial of Richard II at King's Langley in 1400 and that in 1403 Heyworth parted with a small fortune to supplement Henry's outgoings.

Below the surface, and out of sight most of the time, busy as moles, were critics of the established order whom that order had been swift to brand as heretics. Lollards, as they were called pejoratively from a Dutch word meaning 'mutterers', believed that the Church had become too wordly and that the world, as represented by the State, had become too churchy. It was a point of view likely to have attracted adherents in St Albans where, at a time when the heretics were spreading during the first decade of the 15th century, the townsfolk built the Clock Tower, or Curfew tower, in open defiance of the abbey and in its very shadow opposite the abbey's own Waxhouse Gate. Certainly, in 1414 there was a rumour that the Lollards intended to destroy the abbey at the first opportunity and some of the townsfolk, finding an opportunity to support the cause, helped hide near the town a Lollard leader, Sir John Oldcastle, until his discovery and arrest in 1417. Lollard tracts had already been widely distributed in St Albans, although vigorous persecution nationally and the distractions of a renewal by Henry V (1413-22) of the war with France, drove into hiding the forerunners of Protestantism.

The curfew bell itself, cast in 1335 and acquired for the tower from an unknown source, is inscribed: 'Missi de coelis habeo nomen Gabrielis'—'I bear heaven-sent Gabriel's name'. Ordinarily, such bells, known as Gabriel bells after the archangel who greeted the Virgin Mary, were rung to announce the thrice-daily recitation of the Angelus, which includes the 'Hail Mary' prayer. Worcester Cathedral has a similarly inscribed bell dating from the late 15th century.

Heyworth, appointed by the pope as Bishop of Lichfield, kept a soft spot for the abbey after leaving in 1420, sending from his Staffordshire cathedral costly gifts, including cloth of gold for the altar and 10 copes made of the same material. His successor as abbot, John Bostock, a renowned scholar and son of Hugh and Margaret Bostock of Wheathampstead, had studied at Oxford and was prior of the Benedictine college there before his election to the abbacy. Chosen by the English Benedictines in 1423 to represent them at a council of the Church in Italy, he visited Rome, met Pope Martin V and, returning to St Albans, undertook an extensive repair of the abbey and entirely re-built the west front. His friendship with Humphrey, Duke of Gloucester (1391-1447), youngest brother of Henry V, which had begun at Oxford, continued and the duke became a frequent visitor, sharing Bostock's love of books. Indeed, both men encouraged that fondness in others by giving books to libraries: Bostock to the college's library, Humphrey to the university's, a collection which formed the basis of today's Bodleian Library. The duke is buried on the south side of the Chapel of St Alban in the abbey church's only royal tomb, where he had arranged for the annual anniversary of his death to be marked by, among other observances, the paying of 13 poor men to hold commemorative torches.

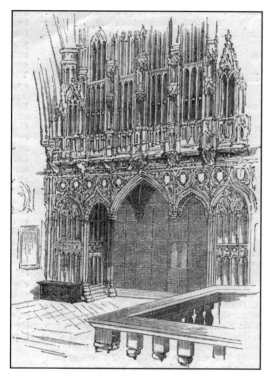

29 *The chantry chapel of Humphrey, Duke of Gloucester (1391-1447), brother of Henry V, is the only royal tomb in the abbey church of St Albans.*

Following Bostock's arrival there had been two severe domestic fires in the town. The first, in 1422, burnt down Lawrence West's house and the second, a year later, destroyed the house and goods of John Hale, a carpenter in Sopwell Lane. Their half-timbered buildings and those of their fellow citizens made St Albans as susceptible to fire as had been Verulamium. Bostock built houses: six in High Street, three opposite the abbey gatehouse, three in Fishpool Street. In spite of fires, the town was growing.

As usual, there was friction between the abbey and the townsfolk who, in 1424, claimed a right to pasture their cattle beside the lanes and roads around the town, but were told by Bostock that they had forfeited that right by having taken part in the uprising of 1381. Less contentiously, in 1425, Thomas Haines requested the abbot's permission to cut turfs at Bernard's Heath for the making of butts so that the town's young men could practise archery. On Nomansland Common in 1437 Bostock's tenants from Sandridge were exercising themselves by tearing down fences around enclosed land. Three years later Bostock astonished his brethren by resigning, blaming ill health, although his litigiousness and the abbey's debts were likely to have been contributory causes. In any case, tired of the responsibility of managing the abbey and its extensive properties, exhausted, too, by the strain of the numerous lawsuits in defence of its rights, he seems to have retired to

30 *The Antelope Inn, known earlier as the Tabard, originally was the abbey's great guesthouse and occupied a site on what is now the corner of Spicer Street and George Street. It was partially demolished in the 1840s.*

his Hertfordshire family home, Mackerye End, and was succeeded by the prior of Wallingford, John Stoke (1441-52).

An unfortunate choice, he failed to maintain monastic discipline, lacked financial acumen at a time when it was especially needed and was accused, unjustly, of being too ready to free his serfs when, in fact, serfdom itself was disappearing. His incompetence brought about in 1448 the priory of Wymondham's independence as a chartered abbey with the prior, Stephen London, formerly a monk at St Albans, elected as its first abbot. In St Albans, upon Stoke's death at Tyttenhanger, the monks unanimously re-elected Bostock to the abbacy.

By then an elderly man, Bostock entered his second term of office at a dangerous time. The Hundred Years' War with France was ending disastrously to be followed, in 1455, by the returned nobles and soldiers finding employment at home with the outbreak of a brutal dynastic struggle for the throne. Fought between descendants of Edward III in rival factions, Yorkist and Lancastrian, the first battle of the struggle (romanticised in the 19th century by Sir Walter Scott as 'The Wars of the Roses') was located in and around St Peter's Street on 22 May 1455. The troops of the mentally unstable Henry VI (1422-61) were routed by those of Richard Mortimer, Duke of York (1411-60). During the butchery a leader of the Lancastrians, Edward Beaufort, Duke of Somerset (b.c.1406), was killed by the Yorkists outside the *Castle Inn,* which stood at what is now the corner of Victoria Street and St Peter's Street. The aftermath for the victorious troops with their experience of the French wars was the plundering of St Albans. To the Yorkist victors went the spoils while the residents, indifferent to the dynastic struggle's outcome, and having witnessed horror in their own streets, had to endure the terror of the ransacking of their own dwellings. The abbey was spared due, in part, to Bostock

31   The George Inn, George Street, *dating from the early 15th century, closed early in the 20th century, although its premises have continued to be used for other purposes.*

plying the soldiers with food and wine. He was successful, too, in pleading for permission to bury the dead who, according to tradition, were buried in a long trench in St Peter's churchyard.

Henry, wounded in the neck with an arrow, sheltered in a baker's cottage until he was discovered and taken to the abbey before being removed to London. Six years later, after the second battle of St Albans on 17 February 1461, when the newly-introduced hand-guns were used, victory went to the Lancastrians, who promptly plundered both the town and the abbey, as well as the convents of St Mary de Pré and Sopwell. They robbed, assaulted and killed indiscriminately during their orgy of celebration. The next month the Yorkist claimant to the throne, Edward, the son of the recently killed Richard, Duke of York, having defeated the

32 Henry VI (1422-71) was taken prisoner at the second Battle of St Albans, 1461, murdered in 1471 and afterwards venerated as a saint for his undoubted piety. This portrait of him is from a late 15th-century rood screen in the parish church at Ludham, Norfolk.

Lancastrians in the North of England, was proclaimed king as Edward IV (1461-83) and Henry eventually was murdered in the Tower of London.

The cost to St Albans of the wars had been considerable and so were their effects. The town, suffering from the violent disruption of its life and trade, went into a brief period of decline. House-plots were left vacant on Romeland Hill. A house in Dagnall Street was demolished and its cellar filled with rubbish. In Chequer Street buildings were demolished or reduced in size. The abbey, too, found it hard to recover from the damages and losses caused by the fighting, had lost estates also and seen many of its tenants ruined. In desperation, Bostock petitioned Edward for help to prevent further impoverishment and, the old abbot hoped, to obtain restitution. In response, Edward did not supply money; instead, he did the next best thing: recognised the means by which the abbey raised money. He caused a charter, first granted in 1440, to be confirmed on 3 November 1461, which re-stated in clearer terms and rendered more effective 'divers liberties, franchises, privileges and immunities' to give the abbey the financial and judicial independence of what virtually amounted to a realm within a realm.

The charter's confirmation crowned Bostock's term of office and, full of years, his sight and hearing having failed, his hands crippled with arthritis, he died in 1465. A locally uneventful decade followed, during which his successor, William Alban, increased the abbey's holdings and continued to free its labourers from their servitude. Two men he freed in Sandridge were father and son: William and Robert Nash.

Alban, whose health had not been good, died in the summer of 1476 and was succeeded by the prior, William Wallingford (1476-92). A prudent abbot, he defended tenaciously the abbey's rights and privileges, and bequeathed as his enduring memorials a chantry chapel near the high altar and the magnificent high altar screen. It was during his abbacy, in 1480, that for the first time books were printed in St Albans by a teacher at the school, where it is probable that the press was housed. Altogether, eight books were printed, including one on pastimes, *The Book of St Albans*, before the press closed down in 1488. Five years earlier, the landlord of the *George and Dragon* in what is now George Street was given permission by Wallingford to use a room at the inn as a chapel where Mass could be celebrated for the convenience of guests. Others, perhaps, in the town would have wanted nothing to do with the chapel: an abbey commission had been set up in 1476 to examine heretics. Three years later, an entirely orthodox widow, Elizabeth Catherine Holstead, became the anchoress at St Peter's Church after a ceremony conducted by Wallingford himself.

'Anchorites' at St Peter's and St Michael's were left bequests of 12d. each in the will of John Ferrers dated 7 October 1488. He left the same sum to the high altars of St Andrew's and St Peter's, and 'To the nuns at Sopwell to pray for my soul, 6s. 8d., and to the shrine of St Alban, 3d. 4d.'. A hermit who lived beyond 'Sopwelmyll' received 12d. and 10s. was to be distributed among the poor on the day of the testator's burial.

At the abbey the 15th century drew to a close with a distinctive and harmonious flourish. Robert Fayrfax (1464-1521), the outstanding Lincolnshire-born composer, was appointed organist and in 1502 received 20s. for setting an anthem. Noted principally for his masses and motets, he also wrote secular music, including instrumental arrangements of jigs and hornpipes. He was buried in the abbey under a stone afterwards covered by the mayor's seat.

There had been an important civic change. At some time before the election to the abbacy of the prior, Thomas Ramryge (1492-1521), it appears that St Albans at last had slipped free of the abbey's close control and that townsmen, not abbey servants, were in the influential posts of town bailiff, representing the abbot, and clerk of the market. In fact, an embryonic town council had existed from the 15th century in the form of the Gild of All Saints. Founded to support two auxiliary chaplains in St Albans, it owned a great deal of land, as well as houses in St Peter's Street, Holywell Hill, Market Place and Fishpool Street. Its surplus revenue went to the poor while its members, all wealthy men, ran the town. Precisely when the municipal take-over occurred is not known.

For the abbey, and for religious houses throughout the country, land and offices were being rented out in an attempt to obtain a secure and stable income which, in St Albans, was not forthcoming. The income continued to drop until in 1519 the abbey fell into debt. Thereafter, in spite of the provisions of Edward IV's charter, a combination of the changing national economic circumstances, plus a widening disparity between the abbey's fixed income from too cheaply leased land and its increasing expenses, made financial recovery doubtful.

New times meant new men. One of them, John Ball, a master of the relatively novel skill of brickmaking who, like his father, shared the same name as a leader of the 1381 uprising, had his occupation proudly inscribed on the 1515 memorial brass to him, his wife and his parents in St Peter's Church:

Here lyeth John Ball brickemaker
which gave to the pson & wardens of
this chirch xs yerely for a ppetuall
obite to be kepte for the soulys of
hym & Elzabeth his wyf and John
Ball his fader & Chrstyan his moder

33 *Hall Place, a large house north of St Peter's Church cemetery, sheltered Henry VI (1422-61) before the first Battle of St Albans in 1455. It was demolished in 1904.*

& the said John deceased the xiii day of Octobre the yere of or Lord MVcXV on whose soules Jhu have mercy Amen.

Only during the previous century had brick come into general use in places, like St Albans, where local stone was scarce.

Scarce, too, were the occasions of untroubled rejoicing during the abbey's few remaining years. To begin with, when Ramryge was succeeded by Cardinal Thomas Wolsey (c.1475-1530) as an absentee abbot—although he did stay overnight in 1529—the dependencies of Wallingford Priory and the convent of St Mary de Pré were suppressed; likewise, too, had been 16 other small houses, to raise money for a college, later Christ Church, Wolsey had founded at Oxford. His fall from power in 1529 and, the following year, death, enabled Henry VIII (1509-47) to put pressure on the monks to elect the prior, Robert Catton, as abbot, 1531-38. By then the process had been set in motion which, as its final outcome, would leave all convents, priories and abbeys, such as St Albans, either demolished, ruined or in profane use.

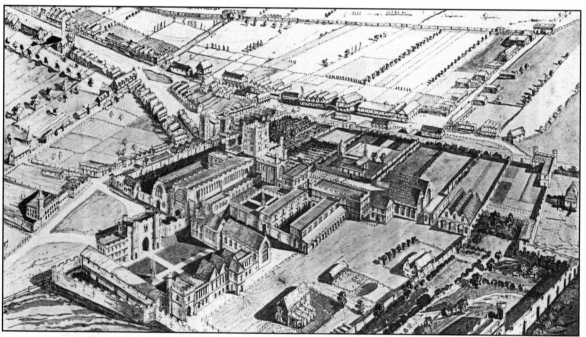

34 *St Albans Abbey as it may have appeared shortly before its suppression in 1539: a conjectural reconstruction by Charles W. Ashdown.*

There still was time during the rule of the last abbots to enjoy the traditional street celebrations and processions with which the Church's year was filled. In one of the processions two monks carried a large, hollow statue of St Alban. As long had been the custom, on its way back to the abbey it was rested at Market Cross and not lifted again until after the abbot, touching it with his crozier, had called, 'Arise, arise, St Alban, and get thee home to thy sanctuary.' The ritual gave a familiar and concluding flourish to the procession. No surprise was caused nor credulity induced by the statue's rolling eyes and nodding head because everybody knew that wires controlled the moving parts: indeed, naughty boys would sneak into the statue, when it stood unattended near the shrine, and play with the wires. Robert Shrimpton, who was mayor in 1588, 1595 and 1605, recollected that when 'young he had many times crept into the hollow part thereof'.

Changes

THE EVENTS leading to the suppression of the monasteries followed in quick succession. Henry's instrument for the plundering and destruction of them, and the taking of their associated properties, was his principal adviser, Thomas Cromwell (*c.*1485-1540). A lawyer, he pushed through Parliament the legislation authorising the suppression, and had in Abbot Catton an accomplice. However, before Cromwell made his frontal attack he obtained for a friend, William Cavendish, leases of abbey property on long and favourable terms in 1534. Two years later, in accordance with the new scheme of things, many traditional holidays were abolished, including that of St Alban on 22 June. From then on it was to be understood that making money would be better than making merry.

The suppression of the smaller monasteries, like Sopwell, Binham and Hertford, and the execution of defiant abbots, persuaded the survivors to yield, letting the king's representatives take everything. Thanks to Richard Boreman, who had been appointed abbot in 1538 on the king's recommendation, the expropriation at St Albans occurred without resistance or bodily injury on 5 December 1539. Boreman and the remaining 38 monks were pensioned: there was nothing for the abbey servants. Twelve days after the suppression the jewel encrusted silver-gilt reliquary of St Alban and the abbey's liturgical vessels made of precious metals were taken for the king's use. This financially valuable plunder amounted to more than 100 ounces of pure gold, 1,000 ounces of parcel gilt and silver and 3,000 ounces of gilt plate. The abbey's priceless

35 Misericord—a tip-up seat with a ledge to rest on when standing: one of the 27 in All Saints' Church, Leighton Buzzard, supposed to have been salvaged from St Albans Abbey after 1539.

collection of books went to the king's library while the delicately carved marble pedestal, on which the reliquary had rested, was destroyed and its fragments used to block arches in the abbey church. The relics of St Alban were taken, some believe, to Cologne.

The next part of the suppression called for the demolition of the monastic buildings and the selling for ready money of whatever could be salvaged. The man of that moment was a professional soldier and military engineer, Sir Richard Lee (c.1513-75). Thanks to his wife, who had winning ways, the king in 1540 granted Sopwell to Lee and St Julian's to Lee's brother, Thomas. Lee himself obtained the grant of the abbey, excluding the abbey church and the great gateway, and helped himself to the stone as it became available to re-build Sopwell as his own Lee Hall. Disliking the nearness of the then London Road, he diverted it and enclosed his park with more stone from the sledge-hammered abbey.

Wars intervened. For the first time in 30 years English soldiers were fighting in France and Scotland, and to Scotland went Lee. His chance came in 1544 after Leith and Edinburgh had been partly burnt and Edinburgh plundered. Among the spoils was a bronze eagle lectern, previously belonging to a bishop of Dunkeld, which Lee generously presented to St Stephen's, and an embossed brass font taken from Holyrood Abbey, which he gave to the abbey church. Vainly describing himself as 'Lee the conqueror', he attached an inscription to the font:

> When Leith, a town of good account in Scotland, and Edinburgh, the principal city of that nation, were on fire, Sir Richard Lee, knight, saved me out of the flames, and brought me into England. In gratitude for this his deliverance, I who heretofore served only at the baptism of the children of kings, do now most willingly offer the same service even to the meanest of the English nation. Lee the conqueror hath so commanded. Farewell.

A century later the font disappeared during the Civil War (1642-51). The lectern, buried for safety in St Stephen's churchyard, was re-discovered in the 18th century and returned to the church, from where its theft in 1985 was blamed on Scottish nationalists.

Among those like Lee in the scramble to secure possession of the abbey's estates were Sir Ralph Rowlett, a merchant and tenant of the former abbey, Sir Richard Pope, who acquired Tyttenhanger, and Sir Nicholas Bacon, who eventually obtained Gorhambury. Both Bacon and Pope had worked amicably together in the suppression of the monasteries and Cromwell's friend, William Cavendish, increased his holdings by obtaining Northaw as well as the manor of Childwick. A John Cox obtained Redbourn Priory.

Little more remained to be done. Zealots during the next hundred years smashed most of what was left of the abbey's statues and stained glass, and defaced its wall paintings along with the paintings and stained glass in the town's three other churches.

So great and violent had been the changes, and so upsetting, that offerings of money at St Peter's decreased to such an extent that the parishioners had to be compelled by law in 1548 to pay as they had in the past. Something remarkable then happened. Instead of trying to save the conveniently sized St Andrew's chapel, which adjoined the abbey church's north-west corner and served the town centre parish, and despite the long years of friction between the town and the abbey, the mayor, John Lockey, and the burgesses accepted Edward VI's offer in 1553 and bought for £400 the recently vandalised and inappropriately vast abbey church to serve the parish and let the chapel crumble. But, as at St Peter's, the parishioners begrudged opening their purses.

In the same year (1553) the king granted the town a charter which, at no cost to the Crown, provided the legal basis for the establishment of a local authority to maintain order

36   The remains of the cloisters on the south side of the abbey church's nave.

37   The Fighting Cocks *public house, originally a pigeon house in the grounds of St Albans Abbey, was re-located around 1600 to its present site at the foot of Abbey Mill Lane. This postcard illustration dates from c.1906.*

in place of the confusion that had followed the suppression of the abbey and to fill the vacuum caused by the consequent abolition of the Gild of All Saints. The charter defined the borough boundaries, stipulated the appointment of council officers and nominated 10 of the 'discreeter and better men' as assistants to help supervise the town's day-to-day affairs alongside the mayor, who also was the clerk of the market. The council is, at first, likely to have met in the Moot Hall, which stood on a site now occupied by the old Town Hall, but soon a timber-framed, up-to-date Town Hall—now W.H. Smith & Son—was built. The citizens were represented nationally by two Members of Parliament. Markets on Wednesdays and Saturdays were confirmed as well as three fairs a year. St Albans had become re-organised. And part of the binding of the council's earliest minute book was a page taken from an illuminated missal: a pathetic reminder of the recent past and fortunate not to have been re-used as wrapping paper or worse.

38   *The Holyrood lectern, St Stephen's Church.*

39 *(below)*   *The ruins of Lee Hall, Sopwell.*

The demands of law and order were served further by magistrates taking over the great gateway as the town's prison. The abbey church's Lady Chapel, cut off by parallel walls of a north-south passageway driven through the church, eventually was handed over to house St Albans School. Its location combined education with eradication as the innovators detested the devotion to the Virgin Mary and sought to suppress it in the town by a requisitional sleight-of-hand.

Religious policy veered again with the accession of Mary I (1553-58) who, nevertheless, found that too much of the Church land and property had gone, in St Albans and elsewhere, for the clock of faith to be put back completely. As a Catholic, she had hoped to revive the abbey, but the extent of the demolition and the unrecoverable loss of its holdings compelled her to abandon that hope.

Outside the abbey's great gateway, and within sight of the ruins, a young Yorkshireman, George Tankerfield, died

40   The Lady Chapel, walled off from the rest of the abbey church in the 16th century, housed St Albans School until 1871.

bravely at the stake on 26 August 1555 for being a Protestant. A cook in London, he was brought from Newgate to St Albans, lodged at the *Cross Keys Inn* and martyred in Romeland. Since nobody from St Albans suffered martydom during that period of persecution, the townsfolk apparently were no more willing to die for the new faith than they had been to put their money into its collecting plates.

41   Death by burning: a 19th-century depiction.

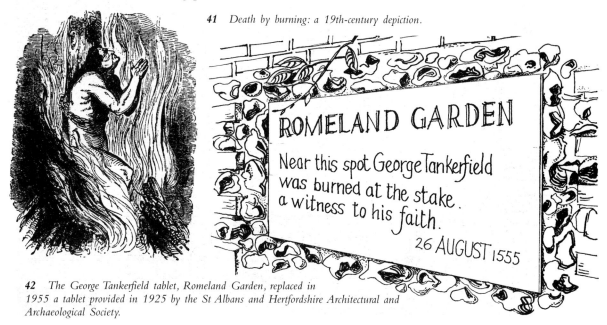

ROMELAND GARDEN

Near this spot George Tankerfield was burned at the stake. a witness to his faith.

26 AUGUST 1555

42   The George Tankerfield tablet, Romeland Garden, replaced in 1955 a tablet provided in 1925 by the St Albans and Hertfordshire Architectural and Archaeological Society.

Money mattered to the Crown. A need for greater efficiency in the handling of its financial resources, and to have those resources of land and property clearly listed, resulted in the so-called Marian survey of 1556 which, for St Albans, recorded the size and general appearance of the town.

Several houses stood between Sandpit Lane and St Peter's Church, including the medieval Hall Place. On the green south of the church, a duck pond caught the eye before Cock Lane (Hatfield Road) was reached where, eastwards, lay the parish pound for stray animals. Westwards, along Catherine Street, were many houses. The gardens of the houses on the east side of St Peter's Street stretched down to the borough boundary, Tonmanditch, in which men and boys practised archery. The *Castle Inn* still occupied the corner of St Peter's Street and Shropshire Lane (Victoria Street), and in Chequer Street, the site of the malt market, were houses previously used by abbey officials. In Dagnall Street there were a 'good number' of houses. There were, too, several houses in French Row, where the nuns of St Mary de Pré had owned a walled garden, and the *Fleur de Lys Inn* with, next door, the *Great Red Lion*, itself bordered by the *Peacock*.

Along the facing road, called the Vintry (High Street), houses on either side continued to Church Street (George Street) where, on the corner of Spicer Street, an abbey guest house had become the *Tabard Inn* and would later be known as the *Antelope*. Further west, curving down to St Michael's, sloped Fishpool Street with its inns and houses on the route leading through St Michael's village to Redbourn and the Midlands.

Most notably of the town's other inns, on the east side of Holywell Hill, whose properties also stretched back to the boundary ditch, were the *Cross Keys*, the *Peahen*, the *Wool Pack*, the *Saracen's Head*, the *White Hart* and the *Dolphin*. The last sign referred to a fourth-century martyr, St Lucien of Antioch, whose soul, according to legend, Christ himself had taken to heaven. Pilgrims staying at the *Dolphin* would have known the meaning of the sign and been reassured. The corner of Holywell Hill and Sopwell Lane, the entrance to the town from London, was dominated by another former guest house for pilgrims, called in 1556 the *Crane Inn,* and now the city's best preserved medieval inn.

Some of the townsfolk still found cause to be reassured, if forlornly, during Mary's reign. Henry Gape, a prosperous tanner and member of a family destined to become prominent, bequeathed a house on Holywell Hill 'to the abbey of St Albans, if it fortune to be made an abbey again or a house of prayer'. It did not fortune as three months after Gape's will, which was dated 28 August 1558, Mary died and with her any chance of the abbey's restoration.

Other well-off citizens remembered the poor. Richard Raynshaw in 1560 left three cottages in Spicer Street adjoining his house, *The Vine*, for the use of 'such honest poor persons as should seem most in need of charity'. In 1579 Thomas Lathbury left a house next to the Clock Tower and another in Dagnall Street for the 'proper use and behoof of the poor people of St Albans'. Thomas and Margaret Hall left nine acres of land at Kingsbury in 1581-82 to give 80 of the poorest in the town 6d. each on Good Friday and Palm Sunday every year. They also left £2 a year to St Albans School.

The school's survival had been precarious. Indeed, after the abbey's suppression it seems to have been closed because the town charter of 1553 authorised the setting up of the school 'within the said church of St Albans or in another convenient place', and put the responsibility for its running and financing on the shoulders of the mayor and burgesses. On the other hand, the charter's mention of the school could have been by way of giving recognition to an already existing, but shaky, establishment. Whatever the case, the real turning point came in 1570 when

Elizabeth I (1558–1603), while staying at Gorhambury House, the home of a favourite, Sir Nicholas Bacon (1510–79), granted his humble petition for a scheme to help pay for the school and the salary of its headmaster. The monies were to be raised from the proceeds of allowing each of 'two discreet and honest persons dwelling within the borough of St Albans' to sell wine and keep a tavern. The privilege was extended early in the following century and lasted until the first quarter of the twentieth.

Elizabeth's favourite, who was Lord Keeper of the Great Seal, helped the school further by drawing up its regulations. The number of pupils was to be no more than 120. Poor men's children were to be accepted first and they would not have to pay the entry fee of 12d. towards 'the repairing of the said school'. Each boy had, though, to be equipped with ink, paper, pens, candles for winter and 'all things at any time requisite and necessary for the maintenance of his study'. The boys were expected to be at their desks from 6a.m. (7a.m. in winter) to 11a.m. and from 1p.m. to 5p.m., except on Saturdays and half holidays, when they could leave at 3p.m. A further stipulation was that each boy should exercise by practising archery and for that purpose needed a bow, three arrows, bow-strings, a shooting-glove and a bracer.

Sometimes rules seemed easier to ignore than to obey. Five men were reported for making a dunghill in Market Place in 1587 and four during the same year were ordered to stop their illegal brewing and selling of strong ale. On 3 March 1587 the town council ruled that the wages of servants, workmen and labourers should remain the same as the previous year and, in November, it instructed the alehouse keepers to sell beer and ale, 'strong and of the best', at three pints for a penny. One of the alehouse keepers, Richard Holland, had his licence withdrawn in February 1588 for 'keeping ill-rule' in his house by allowing 'men to play and banquet upon the Sabbath and Holy Days in time of Divine Service'. Earlier in the year there had been a wave of inconsiderate behaviour: a baker was fined two shillings for leaving a dead horse in Dagnall Street, Thomas Gill left a log outside his house, James Lockey left ashes, John Smith, timber, while John Thompson, Richard Winter and widow Peck made dunghills in Dagnall Street.

A woman 'likely to become a mother', although having found shelter with a joiner, was ordered in April 1588 to 'forthwith quit the borough' so as not to risk being made 'chargeable to the town'. The abbey gone, its charity ended, times could be hard for the poor and the unfortunate. But the municipal heart had not been turned into stone. Firewood was bought for the poor and, at the same time, the council bought equipment to teach them to spin and make worsted. A Dutchman, Anthony Moner, undertook to teach poor children how to spin and, after six weeks of instruction, pay them for their work.

The threat of invasion as the outcome of years of hostility between England and Spain caused the town council to raise money by selling more than three thousand pounds of lead stripped from the abbey church roof for the making of bullets. What replaced the lead is not known. St Albans also paid for the sending of 52 armed men to a great camp at Tilbury, where Elizabeth reviewed the main body of her army in August 1588 after her navy had scattered Spain's mighty invasion fleet into the North Sea and beyond.

For St Albans, the Spanish Armada's conclusive defeat marked the end of alarms and the start of half a century when municipal rather than national preoccupations were uppermost. There still were excitements, such as the holding in the town of the Michaelmas term of the Assize Court in 1594, when residents who refused to contribute towards its setting up were fined. Residents in 1594 were ordered under penalty by the town council to evict poor strangers because, due to the increase in poverty, charity had to begin at home: parishes were being compelled by law to help their own poor, not those from other parishes.

More regulations were invoked in September 1595 when some bakers sold underweight white and wheaten loaves, but it was the alehouse keepers who, once again, caused complaints in 1606. The minutes of the council for 11 April state:

> It was reported that the ale houses and tippling-houses were the cause of much drunkenness and looseness, many people keeping such houses without licence, making proper control impossible. The trade of brewing was also being so extensively carried on in the Borough that the increased consumption of wood caused the price of fuel to be yearly augmented.

It was decided by the virtuous and, maybe, shivering members of the town council that something had to be done: much drunkenness meant less work. 'It was therefore resolved,' the minutes continue, 'that there should be in the future only four beer brewers and two ale brewers in the town.' A fine of 40s. and the forfeiture of the brew was the penalty to be inflicted upon any person breaking the order. And the six men appointed by the council as the money-making brewers included four of themselves, who happened to be the town's most recent mayors.

Far outshining the notable Nicholas Bacon was his son, Francis Bacon (1561-1626) who, when in residence at Gorhambury, made it seem, according to John Aubrey, the 17th-century antiquary and biographer, 'as if the court were there, so nobly did he live'. His sense of style found masterly expression in his *Essays* and other writings, but it was his pioneering of a modern scientific approach for 'the relief of man's estate' that secures him his place in history. A lawyer, courtier, statesman and philospher, he was appointed Lord Chancellor and

Baron Verulam in 1618, was created Viscount St Albans, and fell from power in 1621, spending his final years writing some of his most valuable works. In the same year as his fall he moved from the house built by his father at Gorhambury to one of his own design, Verulam House, located in the north-east corner of the family estate near Bow Bridge on the road to Redbourn. Its remarkable originality and elegance did not save it from demolition around 1657, although the low-lying site may have made it damp and, therefore, unattractive. Bacon's assistant in its building was, wrote Aubrey, 'a Mr Dobson' of St Albans, 'a very ingenious person ... but he spending his estate luxuriously upon women, necessity forced his son William Dobson (1610-46) to be the most excellent painter that England has yet bred'. A portrait painter, his finest works are highly original interpretations of the Baroque style. An alabaster memorial statue of Bacon in St Michael's Church, showing him as he used to sit, was erected by his 'faithful friend and secretary', Sir Thomas Meautys, who died in 1649 and

43 *The life-like statue of Francis Bacon (1561-1626) in the chancel of St Michael's Church was erected by his 'faithful friend and secretary', Sir Thomas Meautys.*

44 *The Pemberton almshouses, opposite St Peter's Church, were founded in 1627 by Roger Pemberton, High Sheriff of Hertfordshire, for six poor women. The engraving dates from the 18th century.*

is buried in the chancel. Bacon's burial place is unknown: he had asked to be buried in the church and there is no reason to suppose that he was not.

As for the drinking establishments surviving the imposition of 'proper control', they were not necessarily safer places. Several people 'suffered much hurt' during 1613 after falling into an open cellar at the *Horseshoe*, in Sopwell Lane. Greater and grander falls inspired James Shirley (1596-1666), the headmaster of St Albans School during the 1620s, to write in the first stanza of a cautionary song:

> Sceptre and Crown
> Must tumble down,
> And in the dust be equal made
> With the poor crooked scythe and spade.

He himself took care to prevent the school's Lady Chapel home from tumbling down by undertaking extensive repairs before leaving to achieve success in London as a poet and dramatist. His departure was prompted, it is said, by his conversion to Catholicism, which coincided with a period of missionary activity by a Benedictine monk and priest, Alban Roe (1583-1642), whose own conversion to Catholicism had begun in St Albans and who, later, was imprisoned in the town for his faith. His execution at Tyburn led to his canonisation. Shirley expressed especial admiration for the Benedictines in *The Grateful Servant*, a play registered in 1629, and it has been concluded that his confessor belonged to the Order. Another of Shirley's plays was a tragedy, *St Albans*, dating from around 1639.

At that time all the crafts and occupations in the town were grouped together in four companies for mutual protection against outside or unauthorised competitors and to uphold standards. A generation later the number of companies was reduced to two: mercers (textile dealers) and innholders. Under those two headings is to be found a roll-call of the town's diverse traders. As well as mercers there were drapers, haberdashers, tailors, dyers, cloth-workers, weavers, glovers and shoemakers. Vintners, apothecaries and barbers provided specialist services. For building work and maintenance there were glaziers, plumbers, bricklayers and tilers. Tinkers, pewterers and braziers mended or made metal hardware of every kind. There

45   Map of St Albans, 1634.

were coopers and carpenters. Bows and arrows were made, and cutlery. There were innholders, tanners, curriers, tallow chandlers, ropers, saddlers and smiths, and bakers, brewers, butchers, cheesemongers, fishmongers and victuallers.

The agreed standards of quality were upheld by tasters whose duty it was to inspect flesh and fish, and other foods. Leather goods were examined for sufficient tanning and preparation. The price of bread, beer, ale, wine and all other victuals could be fixed by the mayor but, in order to protect the town's tradesmen, no outsiders, except victuallers, were allowed to sell goods unless on fair days.

Of the greatest importance in the economic life of the town and the county were the main roads. John Norden in *A Description of Hertfordshire* (1598) implicitly includes St Albans when writing of the benefits brought to the county 'by thoroughfares to and from London northwards ... that maketh the markets to be better furnished with such necessaries as are requisite for Inns for the entertainment of travellers'.

Norden's observations held true in 1637 when the mayor and burgesses petitioned Parliament for St Albans to be excused the payment of a tax because of hardship: 'The town

46 *The cover of an order of service at the Cathedral and Abbey Church of St Alban on the occasion of the 350th anniversary of the death of Alban Roe.*

47 *Trade tokens issued in St Albans during the 17th century included those of, second from top, Henry Gladman, landlord of the George and Dragon; fourth, Thomas Hudgson, corndealer; fifth, Ralph Bradbury, grocer; seventh, John Cowlee, baker; eighth, Richard Finch, of the Swan.*

consists chiefly of inns and victual houses, who drive a trade upon the travelling of passengers, but have had no trade this year, by reason of London having been so grievously visited with the plague.' The decline was temporary and by the same year a regular coach service was running between St Albans and London; from 1657 the long-distance coach became part of everyday life for the town's innkeepers and their staffs.

Like other people, especially the poorer, they long had had to endure the inconvenience of a national shortage of small change until, from 1648, exasperated tradesmen tackled the currency problem by issuing tokens of their own in nearly every town and most large villages in England. Not until 1672 did the Royal Mint begin to issue a copper coinage of farthings and halfpence. In St Albans, among those who issued trade tokens were the landlords of the *Swan*, in Market Place, and the *George and Dragon*, in George Street.

VIII

Civil War

A MAJORITY of the influential men in St Albans, as in the rest of Hertfordshire, had decided before the outbreak of the Civil War in August 1642 to side with the Parliamentarians rather than with Charles I (1625-49). In fact, when it came to the making of a political decision most people in the town and in the county had little or no say, but were expected to grin and uncomplainingly bear the consequences of their betters' decisions, as often they did during the war, when its heaviest burdens fell on them: higher prices, food shortages, compulsory military service (frequently unpaid or with pay long in arrears) and higher taxes. It had not, maybe, mattered to most of the uninfluential people that Charles' taxes had tended to fall unfairly on the better-off whereas, under the Parliamentarians, taxes fell equally on rich and poor alike. Even so, whether or not support for the Parliamentarians was great or small, there were too many different strands in that support, locally and nationally, for it ever to pull other than in separate ways. Policy decisions went to those groups able to pull hardest.

There had from the start in Hertfordshire been outright opposition to the Parliamentarians. Despite the county's declared allegiance, Royalists remained strongly loyal in and around Hertford, Ware, Royston and Hitchin. Sir Arthur Capel, the Member of Parliament for Hertford, died bravely for the king. There were prominent Royalists in St Albans. The mayor, William New, remembering perhaps that 10 years earlier the king had granted the town a valuable charter, and John Howland, the steward (a sort of town clerk), were each imprisoned for their loyalty to the Crown. On the other hand, two well-off Parliamentarians in the town, Alban Cox, who died in 1665, and John Marsh, undertook respectively to train volunteer horsemen and foot soldiers.

Cox, a close friend and political ally of the Parliamentarians' eventual 'chief of men', Oliver Cromwell (1599-1658), became the Member of Parliament for St Albans, served on various local committees during and after the Civil War, regulated the town's religious affairs and successfully repudiated an accusation of having prevented his opponents from voting in the election of 1656.

Successful, too, was a Parliamentarian vicar at St Peter's during the middle of the war: he smashed the medieval stained-glass windows of which he disapproved. Had that church, in the eyes of such a zealot, merited special attention? After all, up until the end of the previous century its churchwardens had refused to part with vestments and sacred vessels obviously dating from Catholic times. Unsmashed, the windows also were reminders of those times, their survival hinting at a hankering for things past. Did it further enrage the iconoclast to wonder if pilgrims still went to Redbourn to pray at the reputed site of Amplibalus' martyrdom and cut pieces of bark from the place's venerated tree to keep as holy relics? 'Many papists' used to go there, 'as lately my own eyes saw,' according to John Shrimpton in his *Antiquities* (c.1631). And had not St Albans harboured Alban Roe, a Benedictine monk and priest hanged, drawn and quartered for his faith shortly before the outbreak of the war?

The war had begun with a bad omen for St Albans. The town was on a route taken in October 1642 by a Parliamentary army which, although itself well-disciplined, foreshadowed the permanent risk of the looting associated with most armies when on the march. A month later that risk was acknowledged by the commander of the Parliamentary army, Robert Devereux, Earl of Essex, who ordered his officers and men to prevent the plundering of Gorhambury House. Thereafter, Parliamentary forces in good and in bad order appeared time and again in St Albans and throughout Hertfordshire. Free quarters had to be provided for the men and their horses. In St Albans, taxes were levied to support the army, prisoners had to be supported out of the public purse, as were sick soldiers when the need arose. Money also had to be found for the town's defences: 'Paid to three men for six days' work done at the town's [north] end,' recorded the mayor's accounts for 1642-43, 'and for mending up the forts there at the rate of tenpence a day ...'.

Early in 1643 those defences were breached effortlessly by the High Sheriff of Hertfordshire, Sir Thomas Coningsbury who, accompanied by other gentlemen, rode into Market Place, where he read a proclamation from Charles offering an amnesty to all who would no longer fight against him. Before anybody could take advantage of the offer Cromwell himself appeared at the head of a troop of horsemen, arrested Coningsbury and took him prisoner to London. Shortly afterwards, perhaps with half an eye on the prevention of further royal blandishments being made public in the town, Parliament installed a garrison in St Albans as an outpost on the northern approaches to London.

Other trouble already had broken out. A Hertfordshire petition to Parliament, presented in January 1643, sought protection for property owners throughout the county 'from the violence and fury of all unruly and dissolute multitudes who endeavour to raise themselves by the ruin of your petitioners'. The alarmist language—'multitudes'—suggests that lowly people had taken to heart, and were trying to achieve, the proclaimed cause of both sides in the war: liberty. But it was plain that liberty meant different things to different people. Sometimes, the lowly people's methods could be direct. In May, 'disorderly, rude persons' at Shenley, near St Albans, removed the gates on common land enclosed by Edward Wingate, a brave captain in the Parliamentarian army.

Matters were not improved when Parliament in July imposed a new system of taxation, excise, on a range of goods, including ale, beer and cider. In December the discontent was such that 300 starving soldiers threatened to pillage St Albans on a market day, but were persuaded to disperse by the Earl of Essex. In February 1644 Hertfordshire civilians retaliated with a petition to Parliament against 'the intolerable burden of Free Quarters of many Horse and Foot'. In May 1646 some two thousand tenant farmers in Bedfordshire and Hertfordshire, among them the names of prominent St Albans families, signed a petition to Parliament against the payment of tithes to the Church of England. Liberty, members of the House of Commons presumably concluded, did not mean licence. 'Tenants,' they quavered, 'who wanted to be quit of tithes would soon want to be quit of rent.' The price of bread doubled.

By the end of 1647 maimed soldiers had been dismissed from the Parliamentary army to beg for a living and those remaining had become mutinous through lack of pay: 10 were jailed in St Albans. But the discontent continued. Victims of the war, people uprooted by it or the dismissed soldiers, wandered in search of work, coming to St Albans, where some were welcomed and where, if undetected long enough by the authorities, they might become entitled to financial assistance from the borough. Accordingly, in July 1647, the town council 'ordered that in future no stranger, be he journey-man or servant, single or married, should remain in the Borough longer than six days without giving an account of himself to the

Mayor.' The officers of the Borough were directed to apprehend strangers and bring them before the Mayor to be sent back to the place of their abode. If they wished to stay they had to procure sureties to prevent the Borough becoming chargeable for them. Every townsman lodging a stranger longer than six days was to be fined 2s. a day for such time as the stranger stopped. The hard times had produced hard rules.

Already that summer Sir Thomas Fairfax, the commander of Parliament's New Model Army, had arrived with the army in St Albans, from where he forwarded to the House of Commons yet another Hertfordshire petition of grievances. Still, for the time being the fighting had finished, and Fairfax's immediate task was to arrange for a party of troopers to go to Royston to bring back the king who, having been handed over to his enemies by the Scots, was being held by the army in the hope of securing a negotiated settlement. Charles rode through St Albans to cheers and the ringing of church bells. It was the last time they would ring for him because the fighting resumed in the spring of 1648 and, less than a year later, he was beheaded.

Before then, 3,000 of his soldiers, taken prisoner in August 1648 after the New Model Army's siege of Colchester, were marched, starving, bare footed and in their shirts, to St Albans and other towns in Hertfordshire. Those who fainted on the road were instantly shot dead. In St Albans they were locked in St Peter's Church and given bread and cheese, for which the townsfolk paid. Then, like their comrades held elsewhere in Hertfordshire, and from which county many of them had volunteered to fight for the king, the prisoners of war were marched off to the ports of the West Country and sold as slaves for the American plantations or the galleys of Venice.

Understandably, the desire for peace ran deep. 'Wearied and wasted with civil war,' wrote Thomas Fuller in *Good Thoughts in Worse Times* (1647), 'we that formerly loathed the manna of peace, because common, could now be content to feed on it, though full of worms and putrified.'

The achievement of a lasting peace, in the opinion of the officers of the New Model Army, meeting in St Albans in November 1648, required the bringing to trial of the king and, as a likely outcome, his execution. Charles' fate was sealed at that meeting in the form of an indictment, called a remonstrance, which, after discussions held in the abbey church, was drawn up at an informal meeting in the *Bull Inn* on Holywell Hill.

There is no record of any protest in St Albans against the king's execution, but three of the county's influential men, among them Alban Cox, examined three Berkhamsted men who had denounced the killing of the king. In June of the same year, 1649, following the failure of the previous year's harvest and consequent widespread hunger and unemployment, the war-weary people of St Albans openly incited soldiers to mutiny and there were riots. The authorities, following many precedents in the Parliamentarians' heartland of East Anglia, provided an entertaining diversion for the townsfolk by hanging Elizabeth Knott and John Palmer as 'notorious witches'.

The war went on until, in 1651, the defeat of a Royalist army at Worcester on 3 September brought about peace and left Cromwell secure as head of a military dictatorship and England a republic. He is unlikely to have endeared himself to St Albans, along with other towns, when in 1652 its charter, granted by Charles 20 years earlier, was revoked in an attempt to purge whatever was left of Royalist control. In the circumstances it is hardly surprising that support for the regime, as for the original Parliamentarians, did not become comprehensive or stay constant, and Cromwell's death in September 1658 was followed by the opening of secret negotiations for a restoration of the monarchy in the person of Charles II (1660-85).

48   *Abbey church passageway entrance, Sumpter Yard, c.1870.*

Taking part in the negotiations was Sir Harbottle Grimston (1603-85), an eminent lawyer and a life-long Member of Parliament for various Essex constituencies, who at first had supported the Parliamentarians as a moderate. Disliking the radical element, he had retired into private life and, after marrying Anne, the widow of Thomas Meautys and a niece of Francis Bacon, acquired Gorhambury in 1652, from where he thereafter kept an eye on St Albans while, at the same time, taking part in matters of national importance. His big moment came when General George Monck, who had fought for Parliament in Ireland and Scotland, stayed in St Albans at the head of an army before entering London in February 1660 to ensure that political conditions would favour the restoration. To further his preparations, Monck enabled Grimston to be elected to the Council of State and in April 1660 Grimston was chosen as Speaker of the House of Commons. Charles was quickly invited to return to England as king. Grimston accompanied the king home from the Dutch town of Breda, later delivering an address of welcome noted for its fulsome and servile tone. His reward that winter was the Mastership of the Rolls of the Court of Chancery. Around the same time he entered into an agreement with gamekeepers in St Albans to keep him supplied with partridge at the rate of 60 brace a year.

Charles II's restoration was welcomed publicly in St Albans at celebrations during which beer and Spanish wine flowed. One innkeeper alone supplied two gallons of sack, another provided wine and tobacco, a third, a gallon of sack, a fourth, a barrel of beer and a fifth, two barrels of beer. In London, people drank the king's health upon their knees in the street which, wrote Samuel Pepys, 'methinks is a little too much'.

But not everybody was happy drinking a health unto his Majesty. Some Protestant nonconformists found that they had little to celebrate: the Cromwellian days of a limited religious toleration were over and, for the new Parliament, religious conformity was what mattered. In the official mind, nonconformity implied, at best, disloyalty or, at worst, treachery. After all, had not sectarians like Baptists and Congregationalists been militant supporters of the Parliamentarians? 'We shall be glad to think them true Englishmen,' wrote John Dryden in the Preface to his poem *A Layman's Faith* (1682), 'when they obey the King, and true Protestants when they conform to the Church Discipline.' To help them conform Parliament restored to the Church of England a position of unchallenged authority in a series of punitive Acts. The Corporation Act of 1661 limited membership of municipal councils to communicating members of the Church of England. The following year, the Act of Uniformity required, among other things, ordination by a bishop for all ministers of religion. As a result, nationally, around two thousand nonconformist clergy were driven from their livings, 57 of them from parishes in Hertfordshire, including the Rev. William Haworth, the minister at St Peter's, St Albans.

His ejection, coupled with the death of a member of his erstwhile congregation, set in motion a train of events which culminated in a tragedy. On 4 May 1662, Elizabeth, the wife of Charles Turrill, was buried in the graveyard at St Peter's, but the new incumbent refused to let Haworth preach at the graveside. Not to be thwarted, Haworth and the mourners decided to hold a memorial service at the abbey church where, rather than risk causing a disturbance inside, they assembled quietly in the walled passageway at the east end. A hymn was sung, the Scriptures read and a prayer offered when, as Haworth started to give his memorial address, an angry officer of the militia, Major Edward Crosby, strode forward, calling the mourners 'rogues' and 'rebels'.

'Why prate you there?' he shouted at Haworth. 'Come down, or I will pull you down.'

'If,' replied the minister, 'you have any authority to command me down, I will obey it, but otherwise, no.'

49 *Abbey church passageway interior, c.1800.*

50 *Waxhouse Gate Lane, leading from High Street to the passageway through the Abbey Church of St Albans, c.1870.*

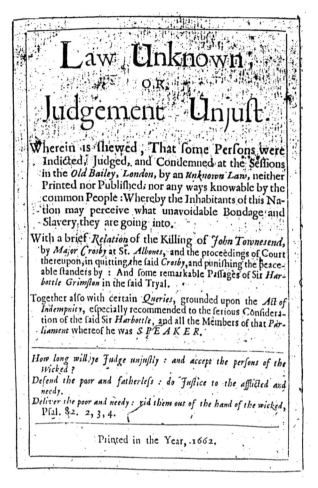

51 *The cover of a pamphlet about John Townsend's killing, 1662.*

Outfaced, Crosby withdrew, threatening to bring re-inforcements, and returned immediately, armed with a cocked pistol and accompanied by Timothy Ratcliffe, a parish constable, who held a fowling-piece. The frightened mourners gathered around Haworth as Crosby advanced. At that moment, one of the mourners, John Townsend, about whom little more is known than his name, stepped between Haworth and Crosby.

'Noble major,' he said with serene politeness, 'pray make no disturbance; consider, it is the Sabbath day.'

'You rogue,' Crosby barked, 'do you tell me of the Sabbath day?' Furious, he lowered the muzzle of his upraised pistol, took aim, fired at point-blank range and shot Townsend dead. He was buried next day in the graveyard at the abbey.

In the subsequent trial at the Old Bailey, Haworth and some of the male mourners appeared on charges of instigating a riot while Crosby was indicted for murder. The foreman of the jury was none other than Timothy Ratcliffe and the judge, Sir Harbottle Grimston. But something went wrong during Crosby's trial. The jury, despite Ratcliffe, found that the indictment of murder was correct: Crosby was guilty. Grimston, appalled, brow-beat the jury into rejecting the indictment, freed Crosby and bound over the 'rioters' to keep the peace. Compelled to leave St Albans, Haworth settled as a pastor of Congregationalists in Hertford.

A week after the trial an anonymous tract, entitled *Law Unknown, or Judgement Unjust*, described the killing of Townsend, related the court proceedings and denounced Grimston for freeing Crosby and punishing the peaceable mourners. 'Some persons,' the tract states, 'were Indicted, Judged, and Condemned at the Sessions in the Old Bailey, London, by an Unknown Law, neither Printed nor Published; nor any ways knowable by the common People: Whereby the Inhabitants of this Nation may perceive what unavoidable Bondage and slavery they are going into.'

Townsend's memorial, and that of similar martyrs, was raised by another and more famous nonconformist:

> Who would true valour see,
>   Let him come hither;
> One here will constant be,
>   Come wind, come weather...

John Bunyan, who included the poem in the second part of his allegorical masterpiece, *The Pilgrim's Progress* (1684), lived in Bedford, and is said to have preached and occasionally lodged in a cottage at Coleman Green, three miles north east of St Albans. Nowadays, only a chimney of the cottage survives.

Nonconformity persisted to flourish in St Albans. Seven years after Townsend's martyrdom around a hundred Presbyterians were meeting every Sunday. Fifty Baptists managed to stay together without a regular place or time of meeting. Sixty Quakers met in a hired house every Sunday and Wednesday. A 'great number' of Congregationalists met in a private house. For them, and for all Protestant nonconformists, freedom of worship was granted under the Toleration Act of 1689.

In the meantime Grimston's function as the watchdog of civic authority had been enhanced. Charles II, in the charter he granted to the town in 1664, referred to 'our beloved and faithful Sir Harbottle Grimston', and appointed him 'to counsel and direct the Mayor and Aldermen'.

The mayor and aldermen tended to be tradesmen: a tanner, an innkeeper, an ironmonger, an apothecary, a draper and a pewterer are recorded as having held office during the years 1665-75. Sometimes they were clumsy. A year before the charter the corporation had ordered the seizure of the goods of two residents of the abbey parish to pay for the repair of a road, but had a change of heart, repaid the money and levied all the parish's inhabitants in amounts varying from 2s. 6d. to 2d. Enlightened self-interest meant that the town should be kept in some sort of order and, to that end, instructions were issued in detail in 1675 on the care and operation of a civic fire engine. An indication of the range of the corporation's responsibilities was a council meeting in 1681 attended by the town's four constables, the two wardens of the two trade companies, viewers of the streets and highways, the flesh and fish tasters, the viewers of the market and the searchers of leather. On the page containing the record of the meeting are some characters in an early form of shorthand. As is well known, Samuel Pepys wrote his indiscreet diary in shorthand.

It was Charles II's charter that referred, for the first time in St Albans, to aldermen rather than burgesses, and which recognised the borough's right to 'hold markets and fairs as well in the waste and open streets and places ... as elsewhere', and to 'erect shambles and stalls and there buy, sell and expose to sale, wares, merchandise, corn, grain, cattle, horses and other saleable things ... and take and levy tolls, stallage and other profits of saleable things'. The rights of the charter's 'ancient and populous Borough' had been reaffirmed.

IX

Remarkably Clear and Fine

HOW 'populous' was St Albans? The population at large had increased gradually during the 17th century and it is probable that it had done so in St Albans. The size of the town, however, was much the same in 1700 as it had been half a century earlier although, of course, more people could have been occupying an almost unchanged number of dwellings. In any case, a population above 4,000 inhabitants is unlikely, and their public concerns, like those more often than not of the town council, were of the perennial kind.

Some of the inhabitants, who refused to pay rent due to the corporation, should be sued, the council decided at a meeting in December 1700, when it also was agreed that unlicensed wine sellers would be prosecuted. The town constables already had been ordered every night to hunt out the criminals of want from

> the houses of all such persons within the borough as were suspected to harbour and lodge vagrants and rogues and other old and disorderly persons, and take up such as they found that they might be punished according to law, and that all such as harboured them were to be suppressed from selling beer or ale.

But the aldermen were not above extending a helping hand. They ordered the overseers of the poor in May 1701 to provide a house for Thomas Sheppard and his family and similarly for Mrs. Nakin, to whom 2s. a week also was allowed towards the support of herself and her children. No doubt, the aldermen could winnow the undeserving from the deserving poor.

The aldermen had a sure sense of their own worth and importance. They had decided in 1700 that the number of people invited to the mayor's annual feast should not exceed 200 and, a year later, granted the mayor £12 towards the cost. Furthermore, and to set a good example, it was agreed that the aldermen take turns, two at a time, with the two bailiffs and two assistants, to 'attend in their gowns upon the mayor' when he went to and from church on a Sunday. To be suitably dignified the procession demanded sobriety, especially as any member of the public found drunk on a Sunday was liable to prosecution. Warrants were issued against 'two persons' for the offence in November 1702.

Time and again the council attempted to prevent or correct unsocial behaviour. Several people found themselves in trouble in December 1702 for cutting down and taking away trees from public waste lands. John Long, a wheelwright, confessed in February 1703 that he had paid for the 'lops and tops' of eight elms growing on waste land in front of a resident's house. Another resident, Nicholas Sparling, was allowed to set up a post in front of his house to keep waggons off the footpath: a precaution the traffic made increasingly necessary in St Albans.

What best to do about the provision or protection of public buildings was a recurrent worry and could lead to confusion. In January 1700, a year after having granted Henry Hunt a 21-year lease of the Clock Tower, the council resolved by eight votes to five to demolish it and to re-build the nearby 16th-century Market House. The speed with which such decisions sometimes were implemented meant that all that happened for two years was nothing until, in January 1702, it was resolved that the Clock Tower should be repaired and let to the highest bidder. What could be fairer? A year later, the repairs having been completed, a lease of 40 years at £5 a year rent was granted by the council to William Marston, an alderman who, some might charitably have supposed, chanced to submit the highest bid. At the same time the corporation ordered £100 to be spent towards the building of a new Market House which, by 1721, had become a well-known landmark.

Equally well known was the aldermanic addiction to very private enterprise. Edward Seabrooke, after his turn as mayor in 1701-2, kept the corporation silver plate and had to be pestered at length into returning it. His example was followed by George Cooke who, after his mayoralty, tried unsuccessfully in 1708 to keep the self-same collection of silver to grace his own table. Together, the mayor and the aldermen could be relied on, as in 1722 and 1732, to secure the return of a preferred candidate in a parliamentary election by enfranchising as many men as were required to obtain a majority but, from about 1743, the council settled on simple bribery. By then, the reputation of St Albans had been confirmed as one of the best towns that money could buy.

But intermittent care was taken to ensure that the markets were conducted according to the rules. Anybody selling grain 'and other things' without paying the tolls risked prosecution, according to a council resolution passed in 1699. In 1702 it was ordered that no corn should be sold before 10 a.m., so as to give all the grain sellers an equal opportunity, and then only if the toll had been paid on the corn grown outside the borough. Two drapers, Nicholas Bradwyn and Francis Halford, were authorised in July 1717 to prosecute 'pedlars and chapmen who sell in the Borough linen, cloths, muslins and such goods belonging to the draper's trade' and 'to have all advantages as could be recovered from the offenders'. But the drapers were unsuccessful in their protectionist endeavours, failing to cover their costs, and the corporation had to pay Halford the 15s. he was out of pocket over the prosecutions. Three years later, in another attempt to protect St Albans' market traders and customers, anybody buying up 'poultry or other goods' to resell them at a higher price was reminded that there were risks in breaking the law on 'forestalling'.

Protection of the traders from the weather was provided in 1720 by the building of a shed or lean-to on the west side of the Clock Tower. Protection against the unsightliness and smell of street rubbish was provided in 1735 by the appointment of Richard Goodson as the town scavenger.

Meanwhile, two men had died in 1723 for whom St Paul's Cathedral is a lasting memorial: its architect, Sir Christopher Wren, and Edward Strong, his chief mason during its building. In St Albans two dwellings are, by tradition, Strong's work: Romeland House and Ivy House, which he built for himself opposite the west door of St Peter's Church, the church where he was buried and is commemorated by a splendid marble tablet.

Stately almshouses under one roof were opened during 1736 in what is now Hatfield Road. The accommodation was for 18 men and 18 women willing to live 'soberly, piously', and each to have four rooms and a garden allotment at the rear of the brick building. Grandly extended over the main entrance were, and remain, the Marlborough arms proclaiming as the benefactress Sarah, Duchess of Marlborough (1660-1744), widow of John Churchill, Duke of Marlborough (1650-1722), one of England's greatest generals. Sarah was born in Sandridge, the youngest of the seven children of Richard and Francis Jennings, among whose ancestors was Sir Ralph Rowlett, a beneficiary of the abbey's suppression. Sarah herself was an an astute

Her Grace the Dutchess of Marlborough

52 *Sarah Jennings, Duchess of Marlborough (1660-1744).*

businesswoman, having made £100,000 when disposing of her shares in the South Sea Company well before it collapsed in 1720, nine years after its establishment to trade mainly in slaves with Spanish America. As newly-weds, John and Sarah Churchill had acquired a neglected mansion, Holywell House, at the foot of Holywell Hill, which they repaired and extended, and where their guests included the future Queen Anne (1702-14). The influential young couple had had the main road outside diverted along what is now Grove Road, and it was not returned to its original course until 1837.

Sarah's interest in politics caused her to intervene in 1737, as she had done before, in a St Albans parliamentary election. The candidate she disliked, Samuel Grimston, second Earl of Verulam, had when a young man written a play, *Love in a Hollow Tree*, which although not performed was published by him at his own expense and, eventually, to his own cost. Savaged by both Alexander Pope and Jonathan Swift, the unhappy author bought in as many copies as he could retrieve and consigned the whole run, he hoped, to oblivion. But Sarah succeeded in obtaining a copy, and had a second edition printed, adding a picture of an ass wearing a coronet accompanied by an elephant dancing on a tight-rope. Copies were distributed, and Grimston, a figure of fun, was laughed to defeat.

There were uplifting events. In May 1739 the Rev. George Whitefield, one of the period's greatest evangelists, and with a voice strong enough in the open air to be heard two

THE MARLBOROUGH BUILDINGS, St. ALBANS.

53 *The 18th-century Marlborough almshouses, Hatfield Road, as depicted in an early 19th-century engraving.*

miles away, preached to 1,500 people in a field in St Albans at seven o'clock in the morning. His popularity as a preacher, in Britain and the American colonies, stimulated a renewal of Christian belief on both sides of the Atlantic.

Another prominent visitor, the Scottish rebel Simon Fraser, Lord Lovat, stayed at the *White Hart*, where William Hogarth painted his portrait before he was taken to London and executed, aged 80 or so, for his part in the 1745 rebellion of Prince Charles Edward. Hogarth had been induced to come to St Albans by a friend, Dr. Joshua Webster (1716-1801), who practised in the town and who, around the time of Hogarth's visit, was writing *Gleanings of Antiquity from Verolam and St Albans*. As well as the antiquities the book includes descriptions of the contemporary town and its countryside, which show Webster to have been a careful, if sometimes caustic, observer:

54 *William Hogarth (1697-1764), the first English-born artist to attract admiration abroad, visited St Albans in 1746. This 19th-century engraving is of Hogarth's famous self-portrait with his dog, Trump, painted in 1745.*

> The town of St Albans is situated upon rising ground and capable as being laid as dry and clean as any town in the Kingdom, but by bad management is a very Dirty one in Winter ... There's a good market for Provision but much hurt by the Corporation suffering London higlers to forestall it before the Town is served ...

Had the corporation been unable to enforce its own publicly declared regulation about price fixing or had there been more very private enterprise? Webster does not say and continues:

> The air about St Albans is remarkably clear and fine ... the Water is no less remarkably pure and wholesome, especially their Well water which is philtered through a very thick strata of chalk ...

As for the surrounding countryside it was

> beautifully diversified with Hills and Vallies affording delightful Prospects and well stocked with Gentlemen's Seats and ancient Buildings ... The Hedges and Fields produce many useful Shrubs and Physical plants in great plenty. The plow'd lands are overrun with Red Poppies ... and the meadows with pulmonaria and Orchis's of Different kinds. About Verolam is found the true Bee Orchis, so very singular in its kind that a stranger unacquainted with it would at first sight take it for a cluster of Bees making so fine a deception that it requires some seconds of time to detect.

Among Webster's friends in St Albans was Dr. Nathaniel Cotton (1705-88), an enlightened carer of the mentally ill, who looked after William Cowper from that stricken poet's first bout of madness in 1763 until patience and kindness had restored him to a precarious sanity

55   *Nathaniel Cotton (1705-88).*

56   *William Cowper (1731-1800).*

by 1765. Cotton treated Cowper in a private asylum, the 'Collegium Insanorum', situated in what is now Lower Dagnall Street and recalled by the name College Street, which occupies part of the site of the long since demolished building. Cotton was a poet, too, and his *Visions in Verse for the Entertainment and Instruction of Younger Minds*, published in 1751, was instantly successful. Written for literate and studious children, it proclaims the advantages of good health and true happiness because Cotton, as a physician and devout Christian, was sure that the wages of sin were death:

> Attend my visions, thoughtless youths,
> Ere long you'll think them weighty truths,
> Prudent it were to think so now
> Ere age has silvered o'er your brow:
> For he, who at his early years
> Has sown in vice, shall reap in tears.
> If folly has possessed his prime,
> Disease shall gather strength in time,
> Poison shall rage in every vein,-
> Nor penitence dilute the stain:
> And when each hour shall urge his fate,
> Thought, like the doctor, comes too late.

The wages of sin had been death for three highwaymen who had robbed the Chester mail coach between St Albans and Barnet in April 1747. One of the trio, Robert Parkinson, was caught as a result of trying to cash two £50 banknotes, and he betrayed his associates, the brothers Thomas and William Bibbie, who were arrested in Bristol as they were preparing to exchange highway robbery for robbery on the high seas as crewmen on board a privateer. The unlucky brothers were taken to Newgate, from where William escaped but, unlucky again, he was killed by a fall while being pursued. The filthy conditions in Newgate put paid to Parkinson. Thomas alone lived long enough to stand trial at Hertford assizes in March 1748 when, found guilty, he was hanged and his corpse suspended in chains near the scene of the disastrous robbery.

57   Collegium Insanorum, Lower Dagnall Street.

Security on the road, despite the dreadful penalty imposed on those who challenged it, continued to be precarious, but the speed of wheeled traffic became faster, though not always safer, as road making improved during the second half of the century. Mid-century, most of the more than fifty inns in St Albans were offering stabling (the *Goat* in Sopwell Lane for 72) as well as beds while, if a fictional incident in Henry Fielding's *Tom Jones* (1749) is based on fact, there were unlikely to be complaints about the food available: 'an excellent shoulder of mutton', at an unnamed inn in the town, 'came smoking to the table' and on which the hero and a friend 'both plentifully feasted'.

The St Albans Turnpike Trust, which had been founded in 1715, kept the Holyhead road from South Mimms to the town 'well mended', according to Daniel Defoe in 1724, and charges collected at the Trust's tollgates to the north west and south east of the town financed its work. Traffic all the time was increasing through St Albans because, besides the coaches, carts and waggons, there were lines of pack-horses as well as innumerable droves of oxen, calves, hogs, sheep, lambs and horses on their way to Smithfield market. In 1765 the Trust built the bridge over the Ver at St Michael's village, which remains the earliest surviving bridge in the county, but it was the Trust's re-routing of the London road in 1796 that crowned its work. Until then the route since the 11th century from London into the town had been along Sopwell Lane, taking a sharp turn right up into the cruelly steep, for the draught horses, Holywell Hill and, near the top, a sharp turn left into High Street and along George Street to an inconveniently narrow Fishpool Street. The new road by-passed Holywell Hill by cutting north west from where Old London Road joins the new one, and caused the demolition of the *Cross Keys Inn* so as to connect with High Street. The new route led to the closure of many of the old coaching inns, which clustered together in Sopwell Lane and on the east side of Holywell Hill, where all that survives of some of them today are their high entrances for the rumbling coaches.

Coaching gave considerable employment to the town, exciting interest and comment. For instance, Thomas Cumber, a St Albans diarist, noted primly in 1785: '22nd

58   Nathaniel Cotton's grave, St Peter's Church cemetery.

59   *St Michael's bridge, built in 1765, and the ford, c.1908. In the distance is the tower of St Michael's Church. The cottages on the far side of the bridge have since been demolished.*

July. At ten, went to see the Liverpool, Manchester, Leeds and Birmingham Mail Coaches come in at exactly a quarter past ten, drove furiously. I think the contractors will find their horses much hurt ...'.

More than horses were being harmed, according to Henry Home in *Sketches of the History of Man* (1774): 'A spring-coach, rolling along a smooth road, gives no exercise; or so little as to be preventive of no disease. It tends to enervate the body, as well as the mind.' Favouring, instead, travel on horseback, 'because it is a healthful exercise', he continued, 'The increase of wheel-carriages within a century is a pregnant proof of the growth of luxurious indolence.' He did not spare his readers a further opinion. 'Cookery and coaches,' he railed, driving his quill as furiously as the despised coaches, 'have reduced the military spirit of the English nobility and gentry to a languid state: the former, by overloading the body, has infected them with dispiriting ailments; the latter, by fostering ease and indolence, have banished labour, the only antidote to such ailments.' The invective was quoted almost word for word by John Adams in *Curious Thoughts on the History of Man* (1790), a compilation of extracts from the works of various authors, which suggests that Home's anxieties were shared.

Across the Channel events had unfolded which led in 1793 to the outbreak of war between Britain and, at first, revolutionary, and then Napoleonic, France. For more than the next two decades the world-wide war would supply in plenty an antidote to indolence. Simultaneously, pressure grew in Britain for social and political reform. 'From what we now see, nothing of reform in the political world ought to be held improbable,' wrote Thomas Paine in the first part of *The Rights of Man* (1791). 'It is an age of Revolutions,' he declared, 'in which everything may be looked for.' The fearful government thought so, too, and in 1794 called into being county armed volunteers as much to quell civil disorders as to oppose any French invasion. Hertfordshire did not deem it necessary to answer the call until 1798, when 10 volunteer infantry associations were formed, including that of St Albans.

Rural St Albans, at first far removed from the immediate repercussions of the war, found its concerns usually unalarming even if sometimes sad. In August 1793 Thomas Robinson had died, aged 66, after working as a waiter at the *White Hart Inn* for 40 years. He, 'by his attention and acquaintance with the antiquities of the place,' reported *The Gentleman's Magazine* shortly afterwards, 'rendered himself useful to all the guests. He left two daughters, one of whom succeeded, in a small shop, her mother, who died about six years ago.' Five years after Robinson's death, John Kent, another admired resident, died at the age of eighty. A plumber and glazier by occupation, he had served the abbey church as clerk for 52 years, and was highly regarded for his knowledge of its history. Between them, a waiter and a plumber-cum-glazier, each had enabled many, who might otherwise have retained a vague and airy understanding, to see the past as possessing a local habitation and a name.

Robinson and Kent's informed location of history among their own familiar surroundings presupposes they would have known that Presbyterians and Baptists had been established in St Albans along with other nonconformists since the 17th century.

The town's first Methodist meeting place—registered on 14 January 1793—was an outhouse at the rear of a house, still standing, on the corner of George Street and the raised footpath to the abbey church. The tenant, David Kent, a Methodist baker, was succeeded as the

60 *The east end of the abbey church, 1793.*

61 *The four steps on the raised path at Romeland led to the town's first Methodist meeting place, 1793.*

tenant by another Methodist, Charles Kentish. Membership increased, and in 1801 larger premises had to be acquired, off St Peter's Street, which sufficed until 1824, when the congregation moved to Lower Dagnall Street, and moved from there in 1841 to new premises on the corner of Upper Dagnall Street and Cross Street, where they stayed until in 1898 their church in Marlborough Road was built. The little out-house survived until earlier this century; now, all that is visible as a reminder to the passer-by are four stone steps leading to a brick wall where once was the meeting place's entrance.

Congregationalists, who had first been recorded in St Albans in 1650, stopped sharing a chapel with Presbyterians in Lower Dagnall Street in 1794 to worship on their own. In temporary premises on the outskirts of the town they opened one of Britain's first Sunday schools for children and, a few months later, moved back with it to the town, fitting up for themselves a barn in Sweet Briar Lane (Victoria Street) until, early in the next century, they opened their present Independent Chapel in Spicer Street.

x

Mysterious Ways

SEVENTY-FOUR OFFICERS and men of the St Albans Volunteer Infantry, each wearing the distinctive red coat of their uniform, stepped out, colours flying, in a review of the county volunteers by George III (1760-1820) at Hatfield Park on 13 June 1800. Their defiant mood, and that of others like them, had been given voice by Robert Burns:

> Does haughty Gaul invasion threat?
> Then let the loons beware, Sir!
> There's wooden walls upon our seas
> And volunteers on shore, Sir!

The threat of invasion, and even its likelihood, passed although the war came visibly closer to St Albans when, high above the town, the Admiralty built in 1807 a signalling apparatus on top of the Clock Tower. Its 'amazing celerity' in helping to convey messages from the Admiralty to Yarmouth was 'truly astonishing' to Solomon George Shaw in his *History of Verulam and St Albans* (1815). Intelligence was sent, he explained, and an answer returned in the short space of five minutes, 'a distance, by the route of the mail, upwards of 200 miles'.

Shaw was astonished because he knew that the time taken to travel the same distance by coach would have amounted to around twenty hours: ten miles an hour being regarded as the 'natural pace'. Tom Brown, for instance, on his way from Islington to Rugby in the 1830s, passed through St Albans on the *Tally-ho* coach, 'a tip-top goer, ten miles an hour including stoppages, and so punctual that all the road set their clocks by her'. Shaw, a stationer, bookseller and binder of Market Place, could not have failed to take an interest in coaching as he knew of its importance in the town's economy. Coaches went daily to London at 8 a.m. from the *Woolpack*, Holywell Hill, from the *George*, George Street, at 7.30 a.m. and from the *Chequers*, Chequer Street, every Monday and Thursday at the awful hour of 2 a.m. The departure times for the return journeys ranged from 2 p.m. to 3 p.m., with the coach to the *Chequers* leaving London at 6 p.m. in the summer and 4 a.m. in the winter.

Shaw sets the scene for the returning coaches:

> On entering the town by the new London road, along High-street, it bespeaks much respectability from the general appearance of the houses and shops situated thereabouts; and there are in other parts of the town, some excellent and comfortable residences.

Next, he presented with the help of simple arithmetic a figure likely to impress his fellow citizens:

> The immense and constant traffic through the town, in consequence of the great north-west road lying through it, affords employment to several most respectable posting

77

62   Market Place, St Albans. The semaphore apparatus on top of the Clock Tower was removed in 1814. The open-sided Market Cross structure housed a pump.

houses and inns, and also many inferior public houses; the mails and stage coaches which run through the town (supposing them to be pretty well loaded) have accommodation for upwards of 600 passengers daily; add to which the number of travellers which pass through by other conveyances, and those on foot, it may reasonably be computed that not less than 1,000 persons pass through this town every day.

The commercial significance of the figure was appreciated by Shaw who, as a shop-keeper himself, had an eye to business and helped it in general as best he could in his *History* with an outright recommendation: 'There are many respectable and well furnished shops, which supply the town and neighbourhood with the necessaries and conveniences of life; but London operates much to the injury of the trading part of the town ...'. Still,

perhaps better butcher's meat is not to be purchased in any market in the kingdom; bread is always half an assize under that of London, and there are two common breweries and also two very respectable inns that brew excellent home-brewed ale. Nor are the articles of grocery, drapery etc. less excellent in their kind, or to be purchased on more moderate terms by the consumer any where.

Shaw was equally generous to the eight 'principal inns' he listed. Among them, the *White Hart*, Holywell Hill, was described as being for families and post coaches, the *Blue Boar*, Market Place, was 'celebrated for home-brewed ale', and the *Crown*, Holywell Hill, was 'a general resort of sportsmen, particularly during the hunting season'. The *Fleur de Lys*, French Row, let saddle horses and single-horse chaises.

Industrial activities, which were approved by Shaw, included the silk mill, established at the foot of Abbey Mill Lane in 1802, and a cotton mill: together they gave 'employment to upwards of 500 persons, mostly children'. The fingers of other children and women were kept busy making straw plait for hat-makers. 'The straw-plat [*sic*] sewing is a source of employment to many females in the town from which they may derive, and also from platting the straws, a respectable and comfortable livelihood.' The town's straw-plait market was 'one of the largest in England, which begins at the ringing of a bell by one of the beadles of the borough and terminates before the commencement of the corn market'.

'There are three fairs annually', Shaw wrote, 'and a public statute for hiring servants.' The largest fair, held at Michaelmas, attracted

> all the gaiety of the country for many miles round; this fair is visited by many shows exhibiting the wonderful and marvellous! but what gives most pleasure and satisfaction is Richardson's portable theatre, and his company of comic and tragic performers: their theatric representations is [*sic*] an indulgence to the sight of the inhabitants of the surrounding villages they but rarely have an opportunity of witnessing, therefore is a source of the highest gratification to their curiosity for dramatic performances, nor does the proprietor seem less anxious to please, than his admirers are to be pleased.

As for the provision of a basic necessity, water, there were two public pumps: one, near the Clock Tower, had been installed at the expense of the Spencer family; the other, known as the Blue Pump, at the south end of St Peter's Street, seldom worked and was of 'very little service'. 'Coals', Shaw noted, turning his attention to another requirement, 'are a scarce and rather expensive commodity at St Albans; the chief supply comes from the Grand Junction Canal at Boxmoor, near Hempstead, from whence there are several miles of land carriage.' All the same, 'a great quantity of Staffordshire coals are burnt here'.

63 Gorhambury House was built during 1778-85. The engraving dates from the early 19th century. An earlier Gorhambury House, built nearby in the 16th century by Sir Nicholas Bacon, Keeper of the Great Seal, survives only as a ruin.

Banks trading in St Albans at the time Shaw was writing included a bank run by the brothers Joseph and Nathaniel Harris, whose notes showed a view of the abbey church. Earlier, the St Albans, Watford, Hemel Hempstead and Hertfordshire Bank had issued £1 notes in 1811 picturing two crossed wheat sheaves in proud acknowledgment of the county's agricultural prowess.

A similar and desirable openness was lacking, Shaw suspected, at the town council: 'There is certainly a great deal of mystery and secrecy attached to the corporation affairs; and there are but very few who have any knowledge at all about them, although it would be reasonable to make, at least, all acquainted with them that are subject to their government.'

What had the city fathers been doing?

There was no denying that they had on occasions worked in most mysterious ways. Apart from increasing to £25 the allowance for the mayor's feast, there were the travels of the plait market to consider. The council had decided in August 1804 that the plait market and the poultry market should be held at the Market Cross; the council then had had second thoughts in October and moved the plait market to School Lane (Waxhouse Gate). Having reminded themselves of the Market Cross, an open-sided octagonal structure near the Clock Tower, sheltering the pump, the city fathers resolved in December to think about removing the Market Cross 'for the purpose of rendering access to the market more easy and commodious to the public'. After thoughts lasting six years they reached the conclusion in January 1810 that the Market Cross was in a dangerous condition and should be taken down. Soon afterwards it was accidentally damaged by a waggon and in March 1810 the waggoner had to

64   *The Silk Mill, established at the foot of Abbey Mill Lane in 1802, survived until 1938. Subsequently, some of the buildings shown on this postcard, c.1905, including the chimney-stack, were demolished and, more recently, the remainder have been turned into flats. The* Fighting Cocks *public house is on the left.*

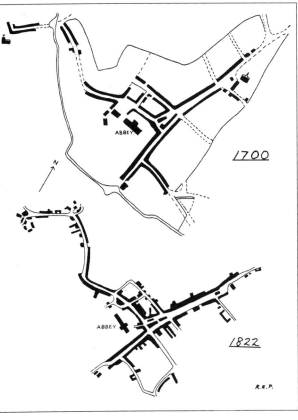

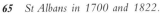

65 *St Albans in 1700 and 1822.*

66 *The Clock Tower in the early 19th century; nearby, surrounded by railings, is a pump.*

hand over £10 for repairs. A year later, as a result of the corporate mind undergoing another convulsion, the Market Cross was demolished.

A physical convulsion shook the town during May 1810, caused by a dispute over payments to men of the Local Militia. A local defence force, it had partially absorbed members of the 240-strong St Albans Volunteer Infantry after that association was disbanded in 1809. Possibly, the disturbances were connected with that re-organisation or to the men's resentment at having to drill on Sundays, thus losing their only day of rest. On top of that there was widespread disaffection over prices and taxes continuing to rise because of the war with France. The events in St Albans, apparently an expression of that disaffection, were among comparable disturbances which flared up throughout the country. For instance, members of the Militia stationed in Devizes mutinied in June 1810 over the army's savage disciplinary punishments and, later the same month, Militiamen at Stamford, encouraged by the townsfolk, forcibly freed two comrades, who had been imprisoned for being absent from parade. During the same month William Cobbett was sentenced to two years' imprisonment for having denounced the flogging of the ring-leaders of a Militia mutiny in Ely over unfair deductions from pay.

In St Albans several of the Local Militia privates had expected to receive various amounts of money, but their officers refused payment. As a result, a sergeant was deputed by the men to speak on their behalf to the commanding officer who, disliking the sergeant's manner and, perhaps, his matter, had him arrested and jailed. The men by then had had more

67 *William Cobbett (1763-1835).*

than enough. Angered, between two and three hundred of them gathered outside the prison, broke open the door and freed the sergeant, according to a London newspaper, *The Star*, in its issue of 30 May.

'The officers assembled as soon as possible, called all the men that would stand by them, with other forces, and repairing to the scene of disorder before the jail, they succeeded in taking into custody 19 of the rioters, without much mischief occurring,' continued the report in *The Star*. Tried before a court martial, five were sentenced to receive 100 lashes and one was ordered 150 lashes. Nevertheless, such was the anger, the trouble continued and officers were alleged to have been threatened with violence. There were noisy meetings, too, but in the end the protest was suppressed.

Despite the dust seeming to have settled, the mayor and aldermen deemed it necessary in October to instruct that their pews in the abbey church should be kept locked to prevent 'improper persons from intruding'. Happier things, though, were in store as one of the council's proudest hours was approaching. In July 1814 members were invited to dine with the Marquis of Salisbury at Hatfield House in the presence of Arthur Wellesley, Duke of Wellington. The chance to swagger and, at the same time, to honour the victorious commander of the British Army, was too good to miss; accordingly, it was agreed to present him with the freedom of the borough and to give him the scroll of the freedom in a gold box costing 50 guineas. A further chance occurred to swagger. Asked to contribute towards the 'relief of the wives and families of British soldiers who had so gloriously fallen at the Battle of Waterloo', which finally had defeated Napoleon, the council in July 1815 granted 20 guineas. Yet again the public purse was opened: £20 in April 1819 being given towards the cost of a new organ at the abbey church.

Change was the characteristic of the 1820s in St Albans, and it was change at an increasingly faster rate, which also heralded the faster and larger changes of the rest of the century and beyond. Clear evidence of the change were the improvements to the road system. George Street already had been widened, in 1814, Chequer Street widened in 1820, Hatfield Road in 1824. The opening of Verulam Road in 1826, and its continuation to Bow Bridge, greatly simplified and improved the route taken by the Holyhead Road on that side of the town; the route on the opposite side had been improved with the opening of the new London Road in 1796. But to avoid paying the tolls on the new Redbourn road farmers were sending their wheat to be sold at markets other than that of St Albans.

William Cobbett, long out of prison and as radical as ever, noted that the farmers' crops around St Albans during the sunny summer of 1822,

> and especially that of the barley, are very fine and very forward. The wheat, in general, does not appear to be a heavy crop; but the ears seem as if they would be full from bottom to top; and we have had so much heat that the grain is pretty sure to be plump, let the weather, for the rest of the summer, be what it may.

The pay of the farm labourers who ploughed the land, and sowed and reaped the harvest, ranged from 8s. to 10s. a week.

Wily farmers notwithstanding, the changes continued. Gas mains were laid in 1824. Water mains followed in 1833. And after what are likely to have been many years of complaint about the inadequacy of the old Town Hall, on the corner of Upper Dagnall Street and Market Place, preliminary moves to vacate it began to be made. 'A more eligible site' for a new town hall was a requirement agreed by the council in 1825. Two years later a proposed site in Romeland was rejected by the council, though the magistrates offered to buy it for a new court house, but were told 'that it was not expedient'. The differences were resolved early in 1828, when the corporation and the magistrates agreed to build a combined town hall and court house: the present old Town Hall, opened in 1831. Its architect, George Smith, received the freedom of the borough for his graceful work.

There had been setbacks. The mayor's undoubted joy at obtaining in 1825 an increase to a very substantial £50 for the annual feast was short-lived as the corporation's funds became insufficient. Consequently, from 1828, the mayor and his guests had had to tighten their belts to manage on a not too paltry £30.

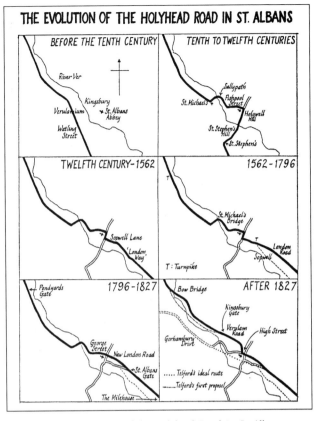

68 *The evolution of the Holyhead Road in St Albans.*

Two men unlikely at any time to have had £30 between them to spend on feasting appeared before the St Albans magistrates in April 1830: Richard Smith and David Thomas, who, having been found guilty of stealing 18 fowls, three ducks and seven rabbits, were each sentenced to seven years' transportation. From the same magistrates Elizabeth Foster received a sentence of 14 years' transportation for stealing two pairs of women's shoes, a linen pocket handkerchief, a length of print, a length of muslin, about a yard of muslin net, 10 pairs of cotton hose, nine stay laces and a quantity of ribbons. George Glover escaped lightly: seven days for stealing a peck of coal. Nathaniel West, convicted of stealing a pair of moleskin trousers, a pair of plush breeches and a pair of worsted stockings, went down for 12 months' hard labour, but escaped and, when recaptured, was awarded seven years' transportation.

People at the brighter end of the social spectrum were the preferred paying guests at the *Verulam Arms*. Built alongside Verulam

70 *Road repairs in the early 19th century.*

70   St Albans Town Hall opened in 1831; this is how it appeared c.1938.

Road soon after the road opened, its position as the first grand hotel available to travellers entering the town from the Redbourn direction gave it, perhaps, an intended business advantage. Nothing else about it seems to have been accidental, either. Claimed an advertisement in *The County Chronicle* on 11 May 1830:

> The Hotel is planned with numerous and spacious apartments fitted up at considerable expense, and affording every accommodation for the reception of Noblemen and families of distinction, with suitable servants' offices, capital cellaring for wine in casks and bottles, beer, ale, and other cellars; a very spacious stable and carriage yard, with stabling for 66 horses; coach houses with lofts and granaries; an abundant supply of excellent water; a tap detached from the house, fronting the road, and possessing every suitable accommodation; pleasure ground stocked with varieties of flowering shrubs, evergreens and fruit trees, with grass plats and flower beds intersected with well-arranged gravel walks and avenue of trees; a productive kitchen garden stocked with fruits and vegetables.

If such a hotel were not entirely suitable for a queen, it was perfectly acceptable for a queen-to-be, Princess Victoria who, with her mother, the Duchess of Kent, lunched there when they were on their way from Scotland to London in 1835.

Arrangements had been made for the less lucky people at the social spectrum's darker end. The new Poor Law of 1834, replacing the old, variable system of poor relief, separately controlled by individual parishes, instituted a uniform, national system of parishes grouped together to form a Poor Law Union, at the centre of which stood the workhouse. Except for the needy old and sick, relief was provided only for its inmates, on condition they worked as told, and applications to be admitted were rejected unless the need was desperate, when husbands would then be parted from wives and parents from children.

'I have seen so many sad things,' Mary Carbery recalled in *Happy World* (1941), an account of her family's comfortable life from about 1860 to 1884 at Childwickbury and the Pré, country houses near St Albans, 'and have grieved for old grannies, parted by workhouse rules from their old men, whose eyelids are burnt red by tears, whose chins quiver when they tell Papa how unhappy they are without a home'. Papa, Henry Joseph Toulmin (1837-1926), a barrister, who served as mayor four times, was chairman of the workhouse Board of Guardians and, his daughter wrote, did all he could 'to lessen the misery of the poor in the workhouse. He insists on their having good fires to sit by, and lets the women wear their own little shawls, and go for walks when they like.' Workhouse children had been allowed since 1839 to walk out two or three times a week 'when the weather is favourable'.

Previously, outdoor as well as indoor relief had been given somewhat more humanely by workhouses like that of St Peter's parish, built in 1764 beside St Peter's Green and nowadays occupied by an estate agent's, or that of St Michael's, built a year later opposite the east end of the church and now the site of the Parish Centre. Two years after its opening the number of inmates at St Michael's workhouse totalled 41: eight men, two of whom, Richard Scott and George Hawkins, were blind; three were lame; 11 women, three of them lame and one consumptive; nine boys, 12 girls, and a lunatic, Hannah Dollamore. Such numbers did not, of course, remain constant: St Michael's had had 58 inmates in 1819 and only 31 in 1829. The figures are likely, though, to be indicative of the numbers relating to the workhouses in the parishes of St Peter's, St Stephen's and the Abbey, each of which, along with St Michael's and the workhouses of Sandridge, Redbourn, Harpenden and Wheathampstead, transferred their inmates to the specially built Union workhouse after its opening in 1838.

Built to accommodate 180 inmates, and nowadays forming part of the City Hospital, it gave its name to Union Lane, which was renamed after the Second World War to commemorate the invasion of France and thereby, as Normandy Road, maintains, albeit by chance, a tenuous French connection: workhouses had commonly been called 'Bastilles'.

In the story of English literature's most famous workhouse foundling, the novel's villain, Bill Sikes, flees after murdering his sweetheart 'and took the road which leads from Hatfield to St Albans' before returning to London. *Oliver Twist* (1837-39) was not the only tale by Charles Dickens with a St Albans interest: an illustration for *Pickwick Papers* (1837) by 'Phiz'—Hablot Knight Browne—includes a view of the abbey church from the north-east. The author himself stayed at the *Queen's Hotel* in Chequer Street; *Bleak House*, the early 18th-century house on the corner of Catherine Street and Normandy Road, has nothing to do with him nor with his novel of that name. The house, built by a Francis Dalton, used to be known as The Daltons or Dalton's Folly: hence Folly Lane. The Dickensian name was substituted whimsically in 1893.

The *Queen's Hotel*, which had been called the *Turf* until about 1852, was built on

71 *Dalton's Folly, Catherine Street, c.1806. The building was given the name 'Bleak House' at the end of the 19th century, although it had no connection with Charles Dickens nor anything to do with his similarly entitled novel.*

the site of the *Chequers* after its new licensee, Thomas Coleman (*c*.1796–1877), a noted trainer, came to St Albans in 1820, and persuaded the owners to rebuild and rename the house. As the *Turf Hotel* it was for the next 25 years at the centre of all kinds of sporting activities on the northern side of London, added to which were the allurements of a good chef, a choice cellar and, especially welcome after a hard day in the saddle, the rare luxury of hot baths. To cap it all, Coleman organised the introduction to England of steeplechasing, which had been enjoyed in Ireland since 1752, when a race between Buttevant and Doneraile church steeples in County Cork gave rise to the word 'steeplechase' and to the sport itself. The St Albans Steeplechase, first run on Nomansland Common in 1830, was, according to Robert Grimston, a son of the sporting James Walter Grimston, 1st Earl of Verulam, instigated by officers of the 1st Regiment of Life Guards while dining at the *Turf*: had they, perhaps, encountered the thrilling sport when on leave in Ireland? Certainly, the Hertfordshire Militia had served in Ireland from 1811 to 1813.

The winner of the St Albans Steeplechase in 1834 was the vicar (1827–50) of St Michael's, the Rev. Lord Frederick Beauclerk, a well-known cricketer and hunter who, to avoid displeasing his bishop, rode under the name of Mr. Brand. Rising costs forced Coleman to discontinue the St Albans Steeplechase in 1839, but in the same year, so quickly popular had the sport become, the first Grand National steeplechase race was run at Aintree.

72   St Albans Grand Steeplechase, 8 March 1832, outside the Turf Hotel, Chequer Street.

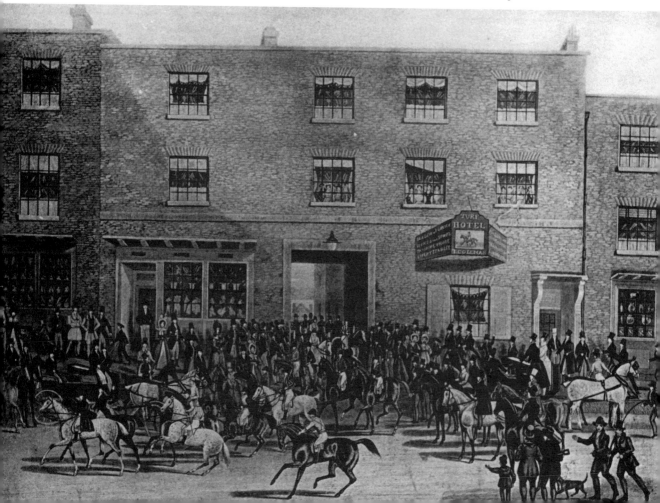

Audiences on Nomansland Common, a venue for flat racing, shooting matches and prize fights, would automatically have included customers of the *Turf*. In 1833 they joined the crowd there to watch a brutal encounter, arranged by Coleman, between Simon Byrne, the champion of Ireland, and 'Deaf' Burke, which lasted for three hours and 16 minutes. Byrne, knocked out, died four days later despite the 'best medical skill', and Burke and his seconds were tried for manslaughter, but were acquitted on the medical evidence: Byrne's death had not been caused by the boxing injuries. Never again, though, would there be a prize fight on Nomansland.

Coleman once more acted at the centre of events when, in 1835, the *Turf* served as headquarters for the Conservatives during the town's first elections under the terms of the Municipal Corporations Act of that year. Earlier, decades of agitation had culminated in the Reform Bill of 1832, extending the vote among the middle class, redistributing the seats more appropriately. The Municipal Act was a logical extension, reforming the franchise for municipal elections. Self-elected councils, like that of St Albans, were swept away; instead, the franchise was granted to ratepayers who had been resident for three years.

True to form, the St Albans aldermen objected. In a petition to the House of Lords before the passing of the Act, they declared that they had under the charters been elected for life and argued that they had a 'right to their privileges as indefeasible as the right of any Peer or office-bearer in the realm'. They regretted that the Bill proposed to displace the present governing body and submitted 'that the proposed plan of Municipal Elections and triennial tenure in Town Councils is in no wise adapted to the genius of the British Constitution', and avowed 'that such a plan will be productive of excitement and party strife in every borough rather than conduce to quiet and peaceable local government'. They further objected to every householder being given the vote and urged either that the voting should depend on rateage or that the municipal franchise should be confined to those who then possessed the Parliamentary franchise.

The tide of reform had proved to be too strong. According to the new legislation St Albans Corporation was to consist of four aldermen, chosen by the council, two of whom were to retire every third year: the days of 'Once an alderman, always an alderman' had ended. There would be 12 elected councillors, four of whom were to retire annually.

The councillors' election in 1835 under the new rules attracted great public interest as no less than 30 candidates were nominated, out of which 11 Conservatives and one Liberal were elected, although the latter headed the poll with 318 votes. After the results were announced 'the town presented a highly animated appearance', reported the *County Press* of Hertford.

> The band perambulated the streets, and a feeling of gratulation seemed to be generally prevalent. At five o'clock 'the elected', amidst an assemblage of friends, sat down to a splendid dinner, served by Mr. Coleman of the *Turf Hotel*, and upon the withdrawal of the cloth, toast and sentiment, the glass and song and high enjoyment bore sway till a late hour.

The hotel survived until the 1980s, when it was demolished.

XI

Full Steam Ahead

THE OPENING in 1838 of the London and North Western Railway to Birmingham via Watford dealt the first of a further three similar, but heavier, blows to the town's coaching trade: in 1858 a branch line from Watford, with its Abbey station, in 1865 another branch line, from Hatfield, with its London Road station and, in 1868, a main line to London from what is now the City station. That direct London link, the culmination of railway hopes in St Albans dating back half-a-century, would before too long help to transform the place from not much more than a bustling village into a booming town. Efforts to beat the railways at their own game by the introduction of steam coaches on the road were frustrated by punitive tolls, despite a steam coach having successively puffed through St Albans at 20 to 25 miles per hour on its way from London to Birmingham in 1835.

Compared with a coach, horse-drawn or steam, the train's advantages of higher and higher speeds, reliability and comfort in the conveyance of passengers, and its speedier and cheaper carrying of goods, outweighed the disadvantages of, for instance, the Watford line's notorious smokiness. 'We left a volume of smoke behind us that would not have shamed a goods-train on the London and North Western,' wrote George Whyte-Melville in *Tilbury Nogo* (1858). But the rail journey from the capital to Birmingham in 1838 took only an incredible four hours and 48 minutes.

An immediate loss of trade had been the price paid by the coaches and coaching inns after the Watford station's opening. Some of St Albans' inns closed, the town's torrent of posting and waggon traffic dwindled to a trickle within a year while, in the 1840s, the long-distance coach routes dried up. Coaches continued to ply between St Albans and London until 1868, and there was a failed attempt at a revival in the 1870s, but the great coaching days had gone. Bravely, the *Wonder* coach ran until at least 1888 and carts, trundling hay to London, manure back, were kept going by a carter, Albert Adams, until around 1890. The town's tollgates, costing more than they earned as a result of the reduction in traffic, had been abolished in 1871.

Typhus fever breaking out in the overcrowded houses of Christopher Place, affecting eight out of its ten families, had been an indication early in 1838 of the need for a public sewerage scheme, but it would take 42 years of recurrent outbreaks of infectious diseases, as well as repeated pleas for remedial action, before a scheme was begun.

'The sewage is clearly a question the corporation ought to deal with; the river is being poisoned and the health of the inhabitants of the town will be affected by the malaria arising from the polluted stream unless a speedy alteration is made,' a public meeting in the Town Hall was told in December 1866. In December 1871, the by then familiar theme was developed with a renewed urgency by a London magazine, *The Illustrated Times*, which described St Albans as having

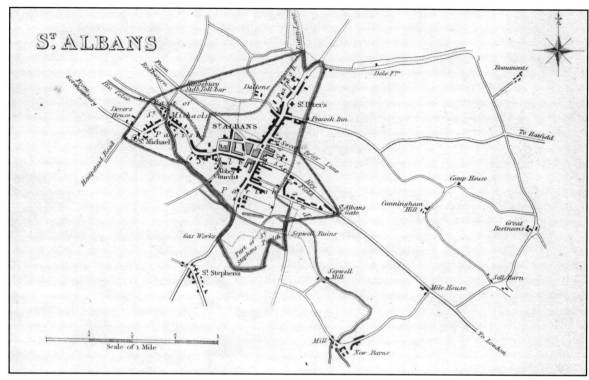

73 *A map of St Albans showing the old (inner) and new (outer) boundaries, c.1840.*

practically no system of drainage, save into cesspools, some of which are actually dug underneath the parlour-floors, because, from lack of main drains and of unbuilt-upon ground, there is nowhere else to which the sewage can be conducted except into the soil on which the houses stand. Within the municipal borough there is a sanitary committee, the members of which do what they can to prevent nuisances from becoming too gross to be endured; what they can do, however, is but little compared to what is needed, and their jurisdiction is limited.

A Public Health Act of 1848 had proved to be insufficiently comprehensive and, in the absence of powers of enforcement, it was not until the passing of the Public Health Act of 1875 that there came a better chance of improvements, although many local authorities, like St Albans, took their time out of consideration of the cost to the ratepayers.

But the risk to health simply would not fade away. An outbreak of smallpox in the

74 *The* Wonder *coach sets off for London down Holywell Hill, c.1893. Established in 1825, the* Wonder *in the 1890s was running only during the summer, but still maintained its celebrity for punctuality and speed.*

town prompted the *Herts Advertiser* (founded in 1855 as *The St Alban's Times and Herts Advertiser*) to add its editorial voice on 27 January 1872 to the ever-lengthening list of calls for action:

> With a dire disease which has already carried off several victims still lurking around us it behoves the ratepayers of St Albans and their governing representatives to take prompt action for securing themselves as far as possible from such an epidemic, that they may not learn too late the value of pure water and effective drainage.

All the same, not until 1884 could *Steven's Almanack and Directory* proclaim a belated civic achievement: 'The contract for the Main Sewer has been completed and house connections are being made in all parts of the city.'

Forty or so years earlier there had been little to shout about in the wake of the typhus fever outbreak and the rapid collapse of coaching with its attendant disruption of trade and employment. Nationally, too, it had been a period of economic depression as well as widespread Chartist agitation for an extension of the vote and, thanks to the Anti-Corn Law League, prolonged and intense pressure in favour of a free trade in wheat imports.

Private joys apart, what there was at such a time to celebrate in St Albans, publicly and without constraint, was a visit in July 1841 of Queen Victoria (1837-1901) and her consort, Prince Albert. As soon as it became known that they would drive through the town on their way from Woburn to Panshanger 'every effort was made to render their entry a triumphant one', according to a contemporary account in the *Hertford Reformer*:

> The worthy mayor (Mr Rumball) convened a public meeting to take into consideration what would be the best means to carry the wishes of the town into effect; and the call was quickly responded to by all the respectable inhabitants, on both sides of politics, whose only ambition seemed to be to outvie each other in the extent of their loyalty.

A committee was formed who, with the mayor, met the royal party outside the *Verulam Arms Hotel* and accompanied them to Chequer Street, where a 120ft.-long triumphal arch had been erected, and where the mayor and committee members waited as their visitors drove away along St Peter's Street. Thousands lined the streets. In the evening, 200 people attended a ball at the Town Hall; 50 tucked in to a dinner at the *Turf Hotel*.

Victoria's return drive through the town on her way to Windsor was, if anything, more welcomed: 'Holywell Hill was covered with brilliant equipages, equestrians and pedestrians of all kinds,' reported the *Hertford Reformer* on 7 August. 'It was like a huge sea as you looked on it from an eminence. Everything bespoke joy and gladness. All, rich and poor—from the peer to the beggar—seemed gratified—and a gratifying sight it was. Laurels, flowers entwined into fantastic wreaths and white satin rosettes were everywhere.' Later, there was a firework display when the town was 'a scene of hilarity and universal merriment'.

The necessary resumption of everyday ways was, perhaps, accompanied by expectations that the example set by the royal couple in visiting St Albans would be followed by many people, who could thereby help make up for the town's loss of trade. There were, however, visitors to St Stephen's Church in October 1841 who had no intention of helping anyone except themselves. The thieves broke in and opened every pew but, it seemed to the surprise of the *Hertford Reformer* on 30 October, they took none of the prayer books. In fact, nothing of any value was taken as the communion plate was kept securely at the vicarage.

Jonathan Swift, in *Gulliver's Travels* (1726), had declared, 'That whoever could make two ears of corn, or two blades of grass, to grow upon a spot of ground where only one grew before, would deserve better of mankind, and do more essential service to his country, than the whole race of politicians put together.' Eighty-eight years after the publication of Swift's satire that essential server was born: John Bennet Lawes (1814-1900) of Harpenden. The direct descendent of a family from the Low Countries which came to England in 1564 to escape religious persecution, he left Oxford without a degree, but from boyhood had shown an interest in chemistry. Inspired by the application of chemistry to agriculture by an eminent German scientist, Justus von Liebig (1803-73), Lawes started field manure experiments on the family estate at Harpenden. With a Congregationalist minister's son, Joseph Henry Gilbert (1817-1901), who had studied under Liebig, he founded the Rothamsted Experimental Station in 1843—Britain's first agricultural research establishment—and manufactured superphosphate, the first artificial fertiliser. Since then, research into soil and plant nutrition has been continuous at Rothamsted while its achievements include the production of the world's most successful range of insecticides.

According to a petition from St Peter's parish, presented to the town council in December 1845, behaviour at the annual Michaelmas fair (around 29 September) had been disorderly. The strait-laced petitioners claimed that the fair gave rise to scenes of profligacy, that the Sabbath was violated, and they asked for a 'stricter superintendance' of the public houses and beer shops. But fairs were good for business—and what was good for business was good for St Albans. 'We are not aware,' the council replied, 'that the progress of the fair is marked by disorder and profligacy although,' as a concession, 'shows and other exhibitions will not in future be allowed to pack up on the Sabbath day and the attention of the borough justices will be called to the petitioners' remarks in regard to the public houses and beer shops.'

There was no hesitation in the invoking of legal proceedings after the municipal elections of November 1846, when a Liberal candidate, Edward Gibson, disputed the return of his

75 *Harvesting, c.1860. The buildings between the harvesters and the then as yet unrestored abbey church are those of the Silk Mill at the foot of Abbey Mill Lane.*

76 *'A burgess's priviledge [sic] to get jolly malty at Election Time'—a cartoon comment on corruption by John Henry Buckingham (1800-81). The spelling of the caption is his.*

77 *'The Guardian of the Morals of the Female Paupers: The Man of Straw.' A John Henry Buckingham cartoon on a mid-19th-century scandal. The building in the background is the Workhouse.*

Conservative opponent, Joseph Russell, on the grounds of their respective votes having been incorrectly given. A scrutiny was refused by the mayor, Richard Kentish (d.1848), acting on the advice of the town clerk, Thomas Blagg (1801-74), a Conservative, whereupon a subscription list was opened to pay the costs of the legal proceedings, which resulted in Gibson being declared duly elected. And even though the council had been reformed might it not have been supposed that the more things changed in St Albans the more they remained the same?

The council did go ahead at a specially convened meeting in 1847 to take the decisions that led to the far-reaching consequences in the town's development: support for a Bill promoted by the London and North Western Railway Company for powers to bring the branch line from Watford to St Albans, and support for the building of the branch line from St Albans to the Great Northern Railway's main line at Hatfield.

Special hopes rose, too, among a handful of people in St Albans on 29 July 1847, when the voters in a Parliamentary election returned Alexander Raphael, a wealthy Liberal and devout Catholic. The hopes were those of his co-religionists who, from 1840, had been attending at a room in the *White Hart Inn* the first public celebrations of Mass in St Albans since the upheavals of the 16th century and who dearly wanted a place of worship of their own, but were too poor to raise the money required. An appeal in the *Catholic Directory* of 1841 for help from 'our more opulent brethren ... to lend a timely support' had fallen on deaf ears. Raphael acted at once, and bought, in 1848, the defunct *Verulam Arms Hotel* (ruined by the railways) plus the adjoining land and property, and started to build the longed-for church with seating for four hundred.

At the same time, Raphael stepped in with financial help to rescue a Catholic college in Bath and for many years had supported places of learning in Austria, Germany and Italy. Near his home in Surbiton, Surrey, he had paid for the building of another Catholic church which, gracefully, was named St Raphael's. But in November 1850, as the walls of his new church were rising, Raphael died after a short illness at the age of seventy-five. No provision having been made for the completion of the church, work stopped, and though the incomplete building was offered to the Catholics of St Albans they could not afford to accept. Instead, the partly-built church was bought in 1856 by a rich widow, Mrs. Isabella Worley (1817-83), of Sopwell House, St Albans, whose benefactions over the years helped many, and she financed the completion, putting the building in trust for the Anglicans as Christ Church, which was turned over to commercial use in 1974.

78 *Sopwell House, c.1806.*

Mrs. Worley was also interested, as had been Raphael, in places of learning, paying for the building of Christ Church School, now the local headquarters of the Royal British Legion. Her interest was in keeping with a long and living local tradition, the nonconformists in particular having been keen to open schools. One of their first in St Albans was the Charity School, founded in 1739 by the St Albans-born Dr. Samuel Clark (1684-1750), the pastor at Dagnall Street Primitive Methodist chapel. The school, which clothed the children, had places for 30 boys and 10 girls, and lasted for almost a century.

Some people would not have approved. For example, Henry Home, the denouncer of travel by coach in *Sketches of the History of Man*, was greatly upset. 'Charity schools at present are more hurtful than beneficial: young persons who continue there so long as to read and write fluently, become too delicate for hard labour and too proud for ordinary labour,' he fulminated in the *History*, declaring, 'Knowledge is a dangerous acquisition to the labouring poor: the more of it that is possessed by a shepherd, a ploughman, or any drudge, the less fitted is he to labour with content.'

In short, to educate was to excite and, therefore, dangerously to incite. But undeterred by Home who, as Lord Kames, was a judge and landowner, the nonconformists opened more schools: one in Cross Street for as many as 130 infants flourished from 1836 to 1888; another, specially-built, had spaces for more than a hundred pupils from 1847 to 1884 at a single-storey building, still standing but much altered, in Spencer Street. Its prime movers had included the Rev. John Harris, of the Independent chapel in Spicer Street, and the Rev. William Upton, of Dagnall Street Baptist chapel, a prominent figure in the town for more than 40 years. The rival Abbey School of the Church of England opened in Spicer Street in 1848, and lasted there until 1970, when new premises in Abbey Orchard were

79 *Christ Church, Verulam Road, 1859.*

opened and the old school was converted into offices and private accommodation. Following the Education Act of 1870 control of the denominational schools was taken by school boards.

Raphael's death in 1850 had caused a Parliamentary by-election, the conduct of which led to a Royal Commission of Inquiry which, in its turn, led to St Albans being disfranchised in September 1852 for bribery and corruption. The voters then were lumped in with those of a county constituency for Parliamentary elections and the town was not refranchised until 1885, although as part of a grotesquely enlarged constituency.

Bribery and corruption for many years had accompanied Parliamentary elections in St Albans, and in elections throughout the country, but St Albans became especially prone to greater corruption by reason of its nearness to London. Previously, the town's aristocratic families, the Grimstons and the Spencer-Churchills, exerted a controlling influence, lubricated with bribery, in favour of candidates, but seats within easy reach of Westminster were proving attractive to wealthy candidates prepared to pay extravagantly for the privilege of proximity. In any case, 'The system had so long prevailed,' the Commission reported, 'and corruption was so widely extended that the moral sense of the inhabitants was deadened and they evinced no shame when they avowed participation in these practices.' The number of voters was small— a little under five hundred out of a population of around seven thousand—and not all took bribes.

As for the town's disfranchisement, private revenge appears to have been the motive that brought it about after one of the election agents, Henry Edwards, a farmer at Bricket Wood and former manager of Muskett's Bank in St Albans, declined to accept the services of a professional election agent, William Gresham, whose practical experience of bribery would have been second to none. In fact, bribery had been denounced by both candidates, Jacob Bell (Liberal) and Sir Robert Carden (Conservative), and it was to Carden's camp that Gresham turned, since Edwards acted for Bell. Now, Bell was determined to enter the House of Commons because, as a leading chemist and founder of the Royal Pharmaceutical Society, in 1841, he believed that chemists needed an informed representative in Parliament to safeguard their interests. So eager was he to win that, like his opponent, only more lavishly, he went along with the town's 'prevailing system' and won the election.

A scurrilous attempt by Gresham to whip up anti-Catholic feeling—Edwards having been Raphael's agent in 1847—had failed to effect the campaign's outcome. But not for nothing was Gresham a professional election agent. Even before polling day he began to make the moves which resulted in a petition being presented to Parliament giving 'notice that Jacob Bell Esq. has by himself and his Agents been guilty of Bribery and Treating, both before and during this election and is thereby incapacitated from sitting in the present Parliament'. Consequently, Bell and the town's other Member of Parliament lost their seats.

The reaction to Gresham's underhand tactics is indicated, perhaps, at an election for the churchwardenship of St Peter's in April 1851 when the voters were urged not to support a contestant who had signed the petition. Furthermore, another signatory, the former mayor John Horner Rumball, and a prominent Carden supporter, Joseph Russell, both of them town councillors, were defeated in the municipal elections of November 1851.

Once again the council was in the throes of reaching a decision. Perplexing the councillors was whether or not to admit newspaper reporters to all meetings of the council and whether or not to admit members of the public on the same occasions. The habits of secrecy proved to be too strong: neither press nor public would be admitted, it was decided in February 1851. Another attempt—to admit reporters—failed in October 1852 and the public were no luckier in February 1853 or in February 1854. Not until May 1854 did a break with tradition occur: burgesses would be admitted.

But where was the railway link for which the council had voted support in 1847? After waiting with exemplary patience, the time came in February 1853 for the council to jog the memories of the directors of the London and North Western Railway Company by sending them a reminder about the proposed branch line from Watford. Steps, replied the railway company in June 1854, were being taken and, in February 1855, to make assurance doubly sure, two councillors, John Mason and Thomas Syrett, were appointed as a committee to draw up a memorial to the directors in favour of a site near the gas works, at the foot of Holywell Hill, as the location for the station. There, three years later, to unprecedented public rejoicing, the town's first train arrived, putting St Albans on the railway map at last.

The celebrations were in keeping with the town's anticipation of the many benefits that would accompany the coming of the railway. Starting at 9 a.m., the church bells rang at intervals till late in the evening; at 1 p.m. a civic procession stepped off from the Town Hall to the station, where a crowd at least 8,000-strong watched; pony races, foot races and many stalls and booths attracted merrymakers to a meadow opposite the station; there was a grand dinner at the Town Hall and, in the newly-built Corn Exchange, a ball lasting till 3 a.m. 'Opening of the St Albans railway', was the heading above a detailed report overflowing with superlatives in *The St Alban's Times and Herts Advertiser* on Saturday, 8 May: 'This great event occurred on Wednesday last [5 May]—and we are bold to aver that our "great" adjective was never more truthfully and justly applied to any other local circumstance which has transpired within the last two or three centuries.'

Wearing white smocks or jackets, and with pink and white ribbons on their caps, 30 navvies—the line's builders—led the civic procession, followed by the men of the St Albans Original Brass Band wearing new caps of crimson and gold and massive gold tassles. Behind them came trade displays, including examples of a bonnet made of 'chaste white Leghorn [plait] of delicate texture and of elegant sloping shape—henceforth to be styled in the trade The St Albans Railway Opening' and another to be known as The St Albans First Class Carriage. The rear was brought up by the beadle, with his staff of office, the superintendent and officers of the borough police, the mace bearer, the mayor, George Debenham, in his official robe, aldermen, the town councillors, the town clerk and 'a very numerous body of Gentlemen and Traders of the town and neighbourhood, two abreast, forming a considerable length, Union Jacks and other flags', and members of the Town Brass Band in their new caps of blue and gold.

About a hundred and ten of the gentlemen and traders, among them 'many of the gentry', attended the dinner in the assembly room at the Town Hall. They heard with approval Councillor Thomas Bowman, proposing a toast to the trade and town, ask rhetorically,

> Where could another town of the size be found that could contribute from £1,000 to £1,500 for a Corn Exchange? Where a town with so many clubs and charities, and yet could contribute from £150 to £160 per year towards a Soup Kitchen [established in 1853], which last winter, distributed 560 quarts of soup per day?

Responding to the toast, the ex-mayor, John Lewis, declared without the slightest fear of contradiction 'that the railway would be of a very great advantage to all. He knew some persons who would now come to reside in the town, and give £200 per year for a house.'

From the start the train service of six trains a day each way to and from London proved insufficient, and in June, as well as increasing the number of trains, six through trains each way every day were introduced, stopping at Watford and Harrow only. 'Thus,' reported *The St Alban's Times*, 'the disagreeable annoyance of change of carriages at Watford will be done away with.'

XII

Sober Excitements, Comical Exertions

COUNCILLOR Bowman's congratulatory remarks at the railway dinner concerning the building of the Corn Exchange saluted an achievement rather than reviewed its genesis. Of course, the civic occasion was neither the time nor the place to tell the story of the Corn Exchange, which owed its conception to the inadequacies of the open-sided Market House and the annoyance caused to farmers unable to stop rain from beating in upon, and spoiling, their sacks of grain. There had been complaints for at least half a century and again in November 1853 those using the Market House asked the council for it to be improved. The council responded by suggesting that subscriptions should be collected to pay for the work. It was further resolved by the council in February 1854 that land it owned in Fishpool Street should be sold at public auction and the money raised be used towards re-building or improving the Market House. But the only real alternative was a new, functional building.

Accepting that fact, the council in October 1855 obtained plans from a Coventry architect, James Murray (1831-63), for a combined Market House and Corn Exchange. They demolished the unsatisfactory Market House but, because the cost of a larger site for the combined building would have been 'exorbitant', built the Corn Exchange alone, to new plans by Murray, on the site of the Market House which, the council agreed, would be built 'elsewhere at some future period', although that future never came. Still, apart from the £65 raised by the sale of the Fishpool Street land, the building's total cost of £1,470 had been raised by public subscription and those who, as it were, had paid the piper felt that they would be able to call the tune.

They were mistaken. Nothing, however, marred the dinner at the Corn Exchange's official opening on 23 September 1857, attended by more than a hundred landowners, tenant farmers and townsfolk who, no doubt, were proud to have done such a good job for themselves. Their justifiable pride preceded their temporary fall. High-handedly, without bothering about consultation, the council decreed in February 1859 that the Corn Exchange's opening hours should be restricted and that no trade would be allowed after 2.30 p.m. The users, ignoring the peremptory regulations, carried on as before until, in December, the peeved council announced that on market days (Wednesdays and Saturdays) no one would be allowed to enter the Corn Exchange after 3 p.m., except to collect grain or samples. The users, not having forgotten that the building belonged, in a sense, to them, objected forcibly on 17 December when, aided by a crowd of supporters, they brushed aside two policemen and entered the building at 3.45 p.m. A court case followed, attended by many farmers, in which William Ransome, of Courser's Farm, Totteridge, George Sanders, of Angell's Farm, Redbourn, and Edward King, a harness maker, of St Albans, were jointly charged with having damaged doors and door frames at the Corn Exchange to the value of £1 2s. 6d. and were fined £1 2s. 6d. with £2 9s. costs or 21 days' imprisonment.

Slow to learn, the council had to be taught another lesson. A crowded public meeting in the Corn Exchange of farmers, corn dealers, traders and others, convened by handbills previously distributed in the town and vicinity, unanimously agreed to boycott the Corn Exchange from 31 December and trade in other premises, thereby inflicting a loss of revenue on the council which, in March 1860, cravenly decided to let the Corn Exchange stay open for as long as the farmers and dealers required. The farmers, whose occupation meant that they knew how to harrow, kept the council waiting for a reply until December. Their terms for a return to the Corn Exchange left no stone unturned: the council would have to pay them the £30 expenses they had incurred in the move, arrange for the use of the premises they had hired and promise not to interfere with the hours of holding the corn market. The council gave way completely on 26 December—its surrender a late Christmas present—and by February 1861 the farmers had returned victorious to *their* Corn Exchange. It remained in use for the buying and selling of grain, among other activities, until the end of the century, when the telephone made corn exchanges redundant, and the building was divided into shops.

Incidents like the forcing open of the Corn Exchange, coupled with the death of a prisoner in one of the old police cells, prompted the council in 1860 to build a single-storey police station—now a shop—behind the Town Hall. There had been a town police force since 1836, when Alexander Wilson was appointed as the first superintendent under the requirements of the Municipal Reform Act. And as police forces, uniform and uniformed, modelled on those first established in London by Sir Robert Peel in 1829, replaced old, military, ways of policing with new, civic, ways, so at St Albans' police station in 1849 did gas light replace candles as a bright sign of the changing times. The new ways of working could be no less exhausting than the old. Peter Jaques had worn himself out by length of service in the town's constabulary and was awarded 5s. a week pension in 1854. Three years later the council resolved to improve their force's efficiency by increasing its numbers to seven: a superintendent, two sergeants, three second-class constables and a constable. The superintendent resigned in 1858 and was succeeded by William James Pike, of Leicester, at £1 10s. a week, with clothes; his duties included those of sanitary inspector, inspector of common lodging houses, and inspector of weights and measures.

The council, having demolished the old Market House, had worked up an appetite for destruction and tried to indulge it. High on its menu was the medieval Clock Tower which, it had been suggested, should be pulled down to save money. Its condition had caused concern in 1852, and some renovation was undertaken but, by August 1855, the council heard evidence that its condition was dangerous and, in November, repairs were recommended. As a start, perhaps, delapidated buildings beside the tower were removed in 1858 and in their place the council resolved by six votes to three in May 1861 to surround (prop up?) the tower with shops. It had taken the councillors nearly ten years to come up with a scheme; if they could take another ten the chances were that the tower obligingly would collapse. But the public outrage that greeted their proposal was immediate, widespread and effective. Eighty-five people living in and around the town, including the Earl of Verulam, signed a petition of protest, supplemented soon after by a persuasive letter from the St Albans Architectural and Archaeological Society. Founded in 1845, and influential from inception, it proposed a public restoration fund, pledging £30 from its own funds, to which the townsfolk added £309. Bowing before the storm, the councillors rescinded their former resolution by five votes to three and the tower, saved at the last moment, was restored by George Gilbert Scott, the noted architect already working sensitively on the restoration of the abbey church.

80   The west front of the abbey church before rebuilding, 1866.

And still the council could not leave well alone. For some time the British and Irish Magnetic Telegraph Company had been negotiating to run their wires through St Albans and, on the understanding that a telegraph office would be maintained in the town, the company was allowed, in August 1867, for £10 a year, to rent as an office the lower room of the tower. It might have been worse. In 1860 two councillors had wanted the police cells to be built near the tower and the lower room to be used as the town's police station. But the restored tower was fitted with a new and costly (£152) clock in 1866. Its old curfew bell, dating from 1335, had been silenced in 1863 after complaints from nearby residents.

Now and again, international affairs attracted municipal attention. During the American civil war, in 1861, the council petitioned the British government not to recognise the secessionist southern states, and sent an address of sympathy to the United States on the assassination of President Abraham Lincoln, in 1865, to which the Americans responded by sending the council a 'finely-bound' volume in acknowledgment.

During the same year, 1865, the town's shop assistants won a small improvement in their working conditions after the publication in *The St Alban's Times* on 2 September of a polite and carefully argued letter to the editor, signed 'The Assistants', which called for early closing:

> In most of our large towns they have 'half holidays'. We do not ask for that, believing that if we did we should not get it at present; but we hope to have it some day. What we want now is 'only an hour' off the Saturday's long and fatiguing labour. The shops are now closed, sir, at eleven and twelve during the summer season, and ten and eleven during the winter (drapers at eleven, and grocers at twelve). Is it too much to ask that all the shops be closed during the winter season at nine, and the summer at ten?

A week later it was reported in the same newspaper that the assistants' appeal had 'had the desired effect' and that the 'drapers, clothiers etc, of the town, have agreed to close on Saturday nights, during the winter months (from November to March inclusive), at Nine o'clock; and during the summer months (from April to October inclusive), at Ten o'clock. The grocers have agreed to close at Ten o'clock all the year round. This,' the report ended, 'is a step in the right direction.'

But five years later, although the drapers, clothiers and outfitters introduced early Saturday evening closing, at 9 p.m. during the winter, the grocers had reverted to their harsher habits of keeping assistants and, perhaps, themselves behind the counter from 7 a.m. to 11.30 p.m. 'Late trading is an expensive evil, and an unhealthy system, and should be wholly and for ever abolished,' wrote a correspondent in the *Herts Advertiser*—as *The St Alban's Times* had re-styled itself—of 15 October 1870.

In its next issue, on 22 October, another correspondent commended the drapers, 'and some others', for agreeing to close early, and declared himself to be

> equally gratified in observing that several grocers and general provision dealers (five, if I mistake not) have had the manly courage to close at eight instead of nine o'clock, and it so happens that five of the number are Nonconformists in principle, and, apparently, dissent from patronising the late hour and drudgery system.

Grocers' youths and shopmen, the letter-writer explained, worked an 87-hour week 'while very many of our mechanics work only 52'.

Early closing seems to have been supported in the town, and by most behind the counter, if an editorial footnote to the second letter accurately reflects public opinion: 'We are glad to inform our correspondent that since his letter was written the grocers generally have agreed to close their shops at eight o'clock.' Furthermore, as Christmas Day that year fell on a Sunday, the town's drapers agreed to close their shops on the Monday and Tuesday 'to give their assistants an opportunity of spending the Christmas holidays with their friends'.

Efforts continued to ease working conditions until, in June 1872, the drapers and other traders announced that they would close at five o'clock for a few weeks to give their employees a chance to enjoy the summer evenings. The grocers again were back to late hours, according to a letter in the *Herts Advertiser* of 1 June 1872, which pointed out that

> if any class of men and assistants really do need, and deserve, a release from toil, it is the grocers, some of whom on Saturdays keep open nearly eighteen hours, which is equivalent to three days of the building trade half-holiday men. I am pleased to hear, that with one or two exceptions, they are, as a body, willing to close, and why it is such a majority should allow themselves to be governed by one or two, is best known to themselves. My advice to them is, 'dare to be humane,' and the public will appreciate your noble sympathy with such a well-merited object.

Quite extraordinary were the antics of some of the shop-keepers in their attempts to ingratiate themselves with the grander customers. Mary Carbery recalled shopping with her mother in the 1870s: 'She sits in the carriage, and out run the shopmen with what she wants. If a helper in the shop gets out first, the owner rushes after him, snatches the tray of ribbons or buttons, jabs the young man with his elbow so that he nearly falls in the gutter, and apologizes to Mama for not having been the first on the spot.' Happy world, indeed!

Keeping an amused and amusing eye on that world was an old Chartist, John Henry Buckingham (1800-81). A former clerk, a sometime brewer, an ex-publican—he had leased the *Vine Inn*, Spicer Street, in 1833—but, about 1859, he hit upon an occupation to his liking: antique dealer. Living frugally, mostly on bread and cheese above his shop in High Street, he took to exercising a talent for landscape painting and his gifts as a cartoonist, using the shop window to tickle the fancy of a delighted public with displays of comic political and social cartoons until shortly before he died. He had also been known to readers of the *Herts Advertiser* as a frequent letter writer on current topics.

Locally and nationally, the farm workers became a topic overnight when, in 1872, under the leadership of a Primitive Methodist lay preacher, Joseph Arch, they formed their first countrywide trade union, the National Agricultural Labourers' Union. There was no question in their own minds, or in the minds of many observers, that they were treated harshly, and deserved better pay and conditions. Edwin Grey, describing Harpenden during the 1860s-70s in *Cottage Life in a Hertfordshire Village*, wrote,

> These hired farm hands, both boys and young men, had to rise at 4 o'clock to feed and water their horses, etc. ... After tending to the horses, etc., came breakfast, the head ploughman came along at 5 o'clock, and at 6 o'clock the men and their teams started off to the fields; they continued to plough until 2 o'clock with a break of half an hour at 10 o'clock for a 'beaver'. By 2 o'clock each team was supposed to have ploughed an acre (ploughing an acre of land being deemed a day's work). The horses would then be shut out from the plough, and they and the men get back to the farm, when the horses would be watered, etc. Then came dinner, after which the horses would be cleaned and combed, stable littered, and the animals fed and made comfortable ... for the night and the men's day's work ended, this was an ordinary day. At harvest and hay times the hours were much longer, the men working sometimes until 9 o'clock or past.

It came, therefore, as no surprise that 500 of the farm labourers from in and around St Albans, with their families, attended a meeting on Nomansland Common in June 1872 and thronged to join the union, whose modest main aims were a weekly wage of 16s. and a nine-and-a-half-hour day. They elected as their local chairman William Paul (1821-1901), of Sandridge, a respected carpenter with sufficient financial independence to risk the farmers' hostility, and who more than anyone, according to E. Giles and R.W. Thrale in *Historic Sandridge* (1952) 'asserted the rights of the artisan class to a share in village government. He broke the tradition that only gentry and farmers should attend vestry meetings.' He was quoted in the *Herts Advertiser* of 8 June as telling the farm workers that the object of their meetings was to raise funds to enable them to form a union, so that they might ask and obtain a fair and proper price for their labours.

A week later a second meeting was held on Harpenden Common, attended by 'no fewer than seven or eight hundred people ... although,' the *Herts Advertiser* reported on 15 June, 'it is true many of them were persons who had evidently come to gratify the curiosity very naturally excited by the novelty of the meeting, and not from motives of personal interest in the matter'. A union official told the meeting that the farmers of Harpenden were willing to increase their men's wages, and that Mr. Dorant, of St Albans, had authorised him 'to receive applications from any of the labourers who wished to emigrate to New Zealand, or any of the colonies, with the view to their obtaining free or assisted passages'.

Among the 'numerous attendance' at the farm workers' meeting on Bernard's Heath in July were 'a considerable number of tradesmen and others from St Albans'. Another meeting, reportedly disorderly, was held at London Colney.

Clearly, the farmers were under pressure, and more pressure was brought to bear by the *Herts Advertiser* in an editorial on 3 August 1872:

That the labourers can show a good case no one can doubt; that their wages must and ought to be increased is equally certain. How they and their families have managed to live on twelve or fourteen shillings per week has often excited our surprise; nor do we believe the employers, as a whole, are adverse to a fair and moderate rise.

And so it proved: agricultural wages rose by an average of 2s. a week throughout the country, although the slightly better times did not last. Huge quantities of cheap wheat were imported from the United States after 1875 and British farming went into a depression from which it did not begin to recover until the outbreak of the First World War in 1914.

Nevertheless, for the farm workers the formation and early successes of their trade union had been instructive, sharpening their desire to take part in national politics and, as a necessary means to that end, their obtaining of the vote. A 'large meeting of agricultural workers was held in the Corn Exchange,' the *Herts Advertiser* reported on 3 March 1873, 'when a resolution was passed asking the House of Commons to extend the borough franchise to the counties of England'. The campaign took another 11 years before the labourers' dogged demand for enfranchisement was met by the Reform Bill of 1884.

Coinciding with the farm labourers' sober excitements of 1872, and overlapping them, were the town council's unintentionally comical exertions concerning a magnificent drinking fountain. The donor was Mrs. Worley, the wealthy widow, of Sopwell House, whose charitable works had become proverbial. She gave clothing and meat every Christmas to hundreds of the poor in St Albans, provided tasty treats for children and, after completing Christ Church for the Anglicans, paid for the building of the vicarage, built a nonconformist meeting place, the Wooden Room, in Lattimore Road, financing its gospel work, and supported various orphanages and hospitals, including the St Albans Hospital and Dispensary on Holywell Hill. It was especially for poor wayfarers tramping to and from London that she offered the town council the gift of the £500 fountain in November 1870.

80 The Wooden Room, Lattimore Road, shortly before its destruction by fire in 1994.

Hesitation, indecision and reconsideration were the continuing responses. The shuffles began on 9 November, when the council appointed a committee—a move indicative of doubts—to consider the offer and did not agree to accept it until certain that the St Albans Water Company would supply the fountain's water free of charge. But a baffling puzzle remained unsolved: where should the fountain be sited? Answers flew backwards and forwards. At the start, on 21 December, the council opted for a position in front of the Clock Tower instead of centrally at Market Cross, overlooking the High Street, near to the site recommended by the fountain's architect, George Gilbert Scott. The matter rested until April 1872, when an anxious deputation of about twenty Market Cross traders, fearing that the placing of the fountain near the Clock Tower would obstruct their businesses, asked the council to follow Scott's advice and, after weighing the pros and cons for two hours, the council voted in favour of a site in front of the Town Hall.

Mrs. Worley objected. 'In giving the matter of the drinking fountain more attention,' she wrote to the mayor, Edward Sutton Wiles (1813-94), on 18 April, 'I think I should prefer it

82 Mrs. Worley's drinking fountain, right, and behind it the medieval Clock Tower, c.1905.

to be placed nearer the Clock Tower in the High Street, as I consider it would be almost useless in St Peter's Street, and would quite defeat the purpose I have in mind, as I wish it to be of benefit to the poor people.' A petition signed by 138 ratepayers supported her objection, and called for the Clock Tower site, while an individual ratepayer, living in the High Street, asked the council to consider putting the fountain on the corner of George Street and Verulam Road.

The argument's outcome mattered, not only to the traders likely to be affected, but to the townsfolk at large, many of whom attended a special meeting of the council, on 23 April, which was reported at length in the *Herts Advertiser:*

> The interest and excitement which have lately prevailed in the town upon this question were again strikingly manifested on this occasion by the presence of a large number of ratepayers, the Council Chamber having been thrown open to the public. At the commencement of business there were but few persons present, but towards eight o'clock there had assembled about seventy or eighty inhabitants, some of whom occasionally gave utterances to expressions either of approbation or disapprobation of the opinions which emanated from the Council. The latter expressions, however, having once or twice assumed the character of hisses, the Mayor courteously requested the ratepayers to refrain from venting their individual feelings, and the proceedings thus maintained a more orderly aspect than they might otherwise have done.

Mrs. Worley's objection, combined with the visible extent of public concern, persuaded the council to rescind its St Peter's Street resolution and again to adopt the site near that proposed by Scott at Market Cross where, in June, the 9ft.-high fountain was opened by the mayor to the loud and long cheers of a large crowd. Mrs. Worley stayed away because, said her friend, Henry Toulmin, 'we who have known that good lady for so many years have always seen that her many good works have been done without any ostentation, and in the most quiet and charming way possible'.

In October 1883, nine months after Mrs. Worley's death, the siting of the fountain came up for further discussion at the town council and it was agreed to relocate it on the site originally proposed by Scott. A councillor noted for his sense of humour, William Hurlock (1840-1925), suggested that the fountain should be put on wheels so that it could be moved from place to place without much expense when the members of the council changed their minds. Wheels were the cause of the fountain's removal in the 1920s owing to the demands of motor traffic, which necessitated street widening, but the fountain was restored and re-assembled, in 1990, as the centrepiece of Victoria Square.

XIII

Enlargement

CHANGES crowded in during the last thirty or so years of the century as St Albans underwent an enlargement faster and greater than for any similar length of time throughout the whole of its previous history. Undoubtedly, many of the inhabitants welcomed the changes, as there was an expectation that a bigger St Albans would be a better St Albans: 'Of late years,' wrote Frederick Mason, in his *Illustrated Handbook* (1884),

> the city, and especially the north-eastern part of it, lying between Bernard's Heath and the Midland [City] Railway Station has very much increased, and is still increasing. A considerable portion of land, known as St Peter's Park, has been planted and laid out for the erection of villas, new roads have been made, and these will form a pleasant addition to the suburbs of the city. Other estates in the same quarter have been sold for building purposes. Altogether a prosperous future appears to lie before the good city of St Albans.

The future had not always appeared to be rosy. There had been the ever-present risk of disease which, in 1872, became actual with an outbreak of smallpox. Part of the trouble was the fault of the town's uncontrolled development, as an editorial in the *Herts Advertiser* of 27 January 1872 explained:

> In the neighbourhood of the Midland [City] Railway-station there has come into existence since the extension of that line almost a second St Albans—an area of land divided and sub-divided by miserable specimens of roads, thickly covered with buildings— many of them attractive villa-residences for middle class people, and many cottages occupied by artisans—the whole in all probability containing about a thousand inhabitants, and most of them erected without the slightest attempt at a system of drainage. Can anything, we ask, be imagined more unfinished, more unsatisfactory and dangerous than this? Numerous inhabitants, most of them belonging to highly respectable classes of society, massed together in blocks of buildings with no drainage but cesspools! There is no disputing the fact that these houses are built without the smallest regard to sanitary convenience and law.

A further fact was that the town's eastern side had overspread the enlarged borough boundary of 1835 and, until an again enlarged boundary was secured, in 1879, the 'second St Albans' lacked statutory control. 'Sanitary law,' the *Herts Advertiser* continued, 'is therefore imperatively in a state of chaos in the extra-municipal part; a land owner is at liberty to break up his land, form badly finished roads, run up ill-conceived and hastily constructed houses with defective drainage, and all in utter disregard of sanitary precautions.'

Dusty streets were another cause for complaint and had been for many years. 'Where are the water carts?' asked 'A Sufferer' in a letter to the *Herts Advertiser* on 21 September 1872.

'The roads are being quickly blown away! Visitors to the town beat a hasty retreat! Every shopkeeper is lamenting that his goods are being ruined! In fact all are suffering from the clouds of dust which, for the last fortnight, have filled our streets and tormented the inhabitants generally!'

Some inhabitants were tormented by the changes to the town and, from time to time, their anguish found violent expression. One such outburst occurred after the closing of the passageway through the abbey church during the restoration work of Sir George Gilbert Scott. A petition to the council signed by 45 residents early in 1874 threatened that unless the boarded up passageway was re-opened they, the petitioners, would consider themselves at liberty to enforce their rights. The following week, on 14 May, the council received another petition, signed by 63 residents, supporting the passageway's closure and the council, perhaps taking into consideration Scott's opinion that the hacking out of the passageway had in the first place been an act of vandalism, resolved that it should remain closed for 12 months to allow the repairs to be completed. The threat, however, of the original petitioners had not been an idle one: on the night of 20 May a crowd tore down the boarding and re-opened the passageway for public use.

But more was at stake for at least one of the protesters, although undeclared at the time, than the protection against change of a long-established right. The hidden promptings were those of the usually outspoken William Hurlock. A successful London draper, who lived in St Albans, he would, at the end of the year, be elected a town councillor, and was and remained a staunch nonconformist. It was his religious outlook that coloured his passageway protest. The passageway closure and the re-uniting of the Lady Chapel with the main body of the abbey church he saw as moves towards a rehabilitation of what he denounced as 'Mariolatry'. To him, any veneration of the Virgin Mary was abhorrent. Later he made public his opinion in a letter to the *Herts Advertiser* on 11 September 1875, when he also expressed indifference concerning the restoration of the Lady Chapel, and described the then recently restored shrines of Alban and Amphibalus as 'no better than the idols of the heathen'. All the same, he led the passageway protest with distinctive style, hiring a brass band to blast home his objections and, though the passageway remained closed, a public right of way was substituted around the east end of the abbey church.

Earlier, the Lady Chapel had been vacated by its occupant for three centuries, St Albans School, which moved into the Gatehouse after that ceased to be used as a prison on the completion, in 1866, of a new gaol opposite the City station. Surrounded by a high, brick wall, the gaol contained 99 cells and was designed to be 'not unnecessarily grim and ugly'. Most of it was demolished in 1931, except for the wall and the gatehouse, which were cleverly incorporated among the offices, erected in 1990, surrounding Victoria Square.

83 The pedestal of the shrine as restored in the 19th century and, in the background, the wooden watching loft, c.1400.

84   Rolling the lawn in Vintry Garden, c.1875.

And when change meant necessary improvement it frequently was sought, even if its achievement were inordinately delayed. There had, for instance, been complaints about the smell caused by a tallow factory on the corner of Verulam Road and George Street, and a petition against the nuisance was submitted to the council in August 1875: 'The stench arising from the tallow, fat and other ingredients is most offensive and intolerable to the surrounding neighbourhood and passers-by, and we trust that you will adopt such measures as may be necessary to abate the nuisance'. Unluckily for the neighbourhood and passers-by the factory's owner, Edward Sutton Wiles, who lived in London Road, was much admired for his kindness and probity, and had been mayor in 1871, and would be again, in 1880 and 1881. He was ordered to abate the nuisance, in 1885, following which the council received a repeated petition of complaint, in 1886, when he was summoned, found guilty of having caused a nuisance and fined. The only reason that the nuisance had been allowed to last for so long was, according to the prosecution, that everyone interested in the matter had such a high respect for Wiles. His factory, re-located at Bernard's Heath, was destroyed by fire in 1911 and, re-built, stayed as smelly as ever.

Charles Woollam (1832-1915), the owner of the Abbey silk mill, and a generous benefactor of the town, carried out in October 1877 a threat he had made in 1874 to prosecute the council for allowing sewage to pollute the Ver. Another petition, signed in 1875 by two-thirds of the ratepayers concerned, requested the lighting of their streets by gas lamps. But the town's inadequacies were glaring: defective drainage, deficient water supply, rudimentary roads and footpaths.

Slowly, the inadequacies were rectified in the course of 10 years, although many of the streets and roads had to wait until 1883 before being paved, kerbed, channelled and improved. Street widening had continued, notably of Sweet Briar Lane which, in 1876, a year before the 40th anniversary of the queen's accession, was re-named Victoria Street. In that street, also in 1876, privately owned public baths, which included a

85   The abbey church of St Albans from Vintry Garden, 1886.

swimming pool, were established after a decade and more of pressure to obtain them, especially 'for the people who are crowded into dwellings too small for thorough ablutions to be performed with decency', as the *Herts Advertiser* of 5 January 1867 had reported.

Two more events ensured that the anniversary year of 1877 would be memorable for St Albans: the town was made a city by royal charter in August as a consequence of the founding of the diocese of St Albans in April. Formed out of the unwieldy diocese of Rochester—of which Hertfordshire and Essex then formed part—the new diocese was created to provide closer episcopal supervision of the area's greatly increased population. The abbey church became a cathedral (although it stayed, and stays, known locally as 'the abbey') and the first bishop was enthroned. Bishop Thomas Claughton (1808-92), an Oxford professor of poetry before becoming vicar of Kidderminster, 1841-67, arrived in St Albans after 10 years as Bishop of Rochester. He took a close interest in the cathedral's sensitive restoration but, a year after his enthronement, the architect responsible, Sir George Gilbert Scott, died and into his place popped an immensely rich barrister and amateur architect, Sir Edmund Beckett, later Lord Grimthorpe (1816-1905).

Solely on account of his wallet he gained official authorisation to 'restore, repair and refit the church' and, said *Murray's Handbook* (1895), 'although there may be differences of opinion as to the character and style of some of the restoration, it cannot be denied that his lordship has at immense expenditure of time and money now placed this ancient building in a thoroughly sound condition'. Charles Kingsley, three years younger than Grimthorpe, almost could have been describing him in *The Water Babies*: 'So they all were setting upon poor Sir John, year after year, and trying to talk him into spending a hundred thousand pounds or so, in building to please them and not himself. But he always put them off, like a canny North-countryman as he was.' Actually, a canny Midlander, Grimthorpe built to his own design, a mile and a quarter north of the abbey church, a home for himself, Batchwood Hall, now a night club.

87   Lord Grimthorpe (1816-1905).

Surely, though, the town's most surprising spectacle during 1877 was that provided by the builders of its first Catholic church to be completed since the 16th century. Cardinal Henry Manning, the Archbishop of Westminster, had laid the foundation stone of SS Alban and Stephen Church on land at 94 London Road donated by Major James Gape (1826-1904), a member of a family long prominent in St Albans, and was present exactly a year later, 22 June 1878, for the opening of the completed portion—all of it, from the digging of the foundations to the laying of the bricks and the finish of the woodwork, having been done entirely by boys under the supervision of an adult builder. The church remained in use until its larger successor in Beaconsfield Road opened in 1905, when it became a garage.

87 *Some of the workmen employed in the restoration work at the abbey church in 1880. The balding man is John Chapple, the Clerk of Works.*

88 *Lord Grimthorpe as an angel in the central porch at the west end of the Cathedral and Abbey Church of St Alban.*

From 1878, when the town council resolved to house the fire engine on the north side of Victoria Street, a string of welcome improvements began to be provided. The engine had been housed previously, for some twenty years, on a site now occupied by St Albans School's war memorial and, before that, since the 17th century, engines of various kinds had been kept at various locations. The late 19th-century engine house was moved at the turn of the century to the south side of Victoria Street, where it remained until a new fire station opened in Harpenden Road in 1964. It also was in 1878 that the townsfolk attending a meeting at the Town Hall supported a proposal to provide a public library, which was incorporated in a School of Science and Art, a spacious building erected opposite the fire station in 1881 by public subscription, and decorated on its frontage by high relief portraits in terracotta roundels of Humphrey Davy, William Hogarth and Francis Bacon. Henry Jenkin Gotto (1818-92), an Oxford Street stationer with property in St Albans, who came to live in the city, improved the appearance of St Peter's Street in 1881 by paying for the planting of lime trees on either side. One good deed deserving another, he was rewarded with the honour of being co-opted to the library committee. Alongside Hatfield Road, on what was then the edge of the town, 18 acres of land were bought in 1882 for use as a cemetery by all religious denominations or none and, to emphasise its inclusiveness, it was dedicated, rather than consecrated, by the obliging Bishop Claughton.

A setback happened in 1883. An offer to the corporation of the unprofitable public baths and swimming pool at a bargain price failed to win the support of ratepayers, who in a poll crushingly rejected acceptance by 1,132 votes to 162 in favour. The upshot was that later in the year the baths were bought by the Salvation Army, refurbished, and opened as its local headquarters, which were re-built in 1911.

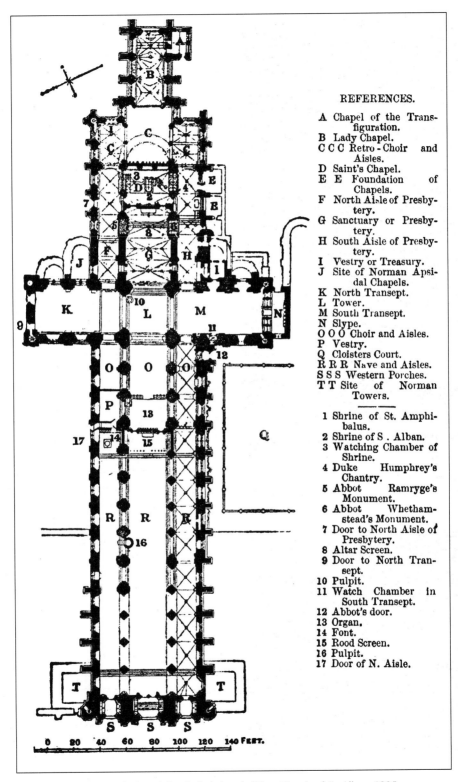

REFERENCES.

A Chapel of the Trans-
    figuration.
B Lady Chapel.
C C C Retro - Choir and
    Aisles.
D Saint's Chapel.
E E Foundation of
    Chapels.
F North Aisle of Presby-
    tery.
G Sanctuary or Presby-
    tery.
H South Aisle of Presby-
    tery.
I Vestry or Treasury.
J Site of Norman Apsi-
    dal Chapels.
K North Transept.
L Tower.
M South Transept.
N Slype.
O O O Choir and Aisles.
P Vestry.
Q Cloisters Court.
R R R Nave and Aisles.
S S S Western Porches.
T T Site of Norman
    Towers.

1 Shrine of St. Amphi-
    balus.
2 Shrine of S . Alban.
3 Watching Chamber of
    Shrine.
4 Duke Humphrey's
    Chantry.
5 Abbot Ramryge's
    Monument.
6 Abbot Whetham-
    stead's Monument.
7 Door to North Aisle of
    Presbytery.
8 Altar Screen.
9 Door to North Tran-
    sept.
10 Pulpit.
11 Watch Chamber in
    South Transept.
12 Abbot's door.
13 Organ.
14 Font.
15 Rood Screen.
16 Pulpit.
17 Door of N. Aisle.

89 *Ground plan of the Cathedral and Abbey Church of St Alban, 1895.*

With a population of almost 11,000, and increasing, St Albans as yet showed few signs of industrial development, except most noticeably for the straw plait trade then at its peak. 'The staple trade of the city is the manufacture of straw hats,' stated Gibbs' *Guide to St Albans* (1884), 'in which women are principally employed, and which therefore accounts for the considerable numerical superiority of women over men in St Albans.' Perhaps that explains why around that time public meetings and discussions in the town were raising the issue of votes for women. A crowded meeting on the subject was held in the Town Hall in January 1884, chaired by the mayor, James Fisk (1837-99), who owned a large drapery store in High Street. He said

> he was astonished that a question so fair and reasonable required so much talking upon. Now, however, they had to agitate if they wanted to get anything done for them. He did not see why female householders should not have the same privileges as men, and he hoped the Government would admit all householders, whether men or women, to the full exercise of the franchise.

It was agitation, allied to direct action, which helped win a battle whose outcome mattered more to the people of St Albans than had any battle fought previously in the town. The campaign began after an unofficial enclosure of some of the common land stretching irregularly eastwards on the south side of Sandpit Lane from near its junction at Stonecross to the railway bridge. The culprits, Frederick Austen, of St Peter's Street, a builder, and John Wells, of Hillside Road, a jeweller and property developer, owned land in Avenue Road which backed on to the common land. Austen had built a house on his land, bought from Wells, who had owned and developed the area, St Peter's Park estate, since 1880, and was completing the building of an estate at Bernard's Heath. The acquisitive pair laid claim to the Sandpit Lane common land early in 1884, demarcating their separate, but adjoining, encroachments distinctively: Austen with a wooden fence, Wells with a wire fence, and the combined length stretched for at least 400ft., enclosing land varying in depth from five feet to eighty.

90 *Common land along the south side of Sandpit Lane was saved from illegal enclosure in 1884. This view from the corner of Heath Road looking towards St Saviour's Church is dated c.1914.*

The first warning of active resistance to the enclosure was given at a town council meeting in March 1884 by a Liberal councillor, William Westell (1831-1901), of Holywell Hill, who as well as being a straw hat manufacturer in St Albans was a friend and political ally of William Hurlock. Each strengthened the other. Westell, having called the council's attention to the encroachment, contended that it was perfectly open to anybody to pull down the fences and he proposed that steps should be taken to get them removed. Hurlock agreed: 'There is no doubt that the whole of this land in Sandpit Lane belongs to the public, and it is a case of clear encroachment.' But, on the advice of the town clerk, Isaac Newton Edwards, it was agreed that legal enquiries should be made before implementing action; thereafter, the dictates of caution affected the council to such an extent that it suffered a prolonged attack of dither.

Resolutions were passed and later rescinded, action was agreed, then postponed or cancelled, and still, after five months, the

91   William Hurlock (1840-1925): a portrait from Ernest Gaskell's late 19th-century Hertfordshire Leaders: Social and Political.

fences remained in place until, in mid-July, among those attending a crowded public meeting in the Corn Exchange to consider the encroachment, it was decided that actions would speak louder than words. The meeting had been called by Hurlock's friend and co-religionist, the Rev. Henry Taylor (1848-1934), the pastor of St Albans Baptist Tabernacle, in Victoria Street, who said, 'I wonder at the audacity of a man who can take such a piece of land from the public. I also marvel at the sweet sleep the neighbourhood and the town council labour under in regard to the matter.'

The sleepers were awakening. A resolution expressing 'indignant protest against the wanton and illegal enclosure' had been passed at the meeting with only one vote against. Next day, a large deputation, headed by Taylor, was received at a meeting of the council in the Town Hall. 'The council are the guardians of the people's rights,' he told them, 'and it is better that they should cause the fence to be removed constitutionally rather than leave it to a hurry scurrying crowd to do the work.' Once more, though, the dithering council voted for the taking of legal advice.

'Pull it down!' members of the deputation shouted. 'Pull it down!'

That afternoon, Wednesday 16 July, fifty or so men, many of whom had accompanied the deputation, tore down part of Wells' wire fence before being dispersed by the police but, while the police were absent changing shifts, returned to continue the clearance. They left Austen's wooden fence until the next evening when, equipped with a long saw, about a thousand protesters surged onto the field of battle in Sandpit Lane and entirely demolished the remaining fence.

Eight of those directly or indirectly involved—all of them living in St Albans—appeared for two days in August before a magistrates' court, the chairman of which was Sir Edmund

Beckett. As well as Westell and Hurlock, the defendants were Edgar Crowhurst, a dealer, William Hilliard, a former lawyer's clerk, Thomas Martin, a one-legged pedlar, and three labourers, William Giddens, Edwin Toms and Harry Wakefield. On the charge of destroying Austen's fence, Westell, Hurlock, Giddens and Toms were dismissed while the others were found guilty, fined £2 10s. each, with costs, or be gaoled for a month; regarding Wells' fence, Westell and Hurlock were, as the leaders, fined £5 each; the others were fined £2 10s. each, or a month, and the costs were ordered to be shared between all eight.

A defence fund had been set up before the trial and, after it, so were the two fences—but not for too long. Complaints were made by the National Footpath Preservation Society to Sandpit Lane's Lord of the Manor, Earl Spencer, who saw to it that the fences were removed, leaving the common land unfenced as it is today. Westell, too, had complained and was thanked by Earl Spencer.

Wells left St Albans, in 1893, to settle in New York as a dealer in works of art and curios. Owning The Mansion, at 1 St Peter's Street, which had been the residence of several mayors, he enterprisingly helped himself to its old oak panelling and Tudor carvings, shipping them to the United States from where, in 1922, he was sailing to England when he died and was buried at sea, aged seventy-eight.

As for Hurlock, he had by no means shot his bolt but proceeded publicly and defiantly to associate himself with a bogey-man of the first magnitude: Charles Bradlaugh. A republican, a radical, an atheist, and prominent for most of the second half of the century as a champion of individual liberties, he had scandalised timid respectability by his advocacy of birth-control. Besides that, although having been chosen by the electors of Northampton, in 1880, to represent them in Parliament, he was denied his seat for more than five years because he wished to affirm rather than take a religious oath. Only early in 1886 had he been admitted to the House of Commons and he was, therefore, a most conspicuous and sulphurous figure to appear in September 1886 as the chief speaker at a Liberal demonstration, chaired by Hurlock in the grounds of his own home, Ver House, at the foot of Holywell Hill.

Bradlaugh arrived to loud cheers, although the attendance was 'moderate', according to the *Herts Advertiser*, and an explanation for that apparent lack of support was offered by the city treasurer, George Walter Blow (1844-1912), a Liberal spokesman, in a letter to Bradlaugh dated 7 October:

> I have no doubt it would have been a satisfaction to you to have been surrounded by the leading Liberals of the division, but they stayed away because you were the principal speaker. If this had been an ordinary demonstration the platform would have been crowded as it was a year ago [for a general election], and the audience would have numbered, as then, 2,500 instead of 900; but your presence was not sufficiently attractive. I ought in fairness to you to say that our absence from the meeting was not because of your attacks upon religion (which I consider will do religion more good than harm) but because of your filthy *Fruits of Philosophy*.

The 45-year-old American birth-control pamphlet had been reprinted by Bradlaugh and his equally sulphurous business partner, Mrs. Annie Besant, in 1877.

◆ **XIV**

'Nice Quiet Place'

MORE hard times had brought hardship although, in 1886, there were hopes that a period of recession was ending. All the same, A.J.O. Gray, a butcher, referred to the deprivations in the *Herts Advertiser* of 5 June while advertising with enlightened self-interest his own contribution towards a lowering of the cost of living:

> Now LAMB—that luscious morsel,
>   Has lately cost so much,
> That artizan or tradesman
>   Never dare this good food touch.
>
> But at the shop in Verulam-street
>   Good LAMB is daily sold,
> Fore-quarters at Eleven pence
>   To young as well as old.
>
> The reason why I sell so cheap
>   Is very quickly told,
> I love my neighbour as myself
>   And care not much for gold.

92   Joseph Halsey (1833-1934) ran a grocery shop in George Street.

To Cardinal John Henry Newman, the most illustrious of the 19th-century Catholics who had at first been Anglicans, St Albans was known as the place where lived and worked an old friend, Henry Bittleston—one of the six priests to whom he had dedicated 'as a memorial of affection and gratitude' his eloquent autobiography, *Apologia pro Vita Sua* (1864). In St Albans, Bittleston served for four years as the parish priest at SS Alban and Stephen Church until his death in July 1886 at the age of sixty-seven. Much loved throughout the district, according to the *Herts Advertiser*, he was buried in the then recently opened Hatfield Road cemetery.

In September, perhaps as an outcome of the Third Reform Bill having extended the franchise, an increased interest in current affairs, and a consequent wider awareness of the need to be able to speak up in public, and speak with confidence, seem to have prompted the formation of the St Albans Debating Society. A corresponding political response to the new possibilities of constitutional involvement in deciding the issues of the day was, during 1886, the opening of a Conservative Club in St Peter's Street and of a Liberal Club in Victoria Street.

The laying of a foundation stone by the mayor, Henry Partridge Smith (1844-1939), for a Cottage Hospital on the corner of Church Crescent and Verulam Road commemorated Queen Victoria's golden jubilee on 21 June 1887 and, at the same time, recognised the need for a larger provision of hospital services to cope with the city's increasing population. Smith, who owned a straw hat factory in Victoria Street, told the large crowd at the stone-laying ceremony that he thanked, on behalf of every child, man and woman in the town and neighbourhood, all who had contributed towards the £3,400 for the building of the hospital. Thanks to the Public Health Act of 1876 local authorities could maintain hospitals from the rates, enabling, in St Albans, the hospital on Holywell Hill, which had sufficed since 1870, to be replaced. A further recognition of the need to provide better facilities was the taking over by the corporation, during May 1888, of baths beside the Ver in Cottonmill Lane.

'Over 6,000 persons patronised the baths during last season,' William Westell told the city council when the baths were being taken over, and he spoke of their great utility as well as their sanitary benefits: 'Public baths under the control of the town council are the more necessary for the advantage of the poorer classes, who are not able to enjoy the luxury of a private bath every day at home, as can the richer inhabitants. Baths are also necessary,' he contended, 'to impart a knowledge of swimming to the inhabitants,' and went on to relate an incident which had occurred at Brighton when a friend of his saved a life through a knowledge of swimming gained at the baths in St Albans.

Knowledge of the notion of neighbourly love, even that as commercial as butcher Gray's, appears to have been lacking among some in the city during the summer of 1888. Two years earlier there had arrived members of the uncompromisingly teetotal Salvation Army—named as such in 1878 by its founder, William Booth, after a decade of Christian endeavour in the East End. His denunciations of alcohol sometimes caused alarm and anger, especially during a recession or, as in 1888, at its ending when lack of work remained the curse of the drinking classes and beer with friends on licensed premises provided a matey means of escape from worries.

93   *The Cottage Hospital—now part of St Albans City Hospital—was built on the corner of Church Crescent and Verulam Road to commemorate Queen Victoria's golden jubilee in 1887.*

Brewers and publicans fearing for their trade also felt alarmed and angry. Those in St Albans, following an example set since 1883 by their counterparts in other towns, raised up a ragtag 'Skeleton Army', as it was called, to stop the Salvation Army from ever being able locally to proclaim the virtues of abstinence. William Hurlock had bluntly told the city council in June 1885 that the opposition to the Army in St Albans 'originated primarily with the licensed victuallers'. Three weeks later, and after there had been a repetition of physical attacks, the mayor, Samuel Monckton White (d.1897), a partner in one of the city's several breweries and president of the Hertfordshire Brewers' Association, offered the council a different explanation: 'the Salvationists have brought opposition upon themselves for the sake of notoriety'.

Among the Army's opponents were those who claimed to be disturbed by the 'noise' its band made when playing outside on the Sabbath. Nearly 500 ratepayers and householders petitioned the council, in June 1888, to enforce a bye-law against the playing of musical instruments in the streets on a Sunday, which time of the week, for the Salvation Army, was perfect: better the day, better the deed. Marching through the streets, its band playing to attract attention, a banner waving, the Army gave the ragtag rowdies an easy target. Punches had been thrown during the previous disturbances, but the fiercest attacks were about to take place. Few, though, of those making up the crowds at the ensuing Sunday skirmishes during June used violence and most seem to have been spectators curious to see what might happen by way of entertainment on an otherwise dreary day. The troublemakers, Hurlock claimed, numbered six, and many of the onlookers were likely to have reacted as did a working-girl in George Gissing's *The Nether World*, published a year later: 'A promenade of the Salvation Army half-puzzled, half-amused her; she spoke of it altogether without intolerance, as did her grandfather, but never dreamt that it was a phenomenon which could gravely concern her.' The same character in the novel went by train from London to St Albans—3s.7d. return.

There had been no trouble during the Salvation Army's marches on the three days before Sunday, 3 June, when early in the afternoon 40 men and women left the Barracks in Victoria Street for another of the day's three marches. Afterwards, surrounded by the crowd, they were holding a service outside the Town Hall when a general scrimmage broke out and a marcher, John Rand, was ducked in a nearby horse trough. The sole cause of the trouble was said by the police to have been William White, of Adelaide Street, who had eight previous convictions. Found guilty by the magistrates of drunkenness and disorderly conduct, he was fined £1 or 14 days, and chose prison. Herbert Booth, a son of the Army's founder, was fined 10s. with 12s. 6d. costs for playing a concertina in front of the Town Hall on the day of the scrimmage. The Army's music was an annoyance, the court was told by a witness—the landlord of the *King William*, in St Peter's Street.

Undeterred, the Salvationists re-emerged into a crowded and anticipatory Victoria Street on the evening of 3 June to find themselves attacked by men the worse for drink. Some of the marchers were knocked down and, most seriously, one of them, a woman, lost an eye. Further ordeals awaited them in St Albans: members were fined, gaoled, but their good work among the poor and needy, and their own resoluteness, eventually pacified the demons of drink, winning respect and acceptance.

Builder demons had to be pacified when, in 1889, land to the south of the cathedral and abbey church went on sale. Public subscriptions raised the £2,100 required to buy it and, saved from a rash of buildings, it remains as part of the Abbey Orchard open space.

School building continued, encouraged by the 1870 Education Act, which established the principle of education for every child and by another Act, in 1876, which instituted compulsory education to the age of twelve. Hatfield Road boys' school, built in 1881, had

94 *A boy wearing a smock c.1895: a photograph by William Henry Lane of 43 St Peter's Street.*

been enlarged four years later and, during the same year, the Abbey School, in Spicer Street, was further enlarged. Alma Road schools for girls and infants dated from 1882—and were to be enlarged in 1890. Before then, in 1889, the St Albans High School for girls was opened in the former hospital on Holywell Hill and would move to new premises in Townsend Avenue in 1908. In Catherine Street, Garden Fields School for girls and infants opened in 1896. Schools built half a century earlier included that of St Peter's for girls and infants in Old London Road (1850), St Michael's for boys and girls (1854) and Mrs. Worley's Christ Church for boys and girls in Verulam Road (1862).

The ever-extending acres of bricks and mortar did not, apparently, dismay Jerome K. Jerome, whose mention of the city in *Three Men in a Boat* (1889) was complimentary, even if slightly tongue in cheek: 'Here, let's go away. I can't stand any more of it. Let's go to St Albans—nice quiet place, St Albans.'

Sometimes, the quiet was that which followed the ending of noisy demolition work as the last wall fell of yet another old building. 'Old houses are being pulled down and acres of what was agricultural land are being built upon,' William Page (1861-1934) told the St Albans Architectural and Archaeological Society in a lecture he gave on 17 May 1893. Secretary of the society for seven years from 1896, Page, an archaeologist and historian, became general editor of the *Victoria History of the Counties of England*. His lecture continued: 'I think I may safely say that the town of St Albans has altered more in the last 30 years than it had done in the previous 300.' Some things, though, stayed more or less the same, and were anything but quiet: 'St Albans on a Saturday night is an entertaining place,' observed *The Lantern*, a short-lived weekly, in its issue of 6 September 1893.

> The primitive street market, with oil lamps flaming away, and the loud cries of the bellicose vendors of all kinds of imaginable wares filling the air, makes it quite captivating. There is a general old-world, quaint air about the place, which appeals forcibly to the stranger. To the Albanian, born and bred, it is quite a matter-of-fact thing; the stranger is instantly struck with the novelty of the affair, and wonders where on earth he has seen anything like it … The town has a charm all of its own on a Saturday night.

To its charm was added, in June 1893, the informal opening of the Sisters' Hospital on a site near the Workhouse and now part of the City Hospital. There was no bunting or a band, but a succession of visitors terribly aware of the prevalence of smallpox and scarlet fever inspected that necessary isolation hospital. Its donor, Sir John Blundell Maple (1845-1903), a London furniture store magnate living at Childwickbury on the town's northern outskirts, gave it in memory of his two young daughters, Winifred and Dorothy, who had died of scarlet fever.

A year later, he surpassed himself by giving to the city the 24-acre Clarence Park. There were cricket and football pitches, which remain, running and bicycle tracks, stylishly over-looked by a still-surviving pavilion, a long since vanished bandstand and a fountain, all located in a public park containing flower beds and 11,000 trees and shrubs. At first, Maple had wanted to do no more than help the St Albans Cricket Club which, although founded in 1876, had its origins in the previous century and seemed to be facing extinction. Its matches were played on Bernard's Heath—pleasant enough though not as secure as an enclosed ground—and the members, despairing of ever being able to obtain land, but unwilling to let their club disappear, put its troubles before Maple. The outcome was, of course, his greatly expanded scheme which, a celebratory supplement to the *Herts Advertiser* stated on 28 July 1894, 'is now the property of the ratepayers of St Albans, and which is unquestionably superior to all other grounds in the county'. Not until 1908 was the St Albans City Football Club formed, and ever since the park has been its home with steadily improved facilities for players and spectators alike.

Part of Clarence Park had been a field bought from Frederick Sander (1847-1920), whose Camp Road orchid nursery was world famous for its size and the great variety of its specimens. Born in Bremen, he settled in St Albans in 1876, opened the nursery a few years later, building a house for himself and family on the same site, and had the honour of being appointed royal orchid grower to Queen Victoria. He published a sumptuous and comprehensive book on orchids containing watercolour plates by Henry Moon (1857-1905), a landscape artist and flower painter, who lived in St Albans. But the trade in orchids waned, and was crippled by the 1914-18 war, although the nursery survived until 1958. A school now occupies the site; opposite, Vanda Crescent recalls an orchid, *Vanda sanderiana*, named after the devotee himself, while nearby Flora Grove is a reminder of the nursery.

Sander's customers had tended to be wealthy whereas those of his near contemporary, Samuel Ryder (1858-1936), were people usually unable to spare more than a few pence at a time for flowers. On that basis, Ryder, the first to sell penny packets of seeds, made a fortune. He, like Sander, had come to St Albans—from Lancashire, where he was born, via Cheshire, where he became a partner in his father's horticultural business—and chose the city, in 1895, because of its location and good railway and postal services. Mayor in 1905, a magistrate and a philanthropist, he indicated the extent of his commercial success by erecting on Holywell Hill, in 1911, offices and floral hall for his seed company in what still is one of the town's most elegant

95 *The Midland—now City—railway station as it was early in the 20th century.*

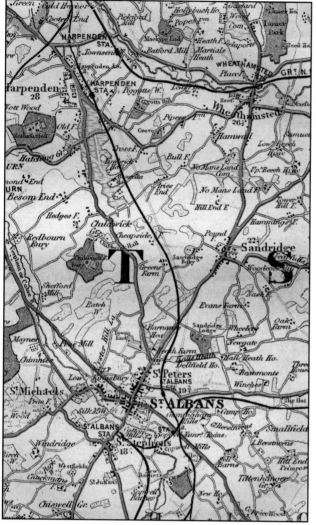

96 *Area map, 1895.*

buildings. He also ran a successful herbal remedy firm, Heath and Heather, from premises near the old City railway station. Today he is most widely remembered by the golfing world. Having taken up the sport to improve his health, he became addicted, playing as often as possible at Verulam Golf Club and, in 1927, proclaimed his love of the game by presenting its internationally famous trophy, the Ryder Cup. His favourite club, a mashie, was buried with him in St Albans Cemetery.

Long before, by the turn of the century, the straw plait cottage industry had been contracting, and was facing extinction, due to the triple impact of machinery, cheaper foreign plait and a fashionable preference for felt hats. Plait manufacture, *Murray's Handbook* (1895) said, 'is not nearly so profitable to the wage-earning community as formerly'. There were alternative ways of earning a living. For example, there were the several boot and shoe factories, and the 100-year-old Abbey silk mill continued to employ about 130 people, mostly women, despite intense foreign competition which, according to the *Herts Advertiser* of 2 February 1901, 'is now too keen to make the work profitable'. However, on the mill shop-floor,

It is quite a pretty sight to see them all [bobbins]—hundreds together— at work, the light noise of the machinery resembling the humming of a myriad of bees, varied only by the gentle movements of the feminine workers as they pass here and there, joining broken threads or extracting imperfections which have brought the reels to a standstill.

Newer industries were being established, especially that of printing, which included the Salvation Army's Campfield Press, in Campfield Road, and Smith's Printing and Publishing Works on the corner of Hatfield Road and Sutton Road. The premises opened in 1897 and, named Fleet Works by the firm, gave the Fleetville district its name. Up until then sheep grazed in the fields on both sides of Hatfield Road. 'On the south side, just past the Cemetery,' a correspondent recalled in the *Fleetville Free Press* of April 1914,

cattle were grazing, and the north side, where Blandford, Glenferrie and all that nest of roads ending with Arthur Road now are, was entirely in the hands of farmers. Everything was peacefully rural ... Hatfield Road, at that time, a quiet country lane where two carts only passed each other with difficulty, has become a busy main road with shops both sides—but only paved on one.

Nearby, Nicholson's raincoat factory at the Beaumont Works in Sutton Road opened in 1900.

The 20th century, confidently heralded in St Albans by the opening, in 1899, of a forerunner of today's Museum of St Albans, started contrarily with an outbreak of smallpox. The most fatal of the infectious diseases, and the most frequently epidemic until largely eradicated by vaccination and 19th-century sanitary reform, its reappearance in London at the end of 1901 prompted the taking of public and private precautions in the town as the disease spread, case by case, into Hertfordshire. Applications by people in St Albans and district, young and old alike, for vaccination and re-vaccination greatly increased. In mid-November the town council assured the residents that arrangements had been made to isolate any smallpox patients. In fact, no definite arrangements were made until after Sidney Haycock, a carpenter of Oster Street, was diagnosed as infected, in January 1902, and taken to the South Mimms Isolation Hospital. It had been decided earlier that smallpox patients could not safely be admitted to the Sisters' Hospital, in whose grounds an emergency isolation ward was prepared only for patients for whom beds elsewhere were unavailable. Unluckily, the carpenter's sister-in-law, a Mrs. Henrietta King, of Park Street, had visited him before he was isolated, caught the disease and was taken to South Mimms while her husband, a railway platelayer, their three-months-old baby, and a sister, remaining at home, were placed in quarantine. As a further precaution their money to pay for shopping brought to them was passed through a bowl of carbolic.

Every opportunity was taken by the council to allay fears and reassure the residents, who were told that the outbreak was under control and not spreading. Almost weekly, further cases occurred. At the end of January, an 18-year-old bricklayer, William Butler, of Fishpool Street, contracted a mild form of the disease after working for the Romeland builder, Christopher Miskin, at the South Mimms hospital. In February, as well as there having been smallpox cases at Hemel Hempstead, Watford, Potters Bar and Aldenham, there were five cases at the City Lodging House, in Sopwell Lane, of which two—one of them the landlord—died. The other victim, a pauper, was buried at night. Those remaining in the house were quarantined while police kept watch around the clock to prevent them from leaving or others from entering, but three more of the lodgers contracted the disease and were taken to the temporary isolation ward near the Sisters' Hospital.

Of concern to the authorities were the many children in the Sisters' Hospital being treated for a simultaneous outbreak in the city of scarlet fever. Permission was sought from their parents to vaccinate the children, especially as the hospital was equipped with only one bath for its 40 patients. More of the townsfolk had been having themselves vaccinated—700 between 1 January and mid-March—and still more in considerable numbers continued to seek re-vaccination. The Lodging House no longer constituted a source of danger, but Mrs. Wells, of Boundary Road, became infected, as did her six-year-old daughter, Eliza, and three other children in the locality. One of them, Mary Smith, aged eight, of Culver Road, died in April. There was a final fatality. One of two infected working men staying at a public house in Fishpool Street died from the disease in June, but the other, and the similarly infected landlady, recovered. By August, the outbreak had as good as ended and so, too, had the scarlet fever epidemic.

Busy behind the scenes had been the mayor, Arthur Edward Ekins (1852-1912), personally supervising the arrangements for isolating those infected at the risk to his own health. A farmer's son, born in the Isle of Ely, he trained as a chemist, took over a chemist's shop in Market Place, in 1876, and after painstaking effort won for himself a distinguished place in his profession. He became the Public Analyst for Hertfordshire, analyst for the Borough of Luton

97 *Arthur Ekins (1852-1912).*

and the Hertfordshire Agricultural Society, was a Fellow of the Chemical Society, a Fellow of the Institute of Chemistry, acted for a time as divisional secretary of the Pharmaceutical Society and was appointed a member of the Council of the Society of Public Analysts. A Conservative, a Freemason, a churchwarden at Christ Church (finding time to be a manager of the church's schools), he also was a director of the temperance Coffee Tavern in Market Place, a member of the Workhouse Board of Guardians, a director of the St Albans Building Society and had, as a shrewd entrepreneur, developed the Beaumont Avenue and Marlborough Road residential areas.

Tribute was paid to him at a city council meeting in November 1902 by a fellow councillor, Arthur Faulkner (1851-1922), the treasurer and financial adviser of Thomas Cook's travel firm and himself a benefactor of the city. To applause, Faulkner said,

He has worked most arduously, and I should like to put this on record, that I believe had it not been for the vigilance of the emergency committee appointed to look into the smallpox question when we were threatened with an epidemic here, and the personal bravery of Mr. Councillor Ekins, that this city would have had a very much more severe visitation of smallpox than we have had. I consider he was most brave in carrying out his duties, ferreting out, and going into danger to find the source from which the smallpox came into this city.

Another danger continued to face the city: the destruction of its historic buildings and, with their destruction, that which gave the city its distinctiveness. The Clock Tower had been saved as a result of a public outcry; the cathedral and abbey church restored—and saved—thanks largely to the architectural fancies of a lawyer-lord. But the need was for sustained, strong pressure, and vigilance remained essential, and would continue to be needed during the rest of the century.

The well-known St Albans topographical artist, Frederic Kitton (1856-1904), made a considered plea for the city's protection when writing on 'Old St Albans and How to Preserve It' in a 1901 issue of *The Home Counties Magazine*:

To deprive St Albans, or any other old town, of its ancient buildings and to substitute for them modern structures, will result in destroying that valuable individuality which should distinguish one place from another; such an act is like the destruction of an ancient missal, the life-work of an industrious monk, and giving us in its place a matter-of-fact version printed in modern type on modern paper ... Some definite and practicable scheme must be initiated if we are to preserve all that is possible of old St Albans; hitherto, bit by bit, it has disappeared, with hardly a hand raised in protest.

In the coming years, more hands would be raised, although not always successfully.

XV

Energetic Steps

NORMALLY law-abiding citizens of St Albans, in common with other like-minded people throughout England and Wales, calmly accepted prison sentences or the seizure of their goods as a result of protesting against the Education Act of 1902. The Act provided for secondary education, placed schools under committees of local authorities and brought denominational schools into the State system which, the protesters believed, put Nonconformists at a disadvantage. Consequently, they organised on a large scale passive resistance to the payment of the education rate—and suffered the penalties of the law.

In St Albans, 37 passive resisters had goods seized and sold in May 1904 to pay the rate and the cost of the court and distraint proceedings. Two months later more passive resisters appeared in court and, also in July, another resister, the outspoken Baptist minister Henry Taylor was threatened with prison but, instead, had furniture taken from his home in Prospect Road to be sold by public auction at the police station. 'Passive Resistance is to the fore again in this City,' said the St Albans and District Free Church Council's *The Free Church Leader* on 20 May 1904, 'and some of our most law-abiding, godly and respected citizens have been warned that they will have to appear this week before the magistrates to show cause why they refuse to pay a rate in the interests of sectarian religion.' The resistance continued—and not always passively—until after a general election in January 1906 when a Liberal government's programme of social reform swept aside the rate protest.

Bread and butter issues had, in any case, been uppermost for many of the city's 16,000 inhabitants. An unusually severe trade depression was to blame: 'It is many years since there was so much distress in the city', reported the *Herts Advertiser* on 10 December 1904,

> and unless things take a material change for the better Christmas will not bring joy and happiness to a good many homes. For some time past, the building trade, in common with the trade all over the country, has been in anything but a flourishing condition, and the slackness is at the present time more pronounced than ever. Bricklayers, carpenters, painters, and labourers have been thrown out of work on all sides, and there is very little prospect of things taking a better turn in the near future.

The Congregational Church in Spicer Street opened its schoolroom to give free breakfasts to 'really deserving' children, starting with about fifty, after which the number quickly rose to more than a hundred. Sunday School children at Trinity Congregational Church sewed clothing for the city's less fortunate children, on whose behalf appeals were made for them to be given boots. At the Salvation Army 120 quarts of soup were served free of charge each Monday, Wednesday and Friday. 'So piteous was the plight of some, that, failing to obtain soup, they begged for bread,' said the Army's local secretary, Geoffrey Longley, of West View Road.

98   *Market Place, c.1907.*

In such circumstances there was evident fellow-feeling among the people of St Albans in May 1905 when welcoming a hundred or so Northamptonshire bootmakers on their march to London to lobby the government against a cut in wages. Met by a delegation, which included a representative of the city's Boot and Shoe Operatives' Union, the marchers were given a meal before attending a large public meeting of support in Market Place. The next month, a 'small army' of unemployed boot and shoe workers from Leicester stayed overnight on their orderly march to London in search of help. A month later, too late for the marchers, the open air swimming pool in Cottonmill Lane was opened on 29 July.

Earlier in the year, the demolition of Hall Place, an historic residence north of St Peter's cemetery, had called attention to a continuing danger. Writing in the *Herts Advertiser* of 4 February 1905, Charles Henry Ashdown (1856-1922), an accomplished historian, commented,

> Considering all points, I am more than ever convinced that in losing Hall Place we lose a connecting link with the past history of our city which is nothing short of a misfortune for the town, and though the loss is now irremedial, yet, perhaps, good may ensue by directing the attention of the citizens to the existing treasures in our midst still remaining to us, and which may be at some future time threatened with similar destruction. The hundreds of visitors to our town do not come to see plate-glass windows or modern red-brick walls; they can see those at home. If St Albans destroys the evidence of its antiquity it ceases to be an attraction for those who now come, even from America, to view them. From the unsentimental point of view of business it is foolish to kill the goose that lays the golden eggs. Every ancient building and landmark remaining is a valuable asset which should be preserved, if at all possible, by the community at large.

Thanks, perhaps, to the controversy over Hall Place, the community at large took energetic steps in 1906 to save St Peter's Street from an act of authorised vandalism. Never before, it was claimed, had the people of St Albans been so deeply aroused. The cause of their anger was the Postmaster-General's insistence that telephone poles should be erected along the street's west side: no other route could be found; the wires, according to official opinion, had to be overhead in the interests of long-distance telephonic communication; besides, officialdom declared, underground wires were unsuitable for technical reasons. The only concession granted was that the poles, instead of being wooden, could be of ornamental iron.

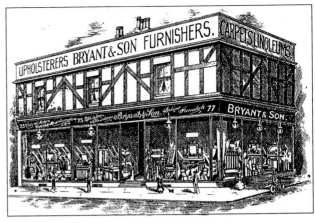

99   Bryant & Son's store in St Peter's Street, 1904.

Neither the argument nor the concession was accepted by the people of St Albans as being adequate because the city's dissatisfaction sprang from the obvious fact that St Peter's Street deserved special protection. Few of the inhabitants were likely to have disagreed with a description in a letter to the *Herts Advertiser* on 10 March 1906:

> This street is picturesque and beautiful by reason of its boulevard appearance; the church at one end; the splendid glimpse of towers and turrets at the other; the unusual width, and the uniformly-broken lines of the houses on either side, hardly two of which are alike. It never fails to arouse the admiration of the stranger.

Another outraged correspondent wrote: 'St Peter's Street, from its width and general picturesqueness, is without doubt one of the most beautiful streets in England, quite apart from its early historic value. Its beauty is so much appreciated that scarcely a week passes during the summer but what one may see an artist at work.' In such a location the telephone poles were, the writer declared, 'national calamities'.

The trouble was that the city council had been bamboozled into granting the Post Office permission to erect the poles and, to make matters worse, had granted the permission in private. Only when the poles were being put up did the agreement come to light in the wake of immediate protest. By then, a council spokesman announced, it was too late to object. 'There is a great agitation,' he said, 'but the people who are raising the agitation are kicking against the pricks and will do themselves no good whatsoever.' The spokesman was mistaken.

In the expectation of attracting attention, if nothing else, objection had been swift and vigorous, the kicks purposeful. A citizens' committee was formed, led by Charles Henry Ashdown, who sent a telegram to the Postmaster-General imploring him to discontinue the erection of the poles. A deputation from the committee was welcomed by the sympathetic mayor, Samuel Ryder, and, equally promptly, a petition signed by 199 prominent residents was sent to the Postmaster-General. According to Ashdown, a master at St Albans School, the petition was 'the most powerfully-supported petition that has emanated from the town for many years'. As he had explained in a letter to the *Herts Advertiser*: 'Many scores of signatures could have been obtained, for everyone is indignant, and some furious, but the object was to invite those to sign who had a large stake in the prosperity of the city, or whose signatures would carry weight in other respects.'

A public protest meeting at the Corn Exchange on Wednesday, 14 March, attracted a 'large and representative' audience when, the *Herts Advertiser* reported, 'genuine indignation was expressed at the disfigurement of the city's boulevard by a government department'. Indicative of the city council's displeasure concerning the outcome of its negotiations with the Post Office was that Ryder chaired the meeting.

The agitation succeeded. By the end of the month the poles had been removed on the orders of the Postmaster-General and, despite the previous 'technical reasons,' the wires were placed underground in St Peter's Street without causing any harm whatsoever to long-distance telephonic communication. 'There is such a force as public pressure,' the *Herts Advertiser* reminded its readers in a celebratory editorial on 31 March. 'That force has been used with decisive effect in this case, and the beauty of our chief street has been preserved. The object was worth working for, and the end has, we venture to think, exceeded the most sanguine expectations of the citizens of St Albans.'

To this day there are no telephone poles in St Peter's Street.

And the pageant of July 1907, when St Albans shared enthusiastically in a craze that had gripped towns throughout England, reflected the St Peter's Street victory. The pageant, re-creating eight notable episodes from the town's past, was performed by 2,000 volunteers on an open-air site in Verulamium, where audiences totalling more than 23,000 watched the six performances. Volunteers, too, made the costumes and properties in a disused straw-hat factory at the corner of Victoria Street and Marlborough Road. Devised and written by Charles Henry Ashdown in the wake of the St Peter's Street success, the pageant was directed by an experienced actor-manager, Herbert Jarman (1872-1919), whose stage career had begun at the age of eighteen. Touring the provinces for many years in parts ranging from Shakespeare to melodrama, he went on to tour Australia, New Zealand and South Africa before assisting in productions at the Lyric, Hammersmith, and made his New York debut in 1912. He lived in London. The pageant's designer, Robert Groves, the head of St Albans School of Art, also designed the pageant's officially approved picture postcards. Black and white, or coloured, and separately showing the eight episodes and the 10 leading characters, the postcards were of a sufficiently high standard for their printing to be carried out in London by the picture postcard specialists, Raphael Tuck & Sons Ltd.

Claude Westell was 11 years old when he acted in the pageant and thereafter remembered the summer of 1907 as 'a season of pageantry'. He wrote in the *Hertfordshire Countryside* of July 1968: 'Centres with any claim to history were caught up in the prevailing fashion and set about enacting scenes from the past in the open air.' Coventry, Bury St Edmunds, the Isle of Wight, Chelsea, Cheltenham, Winchester, Pevensey, Canterbury and Sherborne were among the places succumbing to the passion for a pageant. 'A city as rich

100 *Charles Henry Ashdown (1856-1922).*

in tradition as St Albans could hardly fail to make its offering,' Westell remarked. 'An ideal site lay there for the taking—a lush green meadow on the banks of the River Ver, inside the walls of Verulamium, five minutes' walk from and almost within view of the cathedral and abbey church.' Although looking backwards selectively (no episode about the abbey's suppression, no episode about the Civil War), the very popular pageant clearly made the point that the town was worthy of respect, especially at a time when its inhabitants had reason to believe that both its past and future were under threat. There was more to the pageant than fancy dress.

An episode in the pageant had been given to the uprising of 1381, but in July 1908 a meeting—called by the Social-Democratic Federation and attended by 500 people outside the Town Hall to commemorate the execution in St Albans of a leader of that uprising—was banned as there had been disorder at a similar event the previous year. Among those disappointed were members of the Clarion Cycling Club, who had cycled from London, although as supporters of *The Clarion*, a socialist weekly, they probably were used to hostility. Robert Tressell, in *The Ragged Trousered Philanthropists* (1914), described the readiness of such propagandists to suffer for the cause:

> One Sunday morning towards the end of July, a band of twenty-five men and women on bicycles invaded the town. Two of them, who rode a few yards in front of the others, had affixed to their handle bars a slender upright standard from the top of one of which fluttered a small flag of crimson silk with 'International Brotherhood and Peace' in gold letters. The other standard was similar in size and colour, but with a different legend: 'One for all and All for one' ... The cyclists rode away amid a shower of stones without sustaining much damage.

A woman cycling provided Arthur Melbourne-Cooper (1874-1961) with one of his early films. A son of Thomas Melbourne-Cooper (*c*.1831-1901), St Albans' first professional photographer, Arthur was born at 99 London Road and became a pioneer of the British film industry. He opened his own studios, the Alpha Kinematograph Works, at 14 Alma Road, producing a vast number of films, one of which, *Dreams of Toyland*, made in 1907, probably was this country's first animated cartoon film. A year later, he opened the city's first cinema, the 800-seat Alpha Picture Palace in London Road, on a site where, after a fire, a new cinema was built which, as the Odeon, survived as the town's last cinema until it closed in 1995. Under his own trade name, Alpha, Melbourne-Cooper also published picture postcard views of St Albans—some of them photographs taken earlier by his father.

Pageantry returned in 1909, and with a French accent, as improved relations between Great Britain and France had induced the civic leaders of St Albans and Caen to exchange visits. Links between both towns were longstanding: William the Conqueror had been buried in the Normandy town and Paul de Caen was the first Norman abbot of St Albans Abbey. The exchanges began when a group from St Albans, led by the mayor, Arthur Faulkner, went to Caen early in June and, a month later, the French came to St Albans. Their programme of excursions and events culminated at Clarence Park on Thursday 8 July in a 'Great Demonstration', which involved a pageant of music and dance for 2,500 schoolchildren, whose beautiful singing of the Marseillaise, in French, brought tears to the visitors' eyes. Faulkner, along with his wife, commemorated the exchange of visits by giving the cathedral and abbey church a stained-glass window showing St Alban wearing the uniform of a Roman soldier and Paul de Caen holding a model of the abbey he had re-built.

The new buildings opened in 1911 included an attractive public library at the top end of Victoria Street. Now transformed into a public house, and at the time replacing the public library previously housed opposite in what was the School of Art (now used by a group medical practice), the new library was one of a vast number of public libraries built in the United States, Great Britain and other English-speaking countries with the financial assistance of the Scottish-born American industrialist Andrew Carnegie. In recognition of his generosity he received the freedom of the city when visiting St Albans in October 1911. Diagonally opposite the new library, the Salvation Army citadel was opened in the same year on a site previously occupied by its delapidated barracks.

Around the same time two adjoining houses, 'Farningham' and 'Beckenham', were built in Battlefield Road by Francis Horner (1847-1930), a co-founder of the National Children's Home and Orphanage in 1869, who wished to live near its Harpenden branch rather than remain living in London. Horner and his wife, Ann, occupied 'Farningham' in July 1911 and, at the same time, their daughter, Mary (1876-1940), and her husband, Sydney West, and their children occupied 'Beckenham'. Mary took a deep interest in the work of the National Children's Home, was a member of its general committee and a frequent visitor to the Harpenden branch. Her son, Francis Horner West, was from 1962 the Bishop of Taunton for 15 years.

In an unpublished family history, written in 1962, West recalled St Albans of the early 1900s: 'My mother had to walk all the way into St Albans to do her shopping, although most of the main shops delivered their goods to the door in horse-drawn vans. There were, however, two small shops within easy reach.' One of them was Minter's grocery in Culver Road.

> Young [Billy] Minter (1898-1984) later became an amateur international footballer and played centre-half for St Albans City, which I was to watch every Saturday afternoon as a small boy. He became a great hero of mine and I used to come running back from the shop after seeing him behind the counter crying out to my mother, 'Mummy, Minter was in the shop.'
>
> Cars were comparatively rare in those days. In Sandpit Lane, which was still very rough and full of potholes, they stirred up a lot of dust, which covered the bushes on either side, and pedestrians were well advised to keep out of the way. We always stopped to watch one go by.

Aeroplanes were even rarer. People in Battlefield Road had got up at 4 a.m. in April 1910 to watch the planes taking part in a competition, sponsored by the *Daily Mail*, to fly the 183 miles between London and Manchester in under 24 hours. The winner did it in four hours ten minutes, following the route of the Midland Railway, and received the £10,000 prize. 'At that time the hum of an aeroplane overhead brought people out into their gardens.'

A bye-law, passed by the city council in January 1911, making it an offence to write on pavements, was in answer to clever publicity made by women's suffrage campaigners during the previous summer. They had advertised evening meetings in Market Place by chalking the details upon pavements, thereby attracting large crowds, and at a Saturday market they sold copies of their newspaper, *The Vote*. By July 1913 their supporters in St Albans were numerous enough to provide overnight accommodation for those members of the National Union of Women's Suffrage Societies marching along Watling Street to a rally in London; other members were marching along the Great North Road, the Bath Road and the Portsmouth Road, coming from places as distant as Newcastle, Bangor and St Austell. About fifty people, mostly women, were present during the same month at a meeting in a private house in Battlefield Road when a strong branch was formed of the Church League for Women's Suffrage. In November women were admitted for the first time to a meeting of the St Albans Debating

101 *Two farm workers taking a break from mowing the grass pose for a photographer, c.1910. One of the men sharpens his scythe with a whetstone, the other man's scythe hangs out of the way in the tree.*

Society and, also for the first time, allowed to take part in its debate: 'Is the militant suffragist policy defensible?'. The opposers won by 52 votes to 25, but suffragist activity continued until ended overnight by the outbreak of war between Great Britain and Germany in August 1914.

'St Albans soon became a training centre for London Territorial Regiments,' wrote William Page in *St Albans* (1920).

> After a year's training these troops went abroad and their places were taken by battalions of the Staffordshire, Essex, Leicestershire, West Surrey and other training units. The appearance of these troops changed the whole aspect of the town. Soldiers were billeted in every available house or other building, every hotel was crowded with officers, and every vacant house was commandeered for headquarters or other military purposes. The streets were filled with khaki-clad men, and the sound of the bugle, the sharp words of military command, the rumbling of the transport lorries and the tramp of soldiers soon became too familiar to attract attention.

FOR REMEMBRANCE
1914 ———— 1918
JAMES BAKER   RALPH HALES
WILLIAM BEASLEY   GEORGE HALSEY
BERT EPHGRAVE   CHARLES JAVELEAU
JOHN EPHGRAVE   BERTRAM PARLES
CHARLES FOUNTAIN   PERCY POPE
HARRY CAZELEY   NOAH SWAIN
JESSE CAZELEY   HERBERT WRIGHT
WILLIAM WALDOCK
R.I.P.

102 Sopwell Lane 1914-18 war memorial, 1920.

Less noticeable were the Belgian refugees sheltering in St Albans while near St Michael's was a camp—one of 14 in Hertfordshire—for the German prisoners of war working as farm labourers.

South of St Albans, Napsbury Asylum was taken over entirely as a war hospital from May 1915 to August 1919. Cycling there to visit a patient, the Rev. John Power, the parish priest at SS Alban and Stephen Church, St Albans, was caught in rain, developed pneumonia and died, aged 49, on 1 July 1919.

Corporal Ted Trafford, of Lewisham, had very personal reasons for remembering what seems to have been his last night in St Albans before leaving for the Western Front in 1915. 'Darling,' he wrote from the Somme to his sweetheart and wife-to-be, Pat Randall, 'I suppose it does seem a long while since that eventful night in St Albans. So much has happened that it seems a long time since I last saw your dear face with those eyes of yours—such eyes—just brimming.' Awarded the Military Medal for bravery, he was invalided home after having been wounded and became a senior tax inspector. His letters, lovingly kept by his wife, were published 80 years later by the couple's younger son, Dr. Peter Trafford, a retired Somerset general practitioner.

Frederic Smith, of Ilford, kept a diary after joining the 20th (County of London) Battalion of the London Regiment on 2 September 1914. Aged 19, his military training started at Blackheath from where in November he was drafted to Hatfield for the remainder of his training and, on 11 January 1915, he recorded, 'Battalion moved to St Albans. Billeted comfortably in private house.' The comfort did not last: 'Wednesday, 3 March, Under orders for embarkation. Preparations commence.' Commissioned, and wounded twice in France, he survived to return to his job with the Caledonian Insurance Company.

XVI

Aftermath

AMONG the far-reaching changes brought about by the First World War were those which affected women. Millions of them took over jobs hitherto regarded as the preserve of men who, having been gobbled up by the armed forces, had to be replaced on the home front. As a result, women entered industry in unprecedented numbers, became farm workers, military auxiliaries, ticket collectors, drivers, window cleaners, bakers and chimney sweeps.

In St Albans, as elsewhere, some of them joined the National Union of Women Workers. One of several trade unions exclusively for women, its St Albans branch took as seriously its civic as its trade union duties, sending representatives to a meeting in the Town Hall council chamber in December 1918, a month after the ending of the war, to consider what should be done about the city's acute housing shortage. Also represented at the meeting were St Albans and District Friendly Societies, St Albans and District Trades Council (which had been active since the beginning of the century), Trinity Church Social Group, St Albans Co-operative Society and local branches of the British Women's Temperance Society, and the National Society of Discharged Sailors and Soldiers. The following week the housing shortage came up for consideration at a meeting of the city council when the members, although sympathetic, remained cautious about implementing a housing scheme. New housing, though, continued to be needed. Its financial implications were discussed early in the new year by the Congregational Church Social Service Group and, in March, a meeting of the St Albans

OFFICIAL OF LADY WAR-WORKERS' BUREAU. "What sort of work do you feel fitted for?"
APPLICANT. "I don't quite know, but I want to wear these clothes."

103   Women and war work: a cartoon in Punch.

branch of the National Council of Women heard a lecture on the housing question. At the same time the need for housing stayed prominently before the city council until, at the end of March 1919, its general purposes committee successfully recommended a scheme to provide 100 houses at Townsend.

An editorial in the *Herts Advertiser* of 29 January 1921 commented on the scheme:

Although hampered by the shortage of the necessary labour, the work of construction on the Townsend Housing Site at St Albans is progressing steadily. Of the hundred houses to be erected there, the first two are now roofed in, and half-a-dozen more will be virtually completed by the end of the month—if the roofing tiles, for which the workmen are waiting, come to hand in the meantime. But no hope can be entertained of completing the first twenty-five houses within the time specified in the contract, pressing as is the need for additional housing accommodation. It is a scandal that so much delay and obstruction should have been caused by the Government Department specially charged with the duty of speeding on the work of providing suitable dwellings for the people. Its effect has been, not only to seriously retard building operations, but to discourage many a local authority which set out with a really honest desire to meet, and with a minimum of delay, to combat a very serious situation ... We trust that, as the year proceeds, many of the obstacles that now stand in the way of greater building progress will be removed and that the happy day when there will be houses for all who need them will be speeded forward.

In the same year, 1921, Charles Edward Palmer (1860-1933), a founder of the St John Ambulance Brigade, having moved to St Albans, convened a meeting at the Town Hall, when the first steps were taken to form, in April 1922, a local division of the organisation. Palmer, the author of a standard book on ambulance work, lived at 36 Clarence Road and was buried in St Albans Cemetery.

As 1921 proceeded, unemployment, which since 1919 had been increasing both nationally and locally, increased further, and on 26 February drew editorial comment from the *Herts Advertiser*: 'The fact that there are in the neighbourhood of 450 men definitely out of employment in St Albans at the present time, in addition to about 300 women, and boys and girls aggregating about 90, presents a situation of considerable seriousness and one which calls for speedy and sympathetic attention.'

During February the city council received a deputation of the unemployed and told them that it felt acutely the existing distress and desired to do everything possible towards providing relief. As a start, in March, the council agreed that some of the unemployed should be given the work of widening Waverley Road: from that time until the 1930s similar council relief schemes continued to be needed, bolstered by schemes of private charity. From 1922 voluntary gifts of money and goods enabled the St Albans Christmas Parcels Fund to supply the needy with a dinner at home on Christmas Day; later, the *Herts Advertiser* started a Santa Claus Fund to raise money to give many hundreds of children sound boots and shoes every year.

Seven girls were the only pupils when Loreto College opened as a boarding school in Hatfield Road in January 1922 to begin secondary education for Catholic children in St Albans. By September there were 20 pupils, and in the following year, Marlborough House, previously owned by Samuel Ryder on adjoining land between Upper Lattimore Road and Beaconsfield Road, was bought and became the modern languages department. 'A small but devoted band of nuns laboured hard at transforming the young girls, both Catholic and Protestant, into ladies', wrote Terence Newell recalling St Albans of the 1930s in *Ten of the Best* (1985). 'They seemed to be unaware of the fact that the surrounding walls were not high enough to deter the more energetic and attractive of their French boarders from scaling them in the interests of putting the transformation to a more practical test.' Catholic secondary education for boys had to wait until September 1939, when St Columba's College opened.

Boys and girls equally, as well as their parents, were likely to have welcomed the opening, in 1922, of the city's third cinema, the Grand Palace (later, the Gaumont) in Granville Road. Walking home at night from it or other locations became more enjoyable after the completion, in October 1923, of comprehensive street lighting improvements. Many people, young and old, bathed in joy complete when the next year, 1924, mixed swimming was allowed for the first time at the Cottonmill open-air pool, which opened only during the summer. 'An all-weather swimming bath would be a valuable acquisition,' the *Herts Advertiser* had remarked editorially on 6 October 1923.

Valuable in terms of equality alone was the city council's unanimous election, in November 1924, of its first female mayor, Margaret Wix (1879-1953), after she had served only five years as a councillor. The first woman to be elected to the council, she became its first female alderman, the town's first female Justice of the Peace and the first woman to receive the freedom of the city. She commemorated her year of office by securing enough public subscriptions to establish a fund for the relief of necessitous maternity cases. Her lifelong concerns included education, and the naming of the Margaret Wix junior school, which opened in 1955, was a tribute to that particular concern.

Housing remained a thorn in the side of the post-First World War city. Despite private schemes, and a scheme to provide 150 workmen's dwellings at the Camp, sanctioned by the government in 1925, there remained overcrowding and at least 40 dwellings unfit for human habitation. Public concern was such that a St Albans Housing Enquiry Committee had been formed at the instigation of the Bishop of St Albans, Michael Furse (1870-1955). Subsequently, he was elected president of the St Albans Housing Association, which sought to provide housing and to carry out repairs. No fewer than 600 new houses were known to be needed.

Hundreds had volunteered, the *Herts Advertiser* reported on 15 May 1926, to help maintain essential services in the town during the nine days (4-12 May) of the general strike in support of the miners, who were resisting a cut in wages. St Albans was among the places, such as Berkhamsted, Luton and Watford, where the response to the strike call by the Trades Union Congress was more than 90 per cent, and probably nearing 100 per cent, and where, in St Albans, the reactions to it on all sides were good tempered. About 1,200 of the strikers crowded the cathedral and abbey church on 8 May to attend a special service of intercession for guidance and, the next day, a similar number answered a call by Bishop Furse to attend another service of intercession. He told the congregation to pray for, among other things, the maintenance of constitutional government, for a living wage and a full life for every honest worker.

'No untoward incidents of any kind were reported in St Albans and district during the strike,' the *Herts Advertiser* further stated on 15 May. 'Calm prevailed everywhere, and the conduct of everyone—strikers and others—was exemplary ... So splendid, indeed, was the general behaviour that the few members of the Special Constabulary who had been on duty were withdrawn a few days before the strike ended.' Afterwards, the St Albans and District Trades Council's strike emergency committee became a much needed miners' relief fund committee as the miners held out until December.

The removal in 1926 of the weekly cattle market from outside the Town Hall to a site now occupied by a multi-storeyed car park in Drovers' Way was part of an accelerating process of change in the appearance of St Peter's Street. The chain stores were arriving.

Other changes had been heralded by the council's purchase, in 1930, of 17 acres for housing and 14 acres for a playing field at Cunningham Hall. The prison, too, was bought by the council and handed over to its highways and works department for use as a depot. At the Workhouse—less needed since social insurance began early in the century—the Board of Guardians met for the last time, in March 1930, and its powers were transferred to the county council.

Marching along wide St Peter's Street in April 1930 came a 25-strong contingent of unemployed women—'Hunger Marchers'—heading for a mass meeting in Hyde Park, organised by the National Unemployed Workers' Movement, to put pressure on the government for an increase in unemployment benefit. Mostly married women from the northern cotton mills, although some came from Scotland, they were among a thousand women taking part nationally in the march to London. Those marching through St Albans were welcomed by the Trades and Labour Council at its premises in Alma Road, where the women were fed and lodged overnight. Their leader, Mrs. Rose Smith, a Lancashire textile worker, said before resuming the march, 'The people here have been very kind to us. Indeed, their treatment has been the best we have experienced anywhere in the course of our march'.

The St Albans unemployed numbered about three hundred, said W.H. Hackett, the manager of the city's employment exchange, at a meeting in May 1930 of the two-year-old St Albans Rotary Club. He supposed that the figures (which, in any case, were low) might have been due to the stoppage of subsidies and the general winding up of estates in different parts of the country with the result that men were returning to the city. The principle thing that affected employment, Hackett told the Rotarians, was the question of fashions: the ribbon industry had almost come to grief because of short dresses. But nobody during the depression would have doubted that: 'It was far better to be in Reading than Sunderland, in St Albans than in Llanelly' (C.P. Hill, *British Economic and Social History*, 1985).

Later in the 1930s a long queue of unemployed men formed every morning at the gates of the newly-built Shenley Hospital for a hundred or so of their number to be given a day's work as garden labourers. The garden, designed by a distinguished horticulturist, Stanley Lord (1906-96), and managed by him for nearly fifty years, was renowned as the most beautiful public garden in Hertfordshire. Earlier, government grants helped provide work for the unemployed in the making

104 *The bridge over the Ver at the foot of Abbey Mill Lane in the 1920s before it was re-built in 1931 and Verulamium lake made.*

of the lake at Verulamium, part of which land had been bought by the city council for use as a park. Hockey and cricket pitches, football grounds and tennis courts would complete the scheme at the site where, in July 1930, Dr. (later, Sir Mortimer) Wheeler and his wife, Tessa, started a three-year series of excavations of the Roman city. The result, published by the Wheelers in their report, *Verulamium, a Belgic and Two Roman Cities* (1936), was the first history of a Romano-British town solely to rely on the techniques of controlled archaeological excavation that Wheeler himself had pioneered.

Britain's first naturist club had been opened in Bricket Wood during 1930 by Charles Macaskie (1885-1967), a Scottish electrical engineer, and his wife, Dorothy (1899-1968). Their club's exotic name, Spielplatz, acknowledges modern nudism's German origins, which date back to a rebellion against rigid codes of conduct during the early years of the 20th century. The pioneering club has since been joined by more than two hundred of a similar kind throughout the country.

By the end of 1930 the provision of an up-to-date, indoor, swimming pool was on the council's agenda. Negotiations to acquire a site for the pool already had lasted for nearly twelve months when, in November, a contract was sealed with Edward Hitchcock, a city councillor, for the purchase from him, for £3,500, of property at the St Peter's Street end of Grange Street. A little over a year later the St Albans Ratepayers' Association passed a resolution calling for the cleared land to be sold; whereupon, an offer of £4,000 from London Transport proved to be irresistible, and the central and convenient site became the location of a bus garage. Forty years afterwards the Westminster Lodge swimming pool at last fulfilled the long-held dream. It was too long to wait for the younger residents during a heatwave in July 1932: hundreds of them went swimming at midnight in Verulamium lake. And Cottonmill pool was modernised in 1934.

Concern persisted over the protection of old St Albans. H.M. Alderman, in *A Pilgrimage in Hertfordshire* (1931), wrote, 'French Row near the Clock Tower, and Fishpool Street, leading to St Michael's, are unaltered; but wide St Peter's Street is fast changing for the worse, Georgian work making way for plate-glass'.

The changes were not all for the worse. Modernisation of the street lighting, replacing gas with electricity, had been decided upon by the city council in February 1933. In a similarly buoyant mood, it bought Batchwood Hall and grounds two years later for use as a restaurant and 18-hole municipal golf course. Also in 1935 a new General Post Office opened in St Peter's Street and the city boundaries again were enlarged, bringing its population to around thirty thousand.

But shadows were lengthening. The St Albans branch of the British Union of Fascists had attracted about a hundred people to its first dance at the Victoria Hall, Victoria Street, in April 1934, when many of the men wore the 'Blackshirt' uniform of the movement. Six months later about fifty of their labour movement opponents met in the Central Hall, also in Victoria Street, to elect a delegate from St Albans to attend that year's anniversary celebrations in Russia of the Bolshevik revolution. However, the man elected, John Wemyss, a St Albans branch member of the National Union of Railwaymen, was unable to go because he could not obtain leave of absence from his employers. Two years later, a speaker at the meeting, Ralph Fox, a novelist and literary critic, was killed in action, aged 36, while fighting as a volunteer in the Spanish civil war.

Support in St Albans for the anti-fascist side in Spain was organised by the city's Spanish Aid Committee, which collected money to buy food, clothing and medical supplies. Much of the money was raised by weekly house-to-house collections, collections outside factories and at stalls in the market.

Again the plight of others elsewhere was brought home with the arrival on 29 October 1936 of the 196 men of the 'Jarrow Crusade' marching to London with a petition to Parliament for jobs for the unemployed. They walked briskly into the city, mouth-organs and kettledrums playing, according to the *Herts Advertiser* of 30 October, and were given a civic welcome at the Town Hall by the mayor, the Rev. Benjamin Mitchell, the vicar (1926-41) of St Michael's, who wished them every success. St Albans knew something of the depression, he said, because his predecessor as mayor (William Bird, d.1958) had worked, as few could have worked, in the interests of the depressed areas of the North, and the result was that St Albans knew better about the conditions there than most other cities, quickening both information and sympathy. He hoped that something might result from the march to improve things at Jarrow, and St Albans was sorry indeed that the men had found it necessary to take such a step.

Hot meals and overnight accommodation were provided, visits to the cinemas arranged and a public meeting of support held at the Conservative Hall. A.H. Smith, a baker and confectioner, gave cake.

During 1936 the city's remaining brewery, Adey and White, dating from 1868, closed. St Albans corporation bought the site, demolishing most of the buildings to replace them with a car park which, since 1988, has given way to the Maltings shopping centre. Meanwhile, more schools were being built. The opening of the Townsend Church of England Secondary Modern School at High Oaks in 1936 had been preceeded by SS Alban and Stephen Catholic Infant and Junior School in Vanda Crescent, and followed in 1938 by Beaumont Secondary Modern School in Oakwood Drive and the County Grammar Schools for Boys (Brampton Road) and Girls (Sandridgebury Lane).

105   *Class Three and teacher (back, left) at Camp Road School during the 1930s.*

106 *High Street, c.1938.*

The urgent need for housing was being met, in part, by the building of 100 council houses at Cottonmill and, during the same year, 1938, the city council decided to embark on a £50,000 sewerage scheme to prevent flooding. Verulamium Museum's opening in January 1939, to contain finds from the Wheelers' excavations, came at a time when the country's newspapers were sombre with reports of preparations for war: air raid defence, the formation of a police war reserve, young men joining the Territorials.

When war did break out it came early to St Albans: the first evacuees, from north London, arrived by train three days before hostilities began on 3 September. In the week that followed more trains brought more children, and babies in arms and expectant mothers. 'Householders have responded magnificently to the appeals for accommodation for the evacuees,' the *Herts Advertiser* reported on 8 September,

and there are not many homes in the city and in the villages where there are not some children and mothers billeted ...

The London Transport Passenger Board and the railway company played a big part in the success of the evacuation, while local residents who placed their cars at the disposal of the billeting officials did much to help in the transport of the children from the distributing centres to their new temporary homes ... The tiny tots, many of them literally weighed down with their personal belongings, gas-masks and other oddments, seemed very cheerful as they came off the train. In the first batch on Friday morning, one boy included a football and a pair of fishing boots in his luggage!

XVII

War and Peace

THE EVACUEES and their hosts were more than likely to have been heartened by the news that Flying Officer Kenneth Doran (1915-74), an old boy of St Albans School, had won the D.F.C. for gallantry during an attack on German warships in September 1939, thereby becoming the first member of the R.A.F. to be decorated in the war. Five months later, in January 1940, he received a bar to his award—also the first of the war—for clever tactics and gallant leadership of a bomber formation when attacked over the North Sea.

The evacuees had brought out the best in the people of St Albans who, despite instances of overcrowding and bad accommodation, tried to do their best for the newcomers. By 1940 the many children and adults had been joined by the aged and infirm. Community feeding centres catered for some, and rest centres for young mothers were provided with the help of the churches. Children of school age were, wherever possible, kept off the streets by film shows arranged with the assistance of their teachers. An Evacuees' Welfare Committee, chaired by the Dean of St Albans, the Very Rev. Cuthbert Thicknesse (1888-1971), was established to co-ordinate help and, at its meetings in the Town Hall, determined what needed to be done to make the conditions as easy as possible. A legacy left by Muriel Green (1881-1933), an ardent social worker and co-founder of the St Albans Christian Fellowship, went in 1940 towards the opening of a day nursery, which was named after her, in Lemsford Road; another nursery was opened at 27 Sandpit Lane for children evacuated from, or bombed out of, homes in London.

Their mothers, also having been evacuated to St Albans, did war work, such as making Oerlikon shells, mainly for the Royal Navy, at what had been the Ballito silk stocking factory in Hatfield Road. Opened in 1925, it switched from hosiery to ammunition at the start of the war and by July 1944 had helped produce ten million of the armour-piercing shells. Other women, as during the First World War, served with the city's British Red Cross centre, which had been formed in 1911, and nursed in the hospitals, first aid posts and rest centres. Women serving with the St Albans Auxiliary Fire Service formed an archway of fire axes when Elizabeth Couch, a member of their control room staff at the central fire station, and a journalist, George Davies, who had enlisted in the Royal Army Service Corps, married at SS Alban and Stephen Church in July 1940. They had met while both were working at the *Herts Advertiser*.

Deeply grieved by what he regarded as a setback to human progress caused by the war, William Sibley, a founder member in 1914 of the St Albans branch of the Workers' Educational Association, had died in May 1940 aged sixty-seven. Born in Chesham, and interested throughout his life in all aspects of education, he had for 26 years been a bicycle and perambulator dealer at 9 Verulam Road, but had travelled widely before coming to St Albans.

At Verulamium in September 1940 a thousand or so people hid under trees and hedges when air raid warnings twice interrupted a fête and fair held towards raising money to buy and equip a Spitfire fighter plane. The first of a number of 'War Weapon' events, its £7,500 target was achieved by the end of the following year.

Members of the armed forces, British and those of their allies, were welcomed at a Service Canteen in the Market Hall, off St Peter's Street, staffed by members of the Women's Voluntary Service to whom the grateful customers sent letters of appreciation and regimental Christmas cards. A 'Thank You and Bless You Fund', run by Kathleen Gape, a daughter-in-law of James Gape (see p.107), provided knitted gifts for naval volunteers, and supplied the men with more than a thousand items between January and November 1940. The gifts were distributed by Lt. Stephen Sparrow, who since the start of the war had been serving with the Royal Naval Volunteer Reserve in minesweepers; his father had been a founder of a firm of estate agents, Mandley and Sparrow, of Chequer Street. Similar knitted gifts began to be provided from early in 1941 for the crew of HMS *St Albans*, one of the destroyers sent by the United States to Britain in exchange for leased bases in Newfoundland and the Caribbean.

Bombed out of offices in Holborn during May 1941, the London Trades Council promptly found a temporary home in St Albans and was functioning as usual within 48 hours. A month later Germany invaded Russia and in December Britain and the United States began fighting as allies against Japan. American soldiers, billeted in the city, drilled on a hockey field at Loreto College, where an old gymnasium was used by the pupils as an air raid shelter during daytime raids and as a dormitory at night.

Public air raid shelters had been built at Belmont Hill, in New England Street and Victoria playing fields, on Bernard's Heath and in Clarence Park, while trenches in the St Peter's Street municipal gardens offered basic shelter.

The exceptional needs of the Russian ally evoked an exceptionally generous response after a Red Cross Aid to Russia Fund was

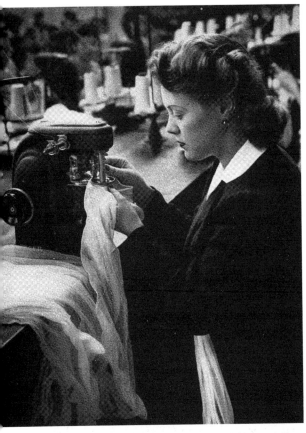

107 Seaming nylon stockings at Ballito Hosiery Mills, Fleetville, in 1949. The factory closed in 1967 and a supermarket was built on the site.

108 St Peter's Street in 1949 showed trees still ringed with white paint to guide road traffic during the Second World War, when it was forbidden for street lights to be lit at night.

launched nationally in mid-October 1941. At the same time, during a crowded meeting on Russia at the Town Hall, under the auspices of the St Albans branch of the League of Nations Union, a delegation from local aircraft factory trade unionists expressed dissatisfaction at the level of arms production, and called for the making of more planes and tanks. An Aid to Russia dance at the Town Hall in February 1943 raised more than £700, and a city flag day for the Russia Fund in October 1944 secured the support of Kitty Davies (1894-1970) as an organiser. A well known St Albans fundraiser, although disabled from birth and confined to a wheelchair, she helped the war effort directly by working at Ballito's.

A year earlier a mass meeting at the Town Hall had protested against the violent and inhuman treatment of Jews in German-occupied Europe. Messages of support were received from various organisations, including the Zionist Federation of Great Britain and Ireland, political parties, and churches and religious bodies. Those on the platform included the mayor, Cyril Dumpleton (1897-1966), the city's M.P., Sir Francis Fremantle (1872-1943), Dean Thicknesse, and Bishop Furse, who referred to the 'massacre of the Jews by the recruited riff-raff of Europe'.

Later during the same year, in April, a rally in Market Square, held by a committee calling for the invasion of Western Europe, sent a telegram to the British forces in North Africa: 'We greet you, our glorious First and Eighth Armies, and pledge ourselves to work as never before to see that a Second Front is opened and maintained in Western Europe so that your courage and your victories are not in vain.'

When the longed-for Second Front was opened and maintained, following the Normandy landings in June 1944, victory, sooner rather than later, was assured. As an early sign, nationally, the nightly 'Blackout' restrictions regarding the concealment of light from every house, street, public building and vehicle were relaxed in September. Wardens had patrolled to ensure that no chink of light showed illegally and people found guilty of negligence were fined. In the darkened streets, driving, cycling or walking was highly dangerous, and more people in the St Albans area were killed as a result of the 'Blackout' than were killed by enemy air raids, against which the restrictions had been imposed at the start of the war.

Another sign, locally, of confidence in the war's outcome was the return home in November of Hastings Grammar School after having been evacuated to St Albans since July 1940. The pupils, billeted with families in the city, had been welcomed at the schoolrooms of the St Albans School, the Boys' County School and the Abbey School, and at rooms in the Abbey Institute. Homework was done in the quiet of the reference room in the old City Library in Victoria Street. For St Albans, the most welcome sign of the way the war was going was the re-hanging in November of the cathedral and abbey church's 12 bells—removed as a precaution four years earlier although their ringing, as those of other churches, had been forbidden except in the event of an enemy invasion.

More than a thousand people—comprising 25 workers from each firm in the city and district doing war work, as well as children—attended a recording for the B.B.C. of its 'Workers' Playtime' radio concert at the Odeon cinema in February 1945. A popular morale strengthener, the show featured comedians, singers and musicians, who performed to war workers at different venues around the country.

Increasingly, the nature of the post-war world was under discussion: the expectation being that Britain, re-built from the ruins of the war, would be a better place for all. Opinion as to the means of its achievement in St Albans was sought early in 1945 from various organisations by the town clerk, S.H. Crane. In its reply St Albans Rotary Club declared that the post-war city should be kept mainly residential with houses as the prerequisite to any development. 'Due regard' should be paid to the city's 'unique and historical characteristics and the preservation of its features.' A 'bold scheme' of slum clearance was required and no industrial undertaking of an obnoxious character should be permitted. Furthermore, hostels should be provided for students and young factory workers, and a modern town hall was 'a necessity'.

St Albans and District Trades Council, representing 3,500 affiliated members, gave its opinion in March: 'The Trades Council considered that St Albans should be regarded not only as a dormitory and residential town but also as an important centre of light industries (particularly light engineering and printing). Development should be planned on the basis of a population not exceeding 60,000.' Like the Rotarians, the trade unionists were 'anxious that the ancient character of such streets as St Peter's Street should be preserved', noting that 'already the street is spoiled by certain shop fronts'.

St Peter's Street, Chequer Street, Market Place and High Street fluttered with celebratory streamers, bunting and flags after Germany's unconditional surrender on 8 May. Most other streets were decorated and street parties—mainly for children—held in many of them. Church bells rang. Floodlighting picked out the city war memorial, the cathedral and abbey church's tower and the Gateway, while in Market Place a big crowd sang and danced around a bonfire until late. Some of the crowd had more to celebrate in July when a general election saw Labour sweep to power, gaining four of the six Hertfordshire seats, including St Albans, which returned Cyril Dumpleton as its first Labour M.P.

The unconditional surrender of Japan, ending the Second World War, followed on 14 August after atomic bombs had destroyed Hiroshima and Nagasaki. The shock waves were felt in St Albans. 'I do not hold a service of thanksgiving in St Albans Abbey,' Dean Thicknesse declared to general surprise, 'because I cannot honestly give thanks to God for an event brought about by the wrong use of force; by an act of wholesale indiscriminate massacre which is different in kind from all the acts of open warfare, however brutal and hideous, hitherto.' His protest, which flatly contradicted the official point of view, received considerable publicity and gave rise to considerable controversy, although most of the people who wrote to him said that they shared his misgivings.

'Crowds,' celebrating the victory over Japan, 'jostled and sang in the Market Square,' the *Herts Advertiser* reported on 17 August; 'fire-works cascaded through the air; strangers linked arms with one another and whirled round together in dizzy circles; youngsters climbed lamp posts, hanging on precariously'. And a service of thanksgiving was held at Marlborough Road Methodist Church, attended by the mayor and members and officials of the council in the presence of a large congregation. At St Peter's Church, a victory peal of 5,056 changes was rung by eight parish members of the Hertford County Association of Change Ringers, whose achievement is recorded by a commemorative window in the church's ringing chamber. A little earlier, Thomas Seymour (1866-1950), of Harpenden Road, had ceased being a bell ringer at the church after 45 years, but did not retire from his building trade work until 1946, when he was eighty.

House-building was an overriding need. Although 646 council houses had been built by 1939, and 570 houses built with subsidies or loans for private ownership, wartime building restrictions, the influx of newcomers and a natural increase meant that by September 1945 there were more than three thousand people in St Albans waiting for suitable accommodation. An editorial in the *Herts Advertiser* on 14 September drew attention to the situation:

> The acuteness of the position created by the dearth of houses is a matter of deep concern, not only for those who are in dire need of living accommodation in this area, but also to those who, taking a general view, regard a happy and contented community as one of the main essentials in the preparations for a durable peace in a well-ordered world.

Happily, private as well as council building schemes were in hand, for it was announced in October that 300 houses were to be built for sale at £1,110 each on the Beaumont estate between Hatfield Road and Sandpit Lane. The city council began a housing programme, which was to provide 4,000 houses in new estates such as Batchwood Drive, Camp Road and New Greens.

Labour gained four seats in the November municipal elections—the first since before the war—and among its seven successful candidates was a life-long resident, Elsie Toms (1890-1982), who was the head of a London secondary school, a subsequent mayor and author of *The Story of St Albans* (1962), an enduring, endearing account of the city's history.

Safeguarding part of that history, a preservation order was placed by the council on properties in French Row, in January 1946, and restoration undertaken, most notably of the 15th-century *Christopher Inn*. History was the inspiration of a millenary pageant in June 1948, when the thousandth anniversary of the founding of the churches of St Peter, St Michael and St Stephen was celebrated in the open at Verulamium. Taking part in the show's nine episodes was a cast of 1,000 with a 200-strong choir and an orchestra of sixty. They were drawn, according to a press release of the time, 'from all ranks in the community... most of them representative of the churches and social and voluntary organisations of all kinds with a good backing of local amateur dramatic societies'. Queen Elizabeth—now (1997) the Queen Mother—attended one of their performances.

A look back at more recent times was presented in *St Albans: The Story of the City and its People*, published by the city council in 1949:

> It is within the last half century that the great development has occurred in local industry, made possible by the coming of abundant and convenient electric power, and during 1940-1944 by the evacuation of individuals and firms from London and the South East ... Clothing made in the City includes hats, embroidery, ribbons, overcoats, stockings, boots and shoes. Foods manufactured are macoroni, suet, and herbal foods. Drinks are represented by lime juice—there is, remarkably, no distillery or brewery ... Musical instruments are manufactured and rubber is processed. Cardboard boxes are made, as well as machinery for making them.

The booklet continues:

> Aircraft manufacture occupies many St Albans citizens, though the factories lie outside the City, at Hatfield and Park Street. The same is true on a smaller scale of jam-making, light metal working, tractor

109 Bill Saunders (left) had worked for 46 years at Sander's orchid nursery when this photograph appeared in 1949. At the microscope is a younger member of the world-famous firm, whose premises were in Camp Road until it closed in 1958.

manufacture, insecticide manufacture, sand and gravel digging, which are carried on in villages around. Chemical work is done in the City and nearby ... Of all the persons living in the City about 20 per cent are engaged in manufacturing industry, 17 per cent are gainfully employed in some other way locally, and 10 per cent are employed in administrative or other professions outside the area; 20 per cent are below working age, nearly 10 per cent are above it. Of those employed locally the men number nearly twice as many as the women.

Since then, closures or removal to other locations of many of the firms, as well as a change in the ratio of men to women at work, have transformed the picture.

But in July 1950 there was a family celebration when Mr. and Mrs. John Farrell, and their two children, became the occupants at 6 Maynard Drive of the council's thousandth post-war house. The family had been on the waiting list for four years.

Their new neighbours and other people living in the area—which adjoined the gas-works—were among the more than five thousand of the city's residents who in August signed a petition, organised by a citizens' committee, protesting against a suggested expansion of the works by the Eastern Gas Board. The objectors, supported by the city council, called instead for a reduction in size of the works and eventual removal altogether because of the noise and smells. Giving evidence in support of the council at a town planning enquiry into the proposal, A.E. Richardson, the architectural adviser to the St Albans Diocese, said,

> I have known St Albans for over 60 years. I have watched its degradation under the frightful progress which we have all experienced ... This is a dollar-earning city which attracts visitors from all over the world, and this is the place it is thought to despoil by the creation of what amounts to a slum industrial centre which no amount of tree-lining will obscure.

The enquiry delayed the enlargement, but still it went ahead and further extensions began in 1955. However, with the introduction of North Sea gas during the 1970s, the objectors had the satisfaction of the last laugh: the site was cleared except for the gasholders, and redeveloped with shops and offices.

To mark the coronation of Elizabeth II on 2 June 1953, the city's main roads and side streets were decorated with flags and bunting, under which parties were held in the streets, and another pageant, 'Masque of the Queens', performed at Verulamium by a cast of hundreds. Others, among the hundreds of volunteers, had made the costumes and scenery. Cyril Swinson (1910-63), the pageant's author and pageant master—as he had been for the preceding one—was the general manager of a London publishing firm, lived in St Albans and wrote children's books and plays.

The next royal occasion for St Albans was at the cathedral and abbey church in April 1957 when Elizabeth II distributed maundy money to old people of the diocese. The first time since the 17th century that the traditional ceremony had been held by the monarch away from London, it attracted a congregation of 3,000 and many more thousands along the Queen's route to and from the abbey.

In the years between the two royal visits builders had been busy throughout the city. At St Albans City Hospital a new physiotherapy department opened in 1954 and three wards were extensively altered to provide higher standards of comfort and hygiene. A ward had been upgraded in 1955 and work on a new chest clinic was nearing completion. New operating theatres, a recovery room, and an extension and improvement of the X-ray department followed. On the other side of the city the Valley Road trading estate had opened in 1955 as new firms continued to come to the area, where there was full employment and many job vacancies,

110 *Cyril Swinson (1910-63), pageant master and author.*

especially for nurses and domestic staff in the surrounding mental hospitals. By 1958, the council's post-war housing programme nearing completion, a large part of the London Road estate was made available for private housing. Car parking already had become increasingly difficult but, in an attempt to ease traffic congestion, work started during 1958 on a by-pass, part of which became a link road to the London-Birmingham motorway when that opened in November 1959.

More than the appearance of the city was changing; traditional attitudes were changing. In March 1957, Mrs. F.A. Gale, a Park Street grocer, became the first woman to be elected as president of the 49-year-old St Albans Chamber of Trade; during the same month, she was welcomed as the first woman to attend an annual dinner of the St Albans Industrial Employers' Association.

A year later that association joined forces with other organisations and individuals, including the chamber of commerce, the trades council, Dean Thicknesse, Sir Mortimer Wheeler and Lord Verulam, to challenge a proposal by the Luton Water Company to pump five million gallons a day from a bore-hole in the Ver. At the head of the opposition were the city and rural councils, along with the St Albans Waterworks Company, which itself was already taking three million gallons a day from the Ver. Redbourn Parish Council expressed its concern, Hertfordshire branch of the National Farmers' Union lodged a formal protest, and Eileen Gibbs, the secretary of the county Natural History Society, said that the many scientists in Hertfordshire should be recruited to help oppose the scheme, because its effects on the Ver valley would be disastrous.

Any moves to protect the Ver were popular, and in February 1958 about a thousand people attended a public meeting in the Town Hall, with an overflow outside listening to the relayed speeches, when all voted for a protest to be sent to the government. An action committee was elected, whose secretary, the publisher Cyril Swinson, lived beside the Ver in Abbey Mill House.

'The Ver is incapable of supplying the water required by the proposal and will lay the Ver dry,' Col. H.C. Bowen, the chief engineer of the Thames Conservatory Board, told the meeting. 'Not for many years,' the *Herts Advertiser* commented on 7 February,

> has any question of local government and similar affairs caught the interest of the public to the extent that this unwelcome proposal has, and there certainly are no signs of apathy over it ... It is inconceivable that the application will be allowed to go through, particularly in the face of the intense local feeling and misgivings that have been aroused.

Ominously, a few days after the protest meeting, the government minister responsible approved a scheme by Welwyn Garden City Urban Council to abstract up to two million gallons a day from two Welwyn boreholes.

In June, by which time 14,000 people had signed a petition against the proposal, an eight-day official inquiry was held at the Town Hall, hearing more than eighty objections. It was agreed that sooner or later Luton would have to get its water from somewhere else; meanwhile, the inquiry decided, it could take no more than two million gallons a day from the Ver. 'There can be no doubt,' Cyril Swinson commented, 'that the volume of local opposition to the scheme must have impressed the minister in some way.'

However, in the absence of sustained opposition sooner became later. Levels of abstraction increased before licensing by the National Rivers Authority began in 1965, although the Ver continued to suffer until in 1976 the Ver Valley Society was formed and started campaigning to save the river. Some twenty years later, after the Ver had dried up, pressure from the society and the N.R.A. resulted in a scheme to pipe water to Luton from a reservoir in Cambridgeshire, enabling the Ver once more to warrant, allowing for poetic licence, its description by Michael Drayton (1563-1631) as 'a famous auncient flood'.

Both the city and the county were about to experience their biggest-ever programme of school building when, in March 1959, the New Greens infants' school was opened to relieve overcrowding at the Margaret Wix junior mixed school. In March 1959 the Fleetville branch library opened, having been suggested by the trades council in 1945, and was the first to be erected with money from the rate fund. A year later, September 1960, the old manual telephone exchange in Marlborough Road, dating from 1922, was replaced by a new, five-storey exchange in Liverpool Road with an automatic dialling system, making it one of the most up-to-date in the country. At the same time the St Albans College of Further Education (now part of Oaklands College) opened in Hatfield Road with accommodation for at least 700 students. New days, too, had dawned for the city's commuters with the introduction of a diesel train service, replacing steam, to and from London, and with an increased frequency—100 trains a week instead of 79— and taking only 28 minutes in either direction.

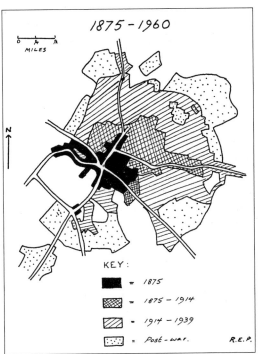

111   *The development of St Albans, 1875-1960.*

The early '60s were notable for a return visit of the Queen Mother to receive the freedom of the city and, a year later, May 1962, the granting of the city's freedom to the Hertfordshire and Bedfordshire Yeomanry (286 Regiment Royal Artillery T.A.) in recognition of its special relationship with St Albans, many of whose citizens had served in its ranks with distinction. On both occasions the freedom ceremonies were conducted by the country's only female town clerk, Betty Entwistle (1913-75), who had been appointed in December 1959, after nearly twelve years as deputy.

XVIII

A Need which Never Ends

ALARMED by fast motor traffic in a built-up area, and anxious to prevent injuries or worse, people living at Chiswell Green had, since early in 1963, been hoping for improved road safety along the Watford Road. Despite a campaign waged on their behalf by a St Albans Rural Council member, William Craik (d.1966), nothing was done until, in October, a 31-year-old pregnant woman and her one-year-old daughter died, and a 10-year-old girl was injured, as a result of being struck accidentally by a car near West Avenue. A few days later the road's speed limit was raised from 30 m.p.h. to 40 m.p.h.

Appalled, several hundred residents met at the end of the month in Chiswell Green Congregational Church, formed an association to strengthen the campaign and received a petition, signed by 589 people, calling for a pedestrian crossing near West Avenue. Craik, a work study engineer, who was elected as chairman, told the meeting, 'We have passed the point of no return.' The determination was that something should be done promptly. To that end, the Chiswell Green Residents' Association kept up the pressure—publicity, letters of protest to the transport and local authorities, a public meeting in the Town Hall—and broadened the campaign by calling for comprehensive road safety measures throughout the city.

The need for better road safety could hardly be denied. At the Batchwood Drive-Harpenden Road junction there had been so many accidents that a dozen public spirited neighbours living nearby met during November at the Batchwood Gardens home of an actress, Beryl Vuolo, to take a course in first aid. Provided by Ruth Tarling, superintendent of the St Albans St John Ambulance Brigade nursing division, it enabled them more proficiently to tend accident victims. One of the neighbours, Sonia Willington, of 1 Batchwood Gardens, had been campaigning for years for traffic lights at the junction, according to the *Herts Advertiser* of 22 November.

Eleven days later, 3 December, a 10-year-old boy on his way home after playing football was accidentally hit by a car near the junction and died the same evening in the city hospital. Soon afterwards, the Ministry of Transport belatedly gave St Albans City Council the long-sought permission to place traffic lights at the fatal junction.

More was granted to the Chiswell Green residents in January 1964 (though not a reduced speed limit until later) following meetings between representatives of the Hertfordshire County Council, the Ministry of Transport and the police: road widening at the Watford Road-West Avenue junction, some dual carriageway provision, central refuges, improved visibility and re-positioned road signs. 'It proves that we have to complain before we get things done,' Craik remarked. 'If they had recognised the fact that Watford Road is dangerous, the deaths might not have happened.'

For people living in and around the city centre a cure proposed in 1964 was likely to have been worse than the condition it sought to change for the better. A road building scheme, planned by the county authorities to relieve traffic congestion, would have meant the demolition of hundreds of houses and the ravaging of the city's appearance. The inner ring road scheme, entirely out of keeping with St Albans, was abandoned after a campaign in which the St Albans Civic Society took a leading part. The society's formation at a crowded meeting in the Town Hall three years earlier, with Elsie Toms and Cyril Swinson among its founder members, was a sign of general anxiety about the city's future, and the ring road opposition a demonstration of the strength of public opinion in defence of an older, small-scale St Albans. The society had been founded with the aims of encouraging high standards of architecture and town planning, and the stimulation of interest in and care for the beauty, history and character of the city and its surroundings.

At the time, Frank Lavery (1900-69), a retired railway employee and secretary of the St Albans Chamber of Commerce, had become the city's first Catholic mayor since the 16th century. He had taken a leading part in the country's first self-build society, the St Albans Mutual Housing Association, which built a total of 24 bungalows at Park Street and St Stephen's but, his main interest being education, he was a governor of many schools until he died.

Pride in St Albans and a desire to help others enjoy finding out about its past prompted the formation of the St Albans Association of Honorary Guides in 1964. It was formed at the suggestion of Beryl Vuolo, and with the help of H.L. 'Dick' Knapp (b.1908), the Youth Hostel Association's national secretary, 1950-68, who lived in St Albans and took an active part in its musical and artistic life. The guides were trained to give talks and conduct walks around the city and Verulamium, while occasionally walks traced, for instance, the medieval borough boundary or the location in the Abbey parish of the street memorials to the parishioners who fell in the First World War. One of the unique memorials, outside 31 Lower Dagnall Street, was deliberately obliterated in 1960. 'It was in a very bad condition,' the house owner explained.

Building work continued during 1964 on the new civic centre, where the City Hall—now re-named Alban Arena—opened in 1968; a start had been made on the development of the 54-acre Westminster Lodge site for a sports centre and indoor swimming pool, and the new police station in Victoria Street was opened in 1966. The opening of the Abbey Theatre by Queen Elizabeth the Queen Mother in 1968 royally rewarded a dedicated group, among whose founder members were the ever lively Cyril Swinson, his equally lively writer brother, Arthur (1915-70), and a family friend, Terence Newell, the subsequent author of the company's history, *Ten of the Best*. Since forming the Company of Ten dramatic society in 1934, following the closure two years earlier of the city's professional County Theatre off St Peter's Street, they had produced consistently attractive shows. The company itself raised the money to design and build the new theatre at the foot of Holywell Hill after losing old premises near Abbey Mill.

A flair for the theatrical was memorably displayed by the Ven. Carlyle Witton-Davies, an idiosyncratic Archdeacon of Oxford and Canon of Christ Church, Oxford, 1957-82. 'It was characteristic,' his obituary in *The Times* on 1 April 1993 recalled, 'that he was one of the last church dignitaries to appear in full fig—attending Dr. Robert Runcie's consecration as Bishop of St Albans as late as 1970 in all the finery of frock coat, apron, breeches and gaiters.' Runcie (b.1921), a popular bishop, became the first from St Albans to be appointed Archbishop of Canterbury, 1980-91.

Earlier, an unlikely pressure group, founded in 1971, established its national headquarters in the city and, seemingly against the odds, saved traditional ales from almost certain

112   Lord Runcie: Rt. Rev. Robert Runcie, Bishop of St Albans, 1970-80, was Archbishop of Canterbury, 1980-91, before retiring to live in St Albans.

extinction. The Campaign for Real Ale, whose founders included two journalists, Michael Hardman and Graham Lees, rented an office above a bicycle shop in Victoria Street, then occupied offices in Alma Road for 19 years before moving to Hatfield Road in 1995. Its winning of widespread support—in addition to 30,000 paying members by the late '70s—as a result of outspoken criticism of the state of British beer, and a sustained programme of public action, persuaded the brewery combines that local beers with local flavours were worth producing and promoting. From its St Albans headquarters the campaign continues to be vigilant, tackles issues such as the preservation of public houses, and publishes an annual *Good Beer Guide* and a monthly newspaper, *What's Brewing*.

Welfare work for old people and the housebound was the driving force in the long and dedicated life of Nan Gazeley (1901-93). Bombed out of her house in Romford during the Second World War, she moved to St Albans. After working in a forces' canteen, she helped found the Old Folk's Welfare Committee, now Age Concern, raised money in 1959 to buy a 'Jaunty Bus' to take the old and house-bound on outings and raised more money to open St Albans House at Worthing in 1972 as a holiday home for the district's elderly. It was closed and sold for lack of financial support two months before her death.

In 1974 the city and district of St Albans was created, bringing together in a single borough St Albans, Harpenden, Bricket Wood, Colney Heath, Redbourn, Sandridge and Wheathampstead with a total population of almost 125,000. Its area of 62 square miles makes the city and district the largest of Hertfordshire's 10 districts, and its road and rail links make it one of the most accessible.

The conjunction in 1977 of the Queen's silver jubilee as monarch, the 900th anniversary of the Norman abbey, and the centenaries of the abbey church as a cathedral and of St Albans as a city called for celebrations which, after careful preparations at the abbey church and throughout the city, were widely enjoyed. They included a thanksgiving service attended by Queen Elizabeth the Queen Mother, concerts, historical lectures, a firework display, theatrical performances and, devised solely for the year of the centenaries, a city carnival whose immense popularity ensured that it became an annual event—one of the largest in England—raising a total of £300,000 for charity over 15 years. A genuine community event, it is organised by the city's Round Table (founded in 1949), helped by the members of many of the city's other charities, with its proceeds going to causes ranging from Guide Dogs for the Blind to the Heathlands School for Deaf Children in Heathlands Drive.

A community event of a very different kind was the long-drawn-out disagreement between the many objectors and the city council over the redevelopment of land east of Chequer Street. There had been disagreement over the use of the site ever since the Chequers cinema closed in June 1962, when plans for a supermarket to replace it were rejected by the council which, in the late '60s, held a competition for a new and larger scheme. Forty-nine proposals were submitted, one of which, from Samuel Properties for a covered shopping centre, was chosen. Work, however, could not be started because of a slump in the property market and, when the situation improved, a new development brief was prepared in 1976. Recognising the growing public opposition to the chosen scheme, the council said it would consider other plans, including one prepared by the St Albans Civic Society which, with a Chequer Street Action Group and other pressure groups, was calling for a scheme more in keeping with the site's historic setting. Strengthening the call, 20,000 people signed a petition in March 1979, but the council, committed to the scheme, mounted an exhibition in an attempt to sway public opinion, although a by-election in the Heath ward a year earlier had delivered a clear enough statement: a Chequer Street Action Group candidate won 803 votes against the winning candidate's 846.

'Chequer Street Action Group members come from all walks of life,' the *Chequer Street Stop Press* reported on 1 March 1979. 'We are housewives, lawyers, copy typists, nurses, shopkeepers and city gents. We are of all the different political persuasions. We are of all ages.' Much the same could have been said of the membership of the other groups, whose tireless champion during the entire campaign was the *St Albans Review*.

At last, in July 1979, the council decided not to proceed with the unwanted scheme. Another development brief was prepared by the council, and of the 34 schemes submitted that from Bredero Consulting won the contract to build what became the £20m Maltings Shopping Centre.

'The Bredero plan for Chequer Street was favoured,' said the *Chartered Surveyor Weekly* on 17 February 1983,

> because of its attention to the particular character of the street frontage—a wide variety of buildings of different ages and styles which form a pleasing whole. Particular care was taken with the entrance to the shopping centre. The entrance skirts the historically valuable Lloyds Bank building on the corner of Chequer Street and Victoria Street, but is still close enough to the junction to form a natural link with the prime shopping area opposite.

Sheltering an enlarged St Albans Central Library, and with its shops attractively ranged on either side of a vehicle-free street, the shopping centre was opened by Diana, Princess of Wales, in 1988.

The scheme was a reminder that, as on previous occasions, many residents expected there to be a considered balance between the new and the old. For one critical outsider, the city's apparently conflicting demands of preservation and alteration were symptomatic of a wider, unresolved, issue: 'In some ways,' wrote Brian J. Bailey in *Portrait of Hertfordshire* (1978), 'St Albans is an epitome of the so-called advance of civilisation and the state of England at present, in which chaos and stress take the place of style and dignity, and pride precedes the fall ... It is as if the city, used to the driving force of a single man, were awaiting another Ulsinus or, worse, another Grimthorpe.'

But again it was the pull of the past—and the past's continuing significance—which inspired the city's remarkable commemoration in 1981 of the uprising of 1381. Among the

113   The Maltings shopping centre was opened on 14 April 1988 by Diana, Princess of Wales.

114   A stainless steel peace tower, donated by a Japanese group, Pax, in memory of the victims of the atomic bombing of Hiroshima and Nagasaki in 1945, was erected at the entrance to Sumpter Yard in 1982. The inscription upon it—in Japanese and English—reads, 'May peace prevail on earth'. Other peace towers have been erected by Pax in Japan, the United States, Germany, France and Bulgaria.

places marking that 600th anniversary, St Albans produced the largest number and most varied of the commemorative events in a programme stretching from March to September. The events included an historical display at the Clock Tower, a St Albans Folk Music Club presentation in words and music at *The Goat*, a pictorial display in the old central library, Cottonmill Clog Morris commemorative dances, a mobile exhibition by Verulamium Museum in St Albans and Harpenden, a talk for children, 'Robin Hood, Rogues and Rebels', by the author, Robert Leeson, and public meetings and lectures. Souvenir posters were on sale at the city museum and the bookshops; St Albans Labour Party offered 'Peasants Revolt' T-shirts at £2 each; Chris Buras, at St Albans Pottery, Spicer Street, made commemorative mugs.

On 31 May, members of the National Union of Agricultural and Allied Workers from all over the country, their banners waving, marched with local people and others from Bernard's Heath to the cathedral and abbey church for a service of remembrance and thanksgiving to commemorate the uprising of 1381. Afterwards, a rowdy meeting in Abbey Orchard field was addressed by Michael Foot, the then Labour Party leader, whose speech was interrupted by a group objecting to British policy on Northern Ireland. A month later, in the abbey church, the Company of Ten presented *This Impatient Nettle*, a dramatisation of the events leading up to the uprising, and a month after that 200 people attended a day-long historical conference at St Albans School on the uprising.

A discordant note was struck in June. The mayor, Kenneth Jenkins (b.1929), a business-man, declined to present the prizes at an exhibition of children's paintings in the Town Hall because he objected to its theme of 'revolt'. In a letter to the organisers, St Albans Co-operative Society, he said there was enough conflict in the world without encouraging children to portray the theme of revolution in paint. 'Ironically,' the *St Albans Review* reported on 11 June, 'the main award of the day, first prize in the senior section, went to Michelle Ward, 15, from London Colney School, for her painting of townsfolk engaged in a jolly game of hooded bluff.' The prizes had, in the disappointing absence of the mayor, been presented by another city councillor, Edwin Hudson (1917-90), a school-teacher, who was among the first in St Albans to suggest that the uprising should be commemorated, and whose lecture, 'The Peasants' Revolt and the Christian Faith Today', was delivered in the abbey church later the same month.

Past and present met again for the building of a new Chapter House on the south side of the cathedral and abbey church. Previous chapter houses had stood on the site, from which the remains of 11 abbots and four monks were removed during preliminary excavations in 1978, and reburied in front of the high altar under a slab of Welsh slate beautifully incised by the St Albans born and bred artist and lettercutter, David Kindersley, assisted by his wife, Lida Lopes Cardozo. Moreover, intact medieval stone blocks found on the site were re-used for the serving counter of the new building's refectory. The exterior's hand-made red bricks, from Bovingdon Brickworks, near Hemel Hempstead, were designed to match the shape and colour of the abbey's re-used Roman tiles. A wall plaque in the

115   Queen Elizabeth II in St Peter's Street after opening the Chapter House, 8 July 1982.

entrance records that Elizabeth II opened the Chapter House on 8 July 1982; afterwards, her walk in bright sunshine along St Peter's Street was a joyous occasion for the thousands of cheering spectators.

The opening in 1983 of an electrified rail service between St Albans and London, reducing the time of the journey to 20 minutes, with a direct connection to the south coast, and the opening in 1986 of the M25 between Bricket Wood and London Colney, completing London's ring-road motorway, made St Albans even more accessible, greatly accelerating its residential and commercial expansion. The accessibility—without any accompanying comprehensive public transport system—led to a corresponding increase in road traffic and, on 31 October 1988, the introduction by the Hertfordshire County Council of a one-way traffic system in the city centre.

Chaos ensued. Overnight, the traffic congestion became worse and shopkeepers, angered at the threat to their approaching Christmas trade, were supported by city councillors in demanding immediate action from the county authorities. Other objectors added their weight: 150 of the residents of Waverley Road and Carlisle Avenue signed a protest petition; 500 put their names to a petition from the St Albans Taxi Drivers' Association and 29,000 signed without hesitation a petition launched in November calling for the one-way system's abolition. The petition's instigator, Steve Blinkhorn, of Marlborough Gate, used the offices of his business research and development firm in The Maltings to distribute the petition forms, which he himself handed in to the county highways committee in January 1989. 'The one-way system', he said, 'promised jam tomorrow, but gave jams today.' Overwhelmed, the county council agreed on 12 January to scrap the scheme—at a cost of more than £775,000.

In the cathedral and abbey church imaginative work was changing the glazing of Grimthorpe's 19th-century rose window in the north transept from a cold, geometrical pattern using clear glass to a blaze of richly-coloured non-figurative stained glass symbolising, according to the artist, Alan Younger, the infusion of matter with spirit. Paid for by Laporte Industries of Luton, chemical manufacturers, to celebrate their centenary, the window took two years to design and make, and was unveiled on 26 September 1989 by the Princess of Wales, making her second official visit to St Albans. Laporte, founded in Yorkshire, moved to Luton in 1898 to supply bleach to the straw hat industry.

Chemicals in the form of a high explosive device were accidentally detonated in the city centre by two I.R.A. terrorists, killing both, shortly before the end of a concert by a

British Army band in the Alban Arena on the evening of 15 November 1991. Nearby, in the Waterend Barn restaurant, Tony Gregory, of Pemberton Close, a veteran freelance photographer with a gift for being in the right place at the right time, was covering the Verulam Cycling Club's annual dinner. 'I dropped what I was doing,' he was quoted as saying by the *St Albans and Harpenden Observer* on 20 November, 'and within 30 seconds of the explosion I was on the scene. I took two or three pictures before the police ushered me, and all passers-by, out of the way.' Dust, broken plate glass and damaged building material had showered the area, but the only other casualty, Andy Jackson, of Alexandra Road, suffered no more than slight leg injuries and a black eye; taken to St Albans City Hospital, he was released after treatment.

116 *Dagnall Street Baptist Church won a Civic Society award in 1990 for the design of its Cross Street Centre.*

But where would he have been taken for treatment a couple or so years later? By that time, a government-inspired reorganisation of the National Health Service had resulted in the transfer to Hemel Hempstead Hospital—nine miles away—of the city hospital's maternity and paediatric departments, and the reduction of its accident and emergency department to a minor injuries unit. The trumpeted reason was to increase efficiency, although a boom in the property market meant that land, like that around the city hospital cleared by the closures, could be expected to sell at inflated prices. As for the public objections, which were instant, large and long-lasting, they made no difference to the prepared outcome. All the same, 'A thousand people marched through St Albans in support of the city hospital on Saturday morning,' the *St Albans and Harpenden Observer* reported on 4 December 1991. On the same date, the *Herts Advertiser* said, 'The rally and march, organised by the St Albans Hospital Action Group, was to keep the proposed fate of the hospital, which health chiefs want to merge with Hemel Hempstead Hospital, in the public eye.' The likelihood of it being overlooked was slight: 57,000 people had signed a petition calling for the hospital to be left alone.

A year later, the activists still were as determined as ever, and 2,500 of them, many carrying placards or posters, greeted a government minister when he visited the hospital in October 1992. 'The streets were so congested that the Under Secretary of State for Health had to abandon his chauffeur driven car and walk the last few metres into the city hospital grounds,' a report in the *St Albans Review* stated on 5 November, and continued, 'Afterwards, Action Group chairman Jim Greening [a former mayor] said, "It was the biggest crowd out in support ever and it was good to see ... If services are slashed the Patients' Charter is a sham".'

'Ill would change be at whiles were it not for the change beyond the change.' The reassurance, offered by William Morris as a

117   Jim Greening, the City of St Albans' last mayor before the formation of the City and District of St Albans in 1974, served as a Fleet Air Arm pilot during the Second World War, then settled in St Albans and worked for the de Havilland aircraft company until retiring in 1985.

118   The Crown Court, Bricket Road, opened in March 1993; its royal coat of arms above the main entrance fills the space between the first- and second-floor windows.

chapter heading in *A Dream of John Ball* (1886–87), links past, present and future in a way similar to that symbolised by the latest restoration of the pedestal of the shrine of St Alban. Undertaken to coincide with the 12th centenary in 1993 of Offa's foundation of the abbey,

119   Beryl Carrington, of St Albans, a journalist with the Herts Advertiser *for 60 years, received an M.B.E. for services to journalism in the Queen's birthday honours list, 1995. Her late brother, Bob, also received the same award for services to journalism as both had followed in the footsteps of their father, Harry, who was editor of the* Herts Advertiser, *1916-47.*

120   Harry Javeleau, a hurdlemaker, in his workshop at 92 Fishpool Street, c.1962. His implements were acquired by Raphael Salaman and are included in the Salaman Collection at the Museum of St Albans.

the work, proposed by the Dean of St Albans, the Very Rev. Dr. Peter Moore (b.1924), had become necessary, despite the care shown during the pedestal's 19th-century reconstruction, because it was gradually falling apart. An appeal co-ordinated by Sir Eric Cheadle (1909-92), a former deputy managing director of the worldwide Thompson newspaper business, raised in three months the £150,000 needed to carry out the work. Foremost among the generous contributors was Queen Elizabeth the Queen Mother, who attended the rehallowing of the pedestal on 6 May 1993. Upon the pedestal, the placing of a finely-embroidered scarlet canopy, representing the medieval original, provided a spectacular finishing touch.

Belief in the value of the past for both the present and the future, and an urge to preserve threatened relics, informed the life of Raphael Salaman (1906-94). Hertfordshire-born, a senior engineer and long resident in Harpenden, he collected and recorded evidence of rural industries, saving from oblivion a mass of old tools until, in the 1960s, their number compelled him to arrange for most of them be put on permanent display at the Museum of St Albans. 'His contribution to cultural history,' an obituary in *The Times* of 3 February 1994 stated, 'also had its source in what has been thought of as a kind of amateurism—if by that is meant a passionate and meticulous following through of a child's curiosity and need to know exactly how and why people have done things as they have.' In the context of local history it is a curiosity, a need, which never ends.

Bibliography

STANDARD works of reference—for example, the *Dictionary of National Biography*, the *Oxford History of England*, the *Victoria County History*—have been consulted as well as various publications and journals, including the *Herts Advertiser*, *Hertfordshire Countryside*, *The Local Historian*, *St Albans and Harpenden Observer*, *St Albans and Harpenden Review* and *Transactions* of the St Albans and Hertfordshire Architectural and Archaeological Society, and the following:

Barbary, James, *Puritan and Cavalier: The English Civil War*, New York, 1977

Bede, *A History of the English Church and People*, trans. Leo Shirley-Price, London, 1955

Bernal, J.D., *Science and Industry in the Nineteenth Century*, London, 1953

Booth, Alan, 'Sam Ryder's Cup', *Official Programme*, 1993 Ryder Cup

Camden, William, *Britannia*, London, 1586

Carbery, Mary, *Happy World*, London, 1941

Carrington, Beryl, *Care in Crisis: Hertfordshire British Red Cross*, Buckingham, 1995

Colville, Mrs. Arthur, *Duchess Sarah*, London, 1904

Corbett, James, *Celebration: The Story of a Parish*, St Albans, 1990

Corbett, James, *Picture Postcards of Old St Albans*, St Albans, 1996

Corbett, James, *Secret City: Hidden History of St Albans*, St Albans, 1993

Cavendish, George, *The Life and Death of Cardinal Wolsey*, ed. R.S. Sylvester, Oxford, 1959

Dean, David, *et al.*, *St Albans c.1820: The Town*, St Albans, 1982

Dickinson, J.C., *The Great Charter*, London, 1955

Duffy, Eamon, *The Stripping of the Altars*, Yale, 1992

Elvins, Mark, *Catholic Trivia*, London, 1992

Fellows, Col. R. Bruce, *Historical Records of Hertfordshire Militia*, Welwyn, 1893

Finberg, H.P.R., *The Formation of England, 550-1042*, London, 1974

Flood, Susan (ed.), *St Albans Wills 1471-1500*, Hertfordshire Record Society, 1993

Foxe, John, *Book of Martyrs*, 1563, London, edn. 1854

Frere, Sheppard, *Britannia*, London, 1967

Gibbs, A.E., *The Corporation Records*, St Albans, 1890

Giles, E. and Thrale, R.W., *Historic Sandridge*, St Albans, 1952

Giles, Rev. J.A. (trans.), *Roger of Wendover's Flowers of History*, Vol.I, London, 1899

Giles, Rev. J.A. (trans.), *Matthew Paris's English History*, London, 1852-54

Gover, J.E.B., *et al.*, *The Place Names of Hertfordshire*, Cambridge, 1970

Gransden, Antonia, *Historical Writing in England II*, New York, 1982

Grey, Edwin, *Cottage Life in a Hertfordshire Village*, Harpenden, 1934

Gutchen, Robert, *et al.*, *Down and Out in Hertfordshire*, Stevenage, 1984

Hebditch, Felicity, *J.H. Buckingham: A Window on Victorian St Albans*, St Albans, 1988

Ingram, Tom, *Bells in England*, London, 1954

Jones, Arthur (ed.), *Hertfordshire 1731-1800*, Hatfield, 1993

Jones, Arthur (ed.), *The Peasants' Revolt in Hertfordshire*, Stevenage, 1981

Jones-Baker, Doris, 'English Medieval Graffiti', *The Local Historian*, vol.23, no.1, February 1993

Kent, E. Stanley, *St Albans in the Early Nineteenth Century*, St Albans, 1929

Kilvington, F.I., *A Short History of St Albans School*, St Albans, 1970

King, Norah, *The Grimstons of Gorhambury*, Chichester, 1983

Lindsay, Jack, *Arthur and His Times,* London, 1958

Morris, John (ed.), *Domesday Book: Hertfordshire*, Chichester, 1976

Morris, John, *Londinium*, London, 1982

Morris, Margaret, *The General Strike*, London, 1976

Newcome, Rev. Peter, *The History of the Abbey of St Alban*, London, 1793

Newell, Terence, *Ten of the Best*, St Albans, 1985

Norden, John, *A Description of Hertfordshire*, 1598, ed. W.B. Gerish, London, 1903

Page, William, *The Marian Survey of St Albans*, St Albans, 1894

Pahl, R.E., 'The Five Sites of St Albans', *Hertfordshire Past and Present*, no.2, 1961

Paris, Matthew, *Chronicles*, ed. trans. Richard Vaughan, Gloucester, 1984

Reynolds, E.V., *The Church and Parish of St Peter*, St Albans, 1982

Richardson, Iseult, *No Shadows Fall: the Story of Spielplatz*, Scarborough, 1994

Roberts, Eileen, *The Hill of the Martyr*, Dunstable, 1993

Rogers, John C., *The Parish Church of St Michael*, London, 1982

Rook, Tony, *A History of Hertfordshire*, Chichester, 1984

Rushbrook-Williams, L.F., *History of the Abbey of St Albans*, London, 1917

Sainsbury, J.D., *The Hertfordshire Yeomanry*, Welwyn, 1994

Scammell, Rev. Canon John, *Guide to the Parish Church*, Leighton Buzzard, n.d.

St Albans Union, *Minute Book*, 1835-41, St Albans Central Library

Scott, A.F., *Every One a Witness*, London, 1975

Scott, Dom Geoffrey, *St Alban Roe O.S.B.*, St Albans, 1992

Shaw, Solomon George, *History of Verolam and St Albans*, 1815

Shrimpton, John, *The Antiquities*, *c*.1631, St Albans, 1966

Swinson, Arthur, *The Quest for Alban*, St Albans, 1971

Tomkins, M., 'The Holyhead Road in St Albans', *Hertfordshire Past and Present*, no.13, 1973

Trafford, Peter, *Love and War: The Letters of Ted Trafford*, Bristol, 1995

White, Donald A., *Medieval History: A Source Book*, Illinois, 1965

Williams, Margaret Harcourt, 'Rothamsted and the Correspondence of Sir John Lawes and Sir Henry Gilbert', *The Local Historian*, vol.23, no.2, May 1993

Index

Aaron of Lincoln, 24
Abbey, St Albans: abbots, 14-18, 21-4, 26-39, 41,
    43-9: angelus bell, 28; arms, 14; attacked, 14, 22,
    24, 34, 38-40; buildings, 22, 26, 27-9, 30, 34,
    36, 41; chapter house, 20, 22, 27; charity, 16, 21,
    36; charter, 46; debts, 44, 47; dependencies, 48;
    diet, 20; foundation, 13; Gatehouse, 41; Lady
    chapel, 34, 53, 57, 105; library, 19, 28, 36, 41;
    nave, 26; Oxford connection, 31, 32, 35, 36, 41,
    43; pre-eminence, 22; privileges, 20, 33, 46;
    provisions, 21; re-building, 18; reliquary, 21, 24;
    rights, 34, 46; scriptorium 19, 20; sued, 32;
    suppression, 49, 50, 69, 125; tolls, 33
Abbey Church, Cathedral and, 107, 141, 146, 149,
    150
Abbey (parish church): 50, 53, 55, 62, 64, 66, 67,
    97, 105, 145, 149
Abbey Mill Lane, 79
Abbey Orchard, 93, 115, 149
Abbey School, 93, 138
Abbey Theatre, 145
Abbots Langley, 20, 27, 39
Abingdon, 34
Adams, Albert, 88
Adelaide Street, 115
Adminius, 3
Adrian IV *see* Nicholas Breakspear
Age Concern, 145
Agricola, 4
agricultural livestock: cattle, 2, 34, 35, 44, 67, 73,
    118; chickens, 21, 80, 83; horses, 61, 67, 73,
    100; oxen, 31, 73; pigs, 1, 14, 18, 21, 73; sheep,
    21, 73, 118; produce: barley, 3, 4, 34, 82; beef,
    20; eggs, 20, 21; fruit, 29; lamb, 113; mutton, 20;
    nuts, 29; wheat, 2, 31, 32, 41, 67, 69, 82, 83, 90,
    101
Alban, 6, 7, 16, 20, 23, 48 (statue), 50 (relics)
Alban Arena, 145, 150
alcohol: ale, 20, 30, 32, 34, 35, 55, 58, 61, 68, 78,
    84, 146; beer, 55, 58, 61, 68, 84, 114, 146;
    cider, 61; wine, 2, 4, 20, 26, 55, 58, 64, 68, 84
Aldenham, 4, 20
aldermen, 67-9, 87
alehouses, 55
Alexander III, 23

Alexandra Road, 150
Alma Road, 116, 125, 132, 146
almshouses, 69
America, United States of, 98, 126, 137
Amersham, Walter, 36
Amphibalus, 23, 24
anchorites, 29, 47
Anglicans, 61, 93, 101, 113, 129
animals (wild): boars, 17; deer, 1; 21; hares, 29, 35;
    pigs, 1; rabbits, 35, 83; wildfowl, 1; wolves, 17
Anne, Queen, 70
Antelope Inn, 54
Arch, Joseph, 100
archery, 44, 54, 55
Armenians, 30
Armorica, 11
Art School, 108, 124, 125
Ashdown, Charles Henry, 122-4
Aubrey, John, 56
Augustine, 12, 14
Austen, Frederick, 110
Avenue Road, 110

Bacon, Francis, 56, 57, 64
Bacon, Sir Nicholas, 50, 55
bailiff, 31, 47, 68
Ball, John, 39
Ballito, 136, 138
banks, 80, 94
Baptists, 64, 67, 75, 111, 121
Barbour, John, 39, 40
Barnet, 29, 38
barons, 22, 26, 27, 29, 31
Batchwood Drive, 140, 144
Batchwood Gardens, 144
Batchwood Hall, 107, 133
baths, swimming, 106, 108, 114
Battlefield Road, 126
Beaconsfield Road, 107, 130
Beauclerk, Rev. Lord Frederick, 86
Beaufort, Edward, 45
Beaumont Avenue, 120
Becket, Thomas, 23, 28
Bede, 12
Bedford, 15

Beech Bottom, 2
Belgic: agriculture, 3; burials, 2; cemetery, 3; coins, 2, 3; enclosure, 1; farmsteads, 2; grave goods, 3; luxuries, 2; pottery, 3; settlements, 2; trade, 2; warfare, 1-4
Bell, Jacob, 94
Belmont Hill, 137
Benedictines, 13, 20, 21, 28, 32, 41, 43, 57, 60
Berkhamsted, 27, 62
Bernard's Heath, 35, 44, 100, 106, 110, 137, 149
Besant, Annie, 112
Bewick, Thomas, 21
Binham, 20, 26, 49
Bird, William, 134
Bittleston, Rev. Henry, 113
Black Lion Inn, 4
Blagg, Thomas, 92
Bleak House, 85
Blow, George Walter, 112
Blue Boar Inn, 79
Bodleian Library, 43
Boudicca, 4
boundary, 29, 35, 38, 52
Boundary Road, 119
Bow Bridge, 56, 82
Bowman, Thomas, 95, 96
Bradlaugh, Charles, 112
Branch Road, 6
bread, 20, 34, 35, 56, 58, 78
Breakspear, Robert, 20
Breakspear, Nicholas, 20
Breauté, Falkes de, 27
bribery, 94
Bricket Wood, 94, 133, 146, 149
bridges, 22, 73
British Legion, Royal, 93
Brittany, 11
Brockley Hill, 4
Bronze Age: hoard, 1; razor, 1
Buckingham, John Henry, 99, 100
Bull Inn, 62
Bunyan, John, 67
burgesses, 19, 31, 32, 34, 35, 67, 94
Bury St Edmunds, 13, 27, 34

Caesar, Julius, 1,2
Caddington, William, 38-40
Camden, William, 24
Camp Road, 117, 120
Campfield Road, 118
Canterbury, 13, 18, 23, 28
Capel, Sir Arthur, 60
Carausius, 8
Carbery, Mary, 85, 99
Carden, Sir Robert, 94
Carlisle Avenue, 150
Carnegie, Andrew, 126
carnival, 146

Cassivellaunus, 1
Castle Inn, 45, 54
Catherine Street, 54, 116
Catholics, 60, 92, 93, 94, 107, 128, 130, 145
Catuvellauni, 1, 2
Cavendish, William, 49, 50
cemetery, 108, 113, 118, 130
charity, 16, 21, 28, 36, 47, 54, 55, 68, 82, 93, 136
Charlemagne, 13
Charles I, 60-62
Charles II, 62, 64, 67
charters, 29, 31, 33, 34, 36, 38, 39, 46, 47, 50, 52, 54, 60, 67
Cheadle, Sir Eric, 152
Chequer Street, 18, 25, 46, 54, 82, 90, 137, 147
Chequers Inn, 25, 86
chess, 25
Childwick, Geoffrey de, 29
Childwickbury, 116
Chiswell Green, 144
Christ Church, 101, 120
Christ Church School, 93
Christina of Huntingdon, 20
Christopher Inn, 140
Christopher Place, 88
Church of England *see* Anglicans
Church Crescent, 114
Church Street, 54
cinemas, 125, 131, 147
City Hall *see* Alban Arena
Civic Society, 144, 147
Civil War, 60-4, 125
Clarence Park, 117, 125
Clarence Road, 130
Clark, Samuel, 93
Claudius, 3, 4
Claughton, Bishop Thomas, 107
Clock Tower, 32, 43, 54, 68, 69, 77, 79, 80, 97, 98, 101, 103, 133, 148
cloth, 21, 25, 27, 69
coaches, 59, 73, 74, 77, 78, 88, 93
Cobbett, William, 81, 82
Cock Lane *see* Hatfield Road
Codicote, 21, 29
Colchester, 3, 4, 62
Coleman Green, 67
Coleman, Thomas, 86, 87
Colney Heath, 146
College of Further Education *see* Oaklands College
College Street, 72
Collegium Insanorum, 72
Colney Street, 1
Cologne, 50
Commerce, Chamber of, 142, 145
Company of Ten, 149
Congregationalists, 64, 66, 67, 76, 91, 121, 129, 144
Coningsbury, Sir Thomas, 61

Conservatives, 87, 92, 94, 113, 134
Constantine, 9
Cooke, George, 69
Co-operative Society, 149
Corn Exchange, 95-7, 101, 111, 123
Cotton, Nathaniel, 71, 72
Cottonmill Lane, 114, 122
Cottonmill Clog Morris, 148
Couch, Elizabeth, 136
council (city): 114, 123, 124, 126, 129-33, 139, 140;
    (city and district): 146, 147; (town): 52, 55, 56,
    58, 61, 67-9, 71, 80, 82, 83, 87, 90-2, 94-8, 101,
    103, 105, 111
Cowper, William, 71, 72
Cox, Alban, 60, 62
Craik, William, 144
Crane Inn, 54
cricket, 86, 117, 133
Cromwell, Oliver, 60-2
Cromwell, Thomas, 49, 50
Crosby, Edward, 64, 66
Cross Keys Inn, 53, 54, 73
Cross Street, 93
Crown Inn, 79
Culver Road, 119, 126
Cumber, Thomas, 73
Cunningham Hall, 131
Cunobelin, 3
curfew bell, 43, 98
cyclists, 125, 128, 158

Dagnall Street, 29, 46, 54, 55, 93
Dagnall Street chapel, 93
Dalton's Folly, 85
Danes, 14-16
Davies, George, 136
Davies, Kitty, 138
Debating Society, 113, 126
Debenham, George, 95
Denmark, 14, 16
Devereux, Robert, 61
Devil's Dyke, 1, 2
Diana, Princess of Wales, 147
Diocletian, 8
ditches, 3, 29
Dobson, William, 56
Dolphin Inn, 54
Domesday (Book), entry for St Albans, 19; survey,
    19, 20
Doran, Kenneth, 136
Drovers' Way, 131
Drayton, Michael, 143
Dumpleton, Cyril, 138
Dunstable, 21, 31, 38

earthquake, 28, 29
Edward I, 31, 32
Edward II, 34, 35

Edward III, 37, 45
Edward IV, 45-7
Edward VI, 50
Edwards, Henry, 94
Ekins, Arthur Edward, 119, 120
Eleanor of Castile, 32
Elizabeth I, 55
Elizabeth II, Queen, 141, 146, 149
Elstree, 4
Ely, 16
enclosures, 35, 38, 44, 61, 110
Entwistle, Betty, 143
epidemic: 28; bubonic plague (Black Death), 37, 59;
    scarlet fever, 116, 119; smallpox, 89, 90, 104,
    116, 119, 120; typhus, 88, 89
Ethelred I, 15
Ethelred II, 16
evacuees, 135, 136

factories, 106, 118, 119, 136, 138, 140
Fairfax, Sir Thomas, 62
fairs, 52, 58, 79, 91
famine, 16, 21, 29, 34, 43, 62
Fascists, British Union of, 133
Faulkner, Arthur, 120, 125
Fayrfax, Robert, 47
fire engine, 57, 108
fires, 4, 6, 27, 28, 44
First World War, 101, 128, 129, 136, 145
fish, 1, 15, 19-21, 28, 34, 58, 67
fishpool, 15
Fishpool Street, 4, 13, 16, 29, 44, 47, 54, 73, 96,
    119, 133
Fisk, James, 110
Fitzwalter, Robert, 26, 27
Flamstead, 17
Flamstead End, 1
Flanders, 34
Fleetville, 143
Fleur de Lys Inn, 54, 79
Flora Grove, 117
Folk Music Club, 148
Folly Lane, 85
football, 117, 126, 133
fountain, 101
Fox, Ralph, 133
France, 20, 22, 26, 33, 37, 45, 50, 74
Fraser, Simon, Lord Lovat, 71
Fremantle, Sir Francis, 138
French Row, 25, 41, 54, 79, 133, 140
Furse, Bishop Michael, 131, 138

Gale, F.A., 142
Gape, Henry, 54
Gape, James, 107, 137
gas, 83, 106, 133, 141
Gaul, 2, 4, 6, 8, 9, 11
Gazeley, Nan, 146

George III, 77
George and Dragon Inn (George) 46, 59, 77
George Street, 41, 46, 54, 59, 73, 82, 103, 106
Germanus, 11, 14
Gibson, Edward, 91
Gilbert, Joseph Henry, 91
gild, 47, 52
Glastonbury, 13
Goat Inn, 73, 148
Goldcliff, Hugh de, 26
golf, 118, 133
Gorham, Cecilia de, 29
Gorhambury, 4, 50, 55, 56, 61, 64
Gotto, Henry Jenkin, 108
Grange Street, 133
Granville Road, 131
Great Red Lion Inn, 54
Great Yarmouth, 28
Green, Muriel, 136
Gregory the Great, 12, 14
Gregory, Tony, 150
Gresham, William, 94
Grimston, Sir Harbottle, 64, 66, 67
Grimston, Samuel, 70
Grimthorpe, Lord (Edmund Beckett), 112, 147
Grindcobbe, William, 38-40
Grove, Robert, 124
Guardians, Board of, 85
Guides, Association of Honorary, 145

Hadrian, 4, 9
Hales, Sir Robert, 38
Hall Place, 54, 122
handmills, 32, 34-36, 38
Harpenden, 85, 91, 100, 146, 148, 152
Harpenden Road, 108, 139, 144
Hatfield, 20, 77, 82, 92
Hatfield Road, 54, 69, 82, 108, 118, 130, 136, 140, 143
Haworth, Rev. William, 64, 66
head cult, 7
Heathland Drive, 140
Henry I, 20, 22
Henry II, 22, 23
Henry III, 27-9, 31
Henry IV, 43
Henry V, 43
Henry VI, 45
Henry VIII, 48, 49
Hertford, 29, 31, 33, 39, 49, 60, 66, 72
Hertfordshire, 1, 11-13, 38, 39, 44, 60, 62, 75, 132
Hertfordshire Brewers' Association, 115
High Street, 44, 54, 73, 101, 103, 110
highwaymen, 72
Hillside Road, 110
Hitchcock, Edward, 133
Hitchin, 60
hoards (coins), 8, 14
Hogarth, William, 71

Holyrood Abbey, 50
Holywell Hill, 15, 22, 25, 29, 41, 47, 54, 70, 73, 79, 95, 101, 114, 116, 117, 145
Honorius, 10
Horner, Ann and Francis, 126
Horseshoe Inn, 57
hospitals, 85, 101, 114, 116, 119, 132, 141, 142, 144, 150, 151
housing, 129-31, 133, 139, 141, 145
Howland, John, 60
Hudson, Edwin, 149
Hurlock, William, 103, 105, 111, 112, 115

Ice Age, 1
Independent Chapel, 93
Industrial Employers' Association, 142
industry, 140, 141
Innocent IV, 28
interdict, 26, 33
Ireland, 64
Irish, 8, 9
Ivy House, 69

Jarman, Herbert, 124
Jarrow Crusade, 134
Jenkins, Kenneth, 149
Jerusalem, 31
John, Bishop of Ardfert, 28
John, King of England, 25-7
John, King of France, 37

Kent, David, 75
Kent, John, 75
Kentish, Charles, 76
Kentish, Richard, 92
King Harry Lane, 3, 11
King William Inn, 115
Kingsbury, 13, 15, 16, 29, 54
Kings Langley, 43
Kitton, Frederic, 120
Knap, H.L., 145

Labour Party, 146, 149
Lanfranc, 18
Lattimore Road, 101
Lavery, Frank, 145
Lawes, John Bennet, 91
Lee, Sir Richard, 50
Lee, Sir Walter atte, 39
Leicester, 4
Lemsford Road, 136
lepers, 21, 24
Liberals, 87, 91, 94, 111-113
libraries, 108, 125, 126, 138, 143, 147, 148
lightning, 28
Liverpool Road, 143
Lollards, 43
London, 3, 4, 9, 21, 28, 34, 38, 53, 61, 64, 88

London Colney, 31, 100, 149
London Road, 50, 73, 82, 106, 107, 125, 126, 142
Lord, Stanley, 132
Loreto College, 130, 137
Louis, Prince, 27
Lower Dagnall Street, 72, 76, 145
Luton, 11, 119, 150

Mackerye End, 45
Magna Carta, 26, 27
Maltings, The, 25, 134, 147, 150
Manderville, Sir John, 37
Manning, Cardinal Henry, 107
Mansel, John, 29
Maple, Sir John Blundell, 116
Marian survey, 54
Market Cross, 48, 80, 101, 103
Market Hall, 137
Market House, 69, 96, 97
Market Place, 47, 55, 59, 83, 119, 121, 126
Market Square, 138, 139
markets, 14, 20, 25, 33, 36, 52, 54, 61, 67, 69, 71,
      79, 116, 126
Markyate, 20, 26
Marlborough, Duchess of, 69, 70
Marlborough House, 130
Marlborough Road, 76, 120, 124, 143
Marsh, John, 60
Mary I, 53, 54
Matilda, Queen, 20, 22
Meautys, Anne, 64
Meautys, Sir Thomas, 56, 54
Mediterranean, 7, 11, 24, 37
Melbourne-Cooper, Thomas, 125
Mercer, Robert, 23
Mercia, 12
Methodists, 75, 76, 139
Middle Stone Age, 1
militia, 81, 82, 86
mills, 19, 21, 29-32, 47, 106
Minter, Billy, 126
Monck, General George, 64
Moner, Anthony, 55
Mongols, 30
monks, 13, 20, 21, 26-8, 30, 32, 35, 37, 41, 48, 49
Montfort, Simon de, 31
Moon, Henry, 117
Moore, Very Rev. Dr. Peter, 152
Moot Hall, 39, 52
Mortimer, Richard, 45
Murray, James, 96
museums, 119, 148, 152

National Children's Home, 126
Napoleonic war, 74, 75, 77, 81, 82
Napsbury, 20, 128
naturists, 133
Neckam, Alexander, 24

New, William, 50
Newell, Terence, 130, 145
New England Street, 137
New Greens, 140, 143
Newman, Cardinal John Henry, 113
Nomansland, 44, 86, 87, 100
Nonconformists, 64, 66, 67, 93, 121
Norfolk, 38
Norman Conquest, 17; Battle of Hastings, 17-19
Normandy, 21, 22
Normandy Road, 85
Norsemen, 16
Norway, 14, 20, 30
Norwich, 13, 28
nuns, 13, 130

Oaklands College, 43
Odense, 16
Offa, 12, 13, 151
Offley, 13
Oldcastle, Sir John, 43
Old London Road, 73, 116
Old Stone Age, 1
Osterhills, 21
Oxford, 24, 31, 35, 36, 41, 43, 47, 91

Page, William, 116
pageants, 124, 125, 140, 141
Palmer, Charles Edward, 130
Paris, Matthew, 28-30
Park Street, 2, 4, 8, 9, 21, 119, 145
passive resisters, 121
Paul, William, 100
Peacock Inn, 54
Peahen Hotel, 29, 54
Pearce, Eustace, 33
Pemberton Close, 150
Picts, 9, 11
Pigeon, William, 26
pilgrims, 13, 19, 23, 24
police, 97, 98
Pope, Sir Richard, 50
population, 67, 68, 110, 146
Post Office, 123, 124
Potters Bar, 4
Power, Rev. John, 128
Prae Wood, 2
Presbyterians, 67, 75, 76
prison, 105, 131
Prospect Road, 121
Protestantism/Protestants, 43, 53, 64, 67, 130
psalter, 20

Quakers (Society of Friends), 67
Queen's Hotel, 85, 87, 90
Queen Mother, Queen Elizabeth the, 140, 143,
      146, 152

railways, 88, 92, 95, 104, 118, 126, 143, 149
Raphael, Alexander, 92-94
Ratcliffe, Timothy, 66
ratepayers, 103, 133
Raynshaw, Richard, 54
Red Cross, 136
Redbourn, 1, 20, 23, 24, 27-29, 31, 36, 39, 40, 50, 54, 56, 60, 82, 85, 96
Richard I, 38-40
Richard II, 43
Rickmansworth, 20 21, 27, 29
roads, 3, 14, 17, 29, 58, 67, 73, 106, 142, 144-6, 149, 150
Robert of London, 27
Robert the Mason, 18, 19
Robinson, Thomas, 75
Roe, Alban, 57, 60
Roger of Markyate, 22
Roger of Wendover, 28
Roman: baths, 3, 4, 6; buildings, 3, 4, 6, 8, 9, 11, 15; burials, 3, 4, 7, 16; coins, 8; farms, 4, 8, 9; fires, 4, 6; forum, 4, 6, 8, 15; gateways, 8, 11; glass, 3, 8, 16; invasions, 1, 3; kilns, 4, 9; lamps, 8; market hall, 4, 6; malting oven, 4; mosaic, 6, 9, 11; oyster shells, 6; pottery, 2, 4, 11; religion, 4, 6, 7, 9, 16; roads, 3, 8, 12; shops, 3, 4, 8, 9; shrine, 7, 11, 12; slaves, 4, 8; temple, 4; theatre, 6-9; town, 3-12, 14; trades, 5; wall, 8; wall paintings, 6, 9, 11; water supplies, 6, 11
Rome, 10, 12, 14, 22, 30
Romeland, 29, 41, 46, 53, 83
Romeland House, 69
Rotary Club, 132, 138
Rothamsted, 91
Round Table, 146
Rowlett, Sir Ralph, 50, 69
Royston, 60, 62
Rumball, John Horner, 94
Runcie, Bishop Robert, 145
rural council, 144
Russell, Joseph, 94
Ryder, Samuel, 117, 118, 123, 124, 130

St Albans Architectural and Archaeological Society, 116
St Albans School, 14, 21, 36, 53-5, 57, 105, 106, 123, 136, 138
St Andrew, chapel of, 14, 47, 50
St Benedict, 13, 20
St Brieuc, 11
St Catherine, 21
St Columba's College, 130
St Germanus, chapel of, 14
St John Ambulance Brigade, 130, 144
St Julian, Hospital of, 21, 22, 36, 50
St Mary de Pré, 24, 45, 48, 54
St Mary Magdalen, chapel of, 14
St Michael's Church, 4, 15, 21, 29, 47, 54, 56

St Michael's village, 15, 73, 128
St Paul's, London, 27, 35, 69
St Peter's Church, 15, 29, 41, 47, 50, 54, 60, 62, 64, 69, 94, 139
St Peter's Green, 85
St Peter's Street, 29, 45, 47, 54, 76, 79, 90, 103, 108, 110, 113, 122-4, 131-3, 137, 139, 144
St Stephen's Church, 15, 21, 33, 50, 90, 145
SS Alban and Stephen Church, 107, 113, 128, 136
Salaman, Raphael, 152
Salisbury Avenue, 3
Salisbury, Marquess of, 82
Salvation Army, 108, 114, 115, 121, 126
Sander, Frederick, 117
Sandpit Lane, 29, 54, 110, 111, 126, 136, 140
Sandridge, 20, 21, 39, 41, 44, 46, 69, 85, 100, 146
Saracen's Head Inn, 54
Saxon: cemetery, 11, 12; church, 12; invaders, 9-11; monastery, 13-16, 18; pirates, 8; settlers, 11, 12
School Lane, 80
schools, 115, 116, 131, 134
Scotland, 34, 50, 64, 84
Scott, George Gilbert, 97, 101, 103, 105, 107
Seabrook, Edward, 69
Second World War, 135-9, 146
serfs, 45, 46
sewers, 6, 88, 89, 90, 104, 106, 135
Seymour, Thomas, 139
Shenley, 20
Shirley, James, 57
Shrimpton, Robert, 48
shrine, 7, 11-13, 22, 23, 31, 36, 47, 105, 151
Shropshire Lane see Victoria Street
Sibley, William, 136
Sigar, 22
silk mill, 79, 106, 118
Simon, Abbot, 23, 24
slaves, 2, 4, 6, 8, 20, 62
Smith, Frederic, 128
Smith, George, 83
Smith, Henry Partridge, 114
Solerno, 24
Sopwell convent, 21, 29, 36, 45, 47, 49, 50
Sopwell House, 93, 101
Sopwell Lane, 41, 54, 57, 73, 119
soup kitchen, 95
Spain, 4, 11, 55, 133
Sparrow, Lt. Stephen, 137
Spencer family, 79, 112
Spencer Street, 93
Spicer Street, 29, 54, 76, 93, 100, 116
Stanefield, 21
steeplechasing, 86
Stephen, King of England, 22
Stokes, Gregory, 31
straw plait, 79, 95, 110, 118, 150
Strong, Edward, 69
Sudbury, Simon, 38

Suetonius, 3
Suffolk, 38
Sutton Road, 119
Swan Inn, 59
Sweet Briar Lane *see* Victoria Street
swimming, 131, 133
Swinson, Arthur, 145
Swinson, Cyril, 141-5

Tabard Inn see Antelope
Tankerfield, George, 53
Tarling, Ruth, 144
Tasciovanus, 2, 3
Taverner, John, 35, 36
taxes, 15, 18, 29, 38, 60, 61
Taylor, Rev. Henry, 111, 121
telephone poles, 123, 124
tenterground, 25
terrorists, 150
Theodosius, 9
Thicknesse, Very Rev. Cuthbert, 136, 138, 139, 142
Thurnoth, 17
tokens, 59
tollgates, 73, 88
tolls, 19, 20, 29, 33, 67, 69
Toms, Elsie, 140, 145
Tonman Ditch, 29, 54
Toulmin, Henry Joseph, 85, 103
Town Backsides, 29
Town Hall, 52, 83, 88, 95, 97, 101, 108, 110, 115, 125, 129, 131, 134, 138, 143-5, 149
Townsend, John, 66
Trade, St Albans Chamber of, 142
trade unions, 129, 131, 133
Trades Council, St Albans and District, 129, 131, 132, 137, 138, 142, 143
trades (medieval): baker, 37, 38; brewer, 25, 37; brickmaker, 47; butcher, 31, 37; clothier, 25; cobbler, 37; cornmonger, 37; draper, 37; dyer, 37; farmer, 25; fuller, 37; hosteller, 37; mason, 18, 19, 26; metalworker, 37; plumber, 37; potter, 25; saddlemaker, 37; saltmonger, 37; skinner, 37; smith, 37; tailor, 37; tanner, 37, 54; taverner, 37; weaver, 37
trades (modern) *c.*1670: 57, 58; *c.*1949: 140, 141; brewers, 56, 78, 79, 115, 134; builders, 56, 107, 110, 119; drapers, 69, 78, 98, 99, 105; farmers, 61, 82, 83, 96, 97, 100, 118, 142; farm workers, 83, 100, 101, 149; grocers, 78, 98, 99; straw-plait, 79, 80, 95, 110, 111, 114, 118, 124; woodworkers, 55, 100, 119, 121; others: 55-7, 68, 75, 77, 98, 99, 108, 113, 118, 131
traffic, 73, 68, 145, 150
transportation, 83
Tresilian, Sir Robert, 39, 40
Turf Hotel see Queen's Hotel
turnpike, 73
Turrill, Charles and Elizabeth, 64

Tyler, Wat, 38
Tyttenhanger, 29, 39, 43, 45, 50

unemployment, 62, 122, 130, 132, 134
Union Lane *see* Normandy Road
Upper Dagnall Street, 76, 83
Upper Lattimore Road, 130
uprising (1381), 147, 148

Valley Road Trading Estate, 141
Vanda Crescent, 117
Ver House, 112
Ver, river, 1-3, 21, 22, 25, 29, 37, 73, 106, 114, 125, 142
Verlamio, 1-4
Verulam Arms Hotel, 83, 84, 90, 92
Verulamium, 3-6, 8-12, 14-16, 18, 124, 125, 133, 135, 136, 140, 141, 148
Verulam, Earl of, 97, 142
Verulam Hill Fields, 7
Verulam House, 56
Verulam Road, 1, 82, 83, 103, 106, 114, 116, 133, 136
Victoria, Queen, 90, 114, 117
Victoria Square, 103, 105
Victoria Street, 45, 54, 76, 106, 108, 111, 113-15, 124, 125, 133, 138, 145, 146
Vikings, 14, 16
Vine Inn, 54, 100
vineyard, 37
Vintry, 54
Visigoths, 10
Volunteers, 75, 77, 81
Vuolo, Beryl, 144, 145

Waeclingas, 12
wages, 37, 55, 83, 101
Walden, 21
Wales, 12, 27, 33
Wallingford, 26, 35, 48
Walsingham, Thomas, 38, 40
Walter of Chichester, 28
Ward, Michelle, 149
Ware, 60
water supplies, 6, 10, 11, 71, 79, 83, 88, 101, 106, 142, 143
Waterend Barn, 150
Watford, 1, 27, 39, 88, 92, 95
Watford Road, 144
Watling Street, 3, 6, 9, 12, 14, 15, 17
Waverley Road, 130, 150
Waxhouse Gate, 43, 80
Webster, Joshua, 71
Wellesley, Arthur, Duke of Wellington, 82
Wells, John, 110-12
Wemyss, John, 133
West Avenue, 144
West, Bishop Francis, 126

West, Sydney, 126
Westell, Claude, 124, 125
Westell, William, 111, 112, 114
Westminster Abbey, 13
Westminster Lodge, 133, 145
Wheathampstead, 1, 85, 146
Wheeler, Sir Mortimer and Tessa, 133, 135, 142
White, Samuel Monckton, 115
Whitefield, Rev. George, 170
White Hart Hotel, 29, 54, 71, 75, 79, 92
Wiles, Edward Sutton, 101, 106
William I, 18, 19, 125
Wilson, Alexander, 97
Willmington, Sonia, 144
Winchelsea, Robert de, 33
Wingate, Edward, 61
witches, 62

Wix, Margaret, 131, 143
Wolsey, Cardinal Thomas, 48
women's suffrage, 126, 128
Wooden Room, 101
woods, 19, 22, 26, 41
Woollam, Charles, 106
Woolpack Inn, 54, 77
Worcester, 62
Workers' Educational Association, 136
workhouses, 84, 85, 116, 119, 120, 132
Worley, Mrs. Isabella, 93, 101, 103, 116
Wymondham, 20, 28, 45

Yeomanry, 143

Zionist Federation, 138